THE LAWYERS WHO MADE AMERICA

No other nation's creation, both politically and socially, owes such a debt to lawyers as the United States of America. This book traces the story of that creation through the human lives of those who played important parts in it: amongst others, of English lawyers who established the form of the original colonies; of the Founding Fathers, who declared independence and created a Constitution; of Abraham Lincoln, Woodrow Wilson, Justices of the Supreme Court and finally Barack Obama. Even Richard Nixon features, if only as a reminder that even the President is subject to the law. The author combines his wide legal experience and engaging writing style to produce a book that will enthral lawyers and laymen alike, giving perhaps a timely reminder of the importance of the rule of law to American democracy.

The Lawyers Who Made America

From Jamestown to the White House

Anthony Arlidge QC

·HART·
PUBLISHING
OXFORD AND PORTLAND, OREGON
2017

Hart Publishing
An imprint of Bloomsbury Publishing Plc

Hart Publishing Ltd
Kemp House
Chawley Park
Cumnor Hill
Oxford OX2 9PH
UK

Bloomsbury Publishing Plc
50 Bedford Square
London
WC1B 3DP
UK

www.hartpub.co.uk
www.bloomsbury.com

Published in North America (US and Canada) by
Hart Publishing
c/o International Specialized Book Services
920 NE 58th Avenue, Suite 300
Portland, OR 97213-3786
USA

www.isbs.com

HART PUBLISHING, the Hart/Stag logo, BLOOMSBURY and the
Diana logo are trademarks of Bloomsbury Publishing Plc

First published 2017

British Library Cataloguing-in-Publication Data
A catalogue record for this book is available from the British Library.

ISBN: HB: 978-1-50990-636-9
       ePDF: 978-1-50990-639-0
       ePub: 978-1-50990-638-3

Library of Congress Cataloging-in-Publication Data

Names: Arlidge, Anthony, author.

Title: The lawyers who made America : from Jamestown to the White House / Anthony Arlidge QC.

Description: Portland, Oregon : Hart Publishing, 2017. | Includes bibliographical references and index.

Identifiers: LCCN 2016058796 (print) | LCCN 2016059676 (ebook) | ISBN 9781509906369
(hardback : alk. paper) | ISBN 9781509906383 (Epub)

Subjects: LCSH: Lawyers—United States—Biography. | Lawyers—United States—History. |
Practice of law—United States—History.

Classification: LCC KF353 .A75 2017 (print) | LCC KF353 (ebook) | DDC 340.092/273—dc23

LC record available at https://lccn.loc.gov/2016058796

Typeset by Compuscript Ltd, Shannon
Printed and bound in Great Britain by TJ International Ltd, Padstow, Cornwall

To find out more about our authors and books visit www.hartpublishing.co.uk. Here you will find extracts,
author information, details of forthcoming events and the option to sign up for our newsletters.

Foreword

THE RT HON LORD JUDGE PC,
FORMERLY LORD CHIEF JUSTICE OF ENGLAND AND WALES

Between 1616 and 1700 some 300,000 people—in those days a huge number—left England to face the enormous hazards and doubtful prospects of crossing the ocean in what were virtually wooden tubs to make new lives for themselves in unaccustomed conditions in the colonies they founded in the Eastern seaboard of the future United States of America. As they departed they took with them what they believed were their rights as Englishmen, not least the ideas about the arrangements for proper government, which had been in ferment in England from the start of the seventeenth century. Half way through it, a civil war, which culminated in the public trial and execution of the King, sent shock waves through the rest of Europe; at its end another King was driven out, and replaced. Events like these established that the monarch was not absolute. He, like everyone else, was subject to the law. Ideas like these, which we take for granted, were once revolutionary. And they all travelled with the colonists to the future United States. There are many explanations for and accounts of the Declaration of Independence and the creation of the United States in 1776, but one, surely, is a determined independence of mind and an adherence to ideas of constitutionality, which was bred in the bone of the original colonists and their descendants.

English lawyers were at the heart of the processes which attended the creation of the colonies. Native born American lawyers were among the leading advocates for a better system of government than dictatorship by a parliament hundreds of miles away across the seas. American lawyers contributed to the long drawn-out process to eradicate slavery. Until recently an American lawyer was the leader of the free world.

Of course the history of the United States was not made exclusively by lawyers. No one suggests that it was. But lawyers were closely connected with many of the seminal moments of that remarkable history. And their involvement in great events and their contribution to them make a fascinating story: so, too, do their own personalities and characters, with their flaws and frailties, their principles and prejudices, and influences outside the law itself. Take John Adams, the second President. Like all those who rebelled against rule from London, if the War of Independence had been lost, he would probably have been hanged for treason. He was not indulging in mere lawyerly talk. Take him again. The views of Abigail Adams come down the centuries to us. Imagine the impact of that wonderful woman on him. Perhaps it is as well that we should be reminded that, although all the characters in this book were lawyers, they were human beings too.

For them all, from 1600 to today, none of the events we look back to as history were already written. Their future had still to come and they were contributing to its making. Without any of them, it might well have been very different. From Walter Raleigh to President Obama, Anthony Arlidge provides us with a series of illuminating insights and thoughtful analysis of the lives and times of the lawyers who over the centuries made America. It makes a captivating read.

Preface

In 2015 I visited an exhibition at the British Library celebrating the 800th Anniversary of the sealing of Magna Carta. It included later constitutional documents which relate back to the Charter. Amongst them was Thomas Jefferson's draft of the American Declaration of Independence, including a passage condemning slavery excised from the final version. I began to read about the background to the Declaration and became fascinated by the interplay of the personalities and issues involved. Those who opposed the actions of the British government started by claiming their rights as British subjects. This was not surprising—the Virginia Charter was drawn by English lawyers and all the early colonists insisted they remained British subjects. Over 50 years ago, I was called to the English bar in the Middle Temple, an Inn of Court intimately connected with the creation of a British Empire in America. It was only the ineptness of the governments of George III that led to Revolution and the creation of the United States of America. As I read, I was struck by what a legal Revolution this was. The failure to abolish slavery under the new Constitution continued to be a sore that infected the growth and reputation of the new nation. It took a lawyer in the shape of Abraham Lincoln to end it, though the baleful effects continue up to the Presidency of another, Barack Obama. The present book is an attempt to tell the remarkable story of the development of an American nation through the lawyers who made it.

I owe particular particular thanks to Robert Olejar, who is both an American attorney and an English barrister. Despite the fact that the legal systems of England and the United States sprang from similar common law roots, many subtle differences have developed; I became conscious I was straying out of my comfort zone. Robert saved me from some howlers and pointed me in the direction of further research. Sir David Eady, an old friend and former High Court judge, made some very useful criticisms and suggested some of the chapters which play a part in the book. My partner, Heather Lockwood, corrected my punctuation (pointing out that her grammar school must have been better than mine) and made useful suggestions designed to increase the drive of the narration and wrestled with footnotes. My publishers, led by Sinead Moloney, were helpful and supportive throughout. In 2014, I had co-authored *Magna Carta Uncovered* with Igor Judge, the former Lord Chief Justice, who has kindly provided a foreword. All errors that appear in this work are mine and none of the above bear any responsibility for them.

I hope readers find as much pleasure in learning more about an astonishing set of men and women as I felt in writing about them.

Contents

Timeline

This Timeline gathers together some of the principal events referred to in the text. As the narrative is written around individual lives, rather than a simple chronological account of the development of the United States, there are inevitable leaps between dates.

1496	John Cabot discovers Newfoundland
1579	Richard Hakluyt senr writes Notes on Colonisation
1575	Walter Raleigh joins Middle Temple
1584	Walter Raleigh granted patent to discover remote places
1587–90	Raleigh's attempts to create settlement in Virginia fail
1588	Defeat of the Armada
1589	Richard Hakluyt jnr publishes an account of English discoveries
1602	Bartholomew Gosnold discovers Cape Cod
1606	First Charter granted to the Virginia Company
1607	English settlers land at Jamestown, Virginia
1609	Second Virginia Charter
1612	Third Virginia Charter
1618	Instructions on behalf of the Virginia Company for the establishment of a representative assembly in Virginia
1620	Pilgrim Fathers settle near Cape Cod
1632	Charles I grants Cecil Calvert Maryland, where a haven for Catholics is established
1638	An Act for the Liberties of the People of Maryland, adopts part of Magna Carta and includes some religious toleration
1641	Body of Liberties approved by the General Court of Massachusetts, partly based on Magna Carta
1681	Charles II grants Pennsylvania to William Penn. He establishes religious toleration there
1682	Pennsylvania Frame of Government adopted
1761	James Otis jnr argues validity of general writs of assistance in the Boston Admiralty Court
1762	Otis asserts that the inhabitants of the American colonies cannot be taxed directly by the British Parliament. as they are not represented in it
1765	British Parliament passes Stamp Act taxing documents; colonists meet in Stamp Act Congress in New York and draw up Declaration of Rights and Grievances
1765	First volume of Blackstone's Commentaries on the Laws of England published

1766	Stamp Act repealed, but Declaratory Act passed stating the right of the British Parliament to tax the colonies
1767	Revenue Act places tax on importation of items into the colonies, including tea
1767	First of Letters from a Farmer in Pennsylvania, written by John Dickinson, appears in the press urging boycott on importation of British goods
1768	Sugar Act imposes duty on sugar imported into the colonies
1773	Tea Act allows the East India Company to sell tea directly to the colonies where their importation is taxed
1773	Boston Tea Party where patriots destroy imported tea
1774	First Continental Congress meets in Philadelphia and agrees further boycott of British goods
1775	First shots fired at Lexington and Concord in April. Washington given command of Continental Army. Battle of Bunker Hill outside Boston. Second Continental Congress meets in Philadelphia in May and sends an Olive Branch Petition to George III, who in August declares the colonies in rebellion
1776	British quit Boston, but defeat Continental Army in Battle of Brooklyn Heights and take New York. In July former Colonies issue Declaration of Independence. British start military campaign against southern states
1777	Articles of Confederation agreed between the now independent colonies
1780	Georgia falls to British
1781	Charleston, South Carolina falls to British, but then English General, Lord Cornwallis, defeated and surrenders at Yorktown
1782	British evacuate Charleston. The Americans have won the war
1787	Constitutional Convention agrees Constitution of the United States to replace the Articles of Confederation
1788	By June sufficient States have ratified for the Constitution to come into effect
1789	Washington becomes first President of the United States
1791	American Bill of Rights ratified. Hamilton becomes first Secretary to the Treasury and creates National Bank
1793	Treaty of Paris agrees peace between Britain and the United States
1795	Hamilton resigns
1797	Adams President
1800	John Marshall becomes Chief Justice of the Supreme Court
1801	Jefferson President
1803	*Marbury v Madison* decided
1804	Hamilton dies in a duel with Aaron Burr
1835	Marshall dies
1860	Lincoln elected President. December 1860–March 1861 the southern states secede from the Union and adopt the Confederate Constitution

1861	Fort Sumpter off Charleston falls to the Confederates and the Civil war has begun
1863	Battle of Gettysburg causes huge casualties on both sides and Lincoln makes the Gettysburg Address
1864	Atlanta, Georgia falls to the Union
1865	Confederate General, Robert E Lee, surrenders with large southern army. Lincoln sworn in for second term as President, but is assassinated a few days later. In December, Thirteenth Amendment abolishing slavery ratified
1866	Fourteenth Amendment ratified guaranteeing equal treatment under the law to all regardless of race
1902	Oliver Wendell Holmes junior appointed Justice of the Supreme Court
1913	Woodrow Wilson President
1914	Britain and Germany at war
1916	Louis Brandeis appointed Justice of the Supreme Court
1917	United States declares war on Germany
1918	Wilson enumerates his Fourteen Points for a lasting peace
1919	Versailles Peace Treaty. In November Congress refuses to ratify it. *Schenck v US* decided
1920	League of Nations established
1924	*Ziang Sung Wan v US* decided
1927	Buck v US decided
1954	Earl Warren appointed Chief Justice; *Brown v Topeka* decided *Roe v Wade* decided
1972	Richard Nixon elected President for a second term
1973	Watergate burglars stand trial. Archibald Cox appointed Special Prosecutor of alleged Watergate conspiracy
1974	Supreme Court rule that President must disclose tapes of conversations with aides. Nixon resigns
1981	Sandra O'Connor appointed Justice of the Supreme Court
1993	Ruth Bader Ginsburg appointed Justice of the Supreme Court
2009	Barack Obama President

1

Prologue: Walter Raleigh

In 1658 a ship left the Temple stairs on the River Thames bound for the Americas. The passengers were all lawyers. Sad to say, before they reached their destination, they had resorted to cannibalism. Curiously the ship's stores had not yet run out. This proved a model for litigation in the New World.

THE SPEAKER WAS Raymond Seitz, United States Ambassador to Britain, addressing an audience of members of the Middle Temple in 1992. From the fourteenth century, trial lawyers in England have trained in the four Inns of Court in London—Inner Temple, Middle Temple, Lincoln's and Gray's Inns. Each Inn tended to draw its members from particular areas and in the case of the Middle Temple this was the west of England. In 1575, at the age of 21, a young man from Devon joined the Inn. He was called Walter Raleigh and his legacy is the United States of America. Largely under Raleigh's influence this college of lawyers was to become a hub of western exploration.

Walter appears to have lived in the Middle Temple for a time. In 1576 he wrote a poem commending *The Steele Glass* by George Gascoigne and signed himself Walter Rawely of the Middle Temple. A practising barrister in neighbouring chambers, called Richard Hakluyt, had already developed a keen interest in exploration; he and his nephew, Richard junior, became the chief advocates of a British empire in America. Raleigh already had a family connection with the Inn.[1] Through his mother, he was half brother to the Gilberts—a well known family of Devonian seafarers. Adrian Gilbert had joined and lived in the Middle Temple from 1562 to 1566. In 1576 Adrian's brother, Humphrey, published a pamphlet advocating a search for a new passage to China[2] and in June 1578 he was granted a patent by Queen Elizabeth to discover remote and heathen lands. Four months later, a fleet of 11 vessels, one captained by Raleigh, set sail westwards. The voyage ended in failure, but Walter's taste for discovery was whetted. He established a settlement on an island off the east coast of America, which he named Virginia after the virgin queen, but sadly that initial attempt failed.

Raleigh had been a favourite of Elizabeth I, but fell from favour when James I became King of England in 1603; he was convicted of high treason and sentenced to death by a fellow member of Middle Temple, Lord Chief Justice Popham. The sentence was not immediately carried out and Raleigh was imprisoned in the

---

[1] See Middle Temple Admission Registers Vol 1.
[2] *Discourse of a discoverie for a new passage to Cataia* (London, Scolar Press, 1576).

Tower of London. Popham took advantage of Raleigh's absence to take over his project of American settlement—an early example of judicial confiscation. Under his supervision the Virginia Company took shape.

Establishing a new colony necessarily involves legal organisation. Popham practised law all his life. By the end of the sixteenth century, however, the Inns had become a social centre for ambitious young men, many of whom, like Raleigh, had no intention of practising as lawyers. Yet so much of the law as they had imbibed served to differentiate the new British Empire from the empires of Spain and Portugal. Claims to overseas territories were based on discovery, but this had to be regularised—should it be a private or public enterprise and who owned what was discovered? Government of a distant colony (America was at least six weeks' sea-voyage away from England) required definition. The Spanish and Portuguese conquered in the name of the King and ruled through Viceroys (literally substitute kings, Spain had two in South America). The English took and claimed in the name of the Queen, but the vehicle for settlement was initially a group of individuals and then a company. The Virginia Company was a joint stock company in which all could invest, an important stage in the development of capitalism. Given the distance between the mother country and colony, the new colonies developed a measure of autonomy and it was another member of Middle Temple, Edwyn Sandys, who drafted the first democratic constitution for Virginia. Sadly the colony proved less profitable than anticipated and 16 years after its inception it failed; the Crown then took direct control, but the Virginia Assembly survived.

From the seventeenth century onwards, 13 separate colonies were established on the east coast of America,[3] colonisation being energised principally by members of minority religious communities in England seeking freedom of worship. Men who had trained in the Inns of Court drafted constitutions for these new colonies, in some instances specifically adopting Magna Carta, and ensured that the English common law ran there. The first fresh charter of liberties in the New World was drawn up by Nicholas Ward, a member of Lincoln's Inn.

The British government treated the new colonies with benign neglect, leaving local assemblies to pay for local government by local taxation. The Seven Years War in the mid-eighteenth century, which resulted in the defeat of the French and to all intents an end to their colonial ambitions in America, left the British government seriously in debt. The attempt of the British parliament to recover some of the cost of the war by directly taxing the colonists, led the latter to claim the privileges set out in the English Bill of Rights in 1689—that they could not be taxed without representation in the English parliament. It was the British government's rejection of this claim that incited revolution. American lawyers were in the van of opposition to the British government, by now many of them home-grown; others, however, continued to train in the English Inns of Court and ironically, when ties were severed with England, five members of the

---

[3] Delaware only declared itself an entity after the Declaration of Independence—below Ch 12.

Middle Temple signed the Declaration of Independence and seven the United States Constitution.

Looking at these revolutionaries as a group provides some interesting insights. Many of them were surprisingly young. The Revolution gave them a huge opportunity for social advancement—a significant number were born in log cabins in frontier territory. It also made them international super-stars—who has not heard of John Adams or Thomas Jefferson? But for the struggle for independence, they would have ended up as successful, but swiftly forgotten, provincial lawyers dabbling in local politics. Their initial aim was not independence, but to secure for themselves the rights which Englishmen in England enjoyed. They were strongly influenced by the publication of a *Commentary on the Laws of England*, written by William Blackstone, the first Professor of English Law at Oxford University, and published in America just a few years before independence. They were advocates of the benefits of English common law and the British Constitution and tried to replicate it (without a king) when they drafted their own constitution. They were also clearly affected by the ideas of the eighteenth century European Enlightenment, particularly the application of reason to solving human problems. Many of them were taught in America by Scots, who brought with them the enlightened views adopted in Edinburgh by the likes of Hume. Most of the British colonies in America were established by religious minorities in England seeking territory abroad, where they could worship freely without persecution from the government. Yet many of these men in the van of American revolution rejected—in some cases privately—traditional religious views in favour of deism or Unitarianism. There were, of course, others who were not practising lawyers, such as Mason and Madison, who played decisive roles in the revolution, but even they, as part of a general education, were well aware of English legal traditions. These were heady times—here was a clean slate upon which the draftsmen of the Declaration of Independence and the Constitution of the United States could attempt the perfect organisation of a new republic. America had a very legal revolution.

There was, however, a problem left unsolved which was to tear the new nation apart—there were African slaves in most states, but preponderantly in the southern ones, farming labour intensive crops. The Declaration of Independence, drafted by Jefferson, declared all men to be born free and equal and consistent with this asserted the evil nature of the slave trade; this assertion was removed at the instigation of the southern states. To the constitution makers unanimity was paramount.

The new Constitution created a federal Supreme Court. In the early nineteenth century, John Marshall was Chief Justice for some 35 years and decisively steered the Constitution towards federal power. The Supreme Court adopted the power to declare acts of Congress and States unconstitutional and also produced opinions which contributed markedly to social change, for instance in the areas of racial segregation and abortion. Particular Justices of the Supreme Court are here selected to demonstrate the workings of the Supreme Court, including the first two women to be appointed.

It took the American Civil war to end slavery. Abraham Lincoln, the President who waged and won that war, practised as a lawyer before and after entering politics. Slavery and its aftermath are themes which run through American history and have still not been resolved. It was to a great extent through the courts that racial and sexual equality were achieved.

People who fled Europe to become citizens of the United States were naturally reluctant to involve themselves in the affairs of Europe. Woodrow Wilson, who became President shortly before the First World War, practised at the bar for a short time, but then became an academic lawyer; he was to lead America out of isolation on to the world stage. He suggested at the Versailles Conference at the end of the First World War that all peoples should be entitled to self determination—a view at odds with the European view that nations were entitled to empire. It took time for Wilson's views to be adopted. The United States has wrestled ever since with its role as putative policeman of the international community.

The constitutional conflict in England in the seventeenth century revolved round the question whether the King could rule as he chose by divine right, or, whether he, like his subjects, was subject to the law. The American Constitution established three separate branches of government—Executive, Legislative and Judicial. In the mid 1970s some members of the Republican Party organised a burglary of the Democratic Party headquarters in the Watergate Building in Washington in order to find out the latter's election tactics. President Nixon was aware of this, as was apparent from tapes made of conversations with his aides. Political pressure forced Nixon's Attorney General to appoint a Special Prosecutor, Archibald Cox, who demanded the tapes. The President claimed executive privilege. In the end he was forced to reveal them and this forced his resignation. The President too was under the law.

History is made by people. Lawyers are people too, though some do their best to hide it. The choice of individual lawyers who contributed to the establishment and continuing development of the United States of America is necessarily personal. No doubt some have been omitted, who should have been included. Although legal definition often appears at the forefront of the argument, other more general influences can be seen. The cry in the mid-eighteenth century of 'no taxation without representation' came from colonists with a growing confidence to transact their own affairs and that confidence grew even stronger after independence, particularly when the United States displaced Britain as the most prosperous nation in the world. Now Presidents find themselves embroiled in international disputes that few could have foreseen. This book traces, through the lives of some of the principal players in the courts and politics, the growth and definition of the modern United States of America. It is a truly amazing story.

2

Maps and Explorers:
Richard Hakluyt

RICHARD HAKLUYT WAS admitted as a student in the Middle Temple in 1555 and thereafter lived and practised as a barrister in his rooms, or chambers, there during the legal terms, returning to his home in Herefordshire in vacation. He had a nephew, also called Richard, born in 1554. His parents died when he was young and Richard senior became his guardian and sent him to Westminster School.[1] In 1589 Richard junior wrote to the Queen's principal secretary, Sir Francis Walsingham:

> I do remember that being a youth and one of Her Majesties scholars at Westminster, that fruitful nurserie, it was my happe to visit the chambers of M Richard Hakluyt my cosin, a Gentleman of the Middle Temple well knowen unto you, at a time when I found lying open upon his boord certeine books of Cosmographie, with an Universal Mappe; he seeing me somewhat curious in the view thereof, began to instruct my ignorance ... from the Mappe he brought me to the Bible and turning to Psalm 107 ... I read that they which go down to the sea in ships and occupy the great water see the works of the Lorde.[2]

Uncle Richard had difficulty storing his universal map. The principal mapmakers at this time were Abraham Ortelius from Antwerp and Gerardus Mercator, also Flemish, but now working in Germany. Shortly after his nephew's visit Richard senior wrote to Ortelius:

> For as much as men usually live in houses which are neither spacious enough nor light enough to place or spread out conveniently a large world map *in rem*, it will be most gratifying to many to have a map thought on the following lines: namely that when spread out to its full extent it is quite fit and suitable for a hall or other spacious place of that kind and also when rolled up at each end on two smooth revolving rods it lies conveniently on a table three or four feet square.

Such a map was never made, for Mercator invented a new way of projecting maps and in 1570 Ortelius published his *Theatrum Orbis Terrarum* (Theatre of the Globe), the first atlas. Later, Richard junior published a copy of a map by Ortelius, corresponded with Mercator and became a friend of his son.[3]

---

[1] See Intro to R Hakluyt jnr, *The Principall Navigations, Voiages and Discoveries of the English Nation,* (London, George Bishop and Ralph Newberie, 1589); (Harmondsworth, Penguin, 1982).

[2] ibid.

[3] See EGR Taylor, *The Original Writings and Correspondence of the two Richard Hakluyts* (London, The Hakluyt Society, 1935) Docs 7 and 26.

From the time he was admitted to the Middle Temple, Richard senior was interested in exploration and particularly in expanding English trade. The Muscovy Company was incorporated during the early 1550s. In 1555, under its patronage, Willoughby and Chancellor sailed round the North Cape hoping to find a north east passage to Asia. Chancellor eventually reached Moscow and established trade links with Russia. Richard senior wrote him guidance on how to seek intelligence.[4] In 1580 he sent similar instructions to Pet and Jackman before they sailed to seek the same passage.[5] In 1579 he wrote notes to Master Hubblestone, a dyer who was travelling to Persia, expressing concern that, whilst England produced the finest quality wool, English merchants did not have the ability to finish it well. He asked Hubblestone to find out how the Persians dyed wool.[6]

In 1578 he wrote *Notes on Colonization*, giving advice on how to choose a site for settlement: 'it behoveth that all humanities and curtesie and much forbearing of revenge to the inland people be used, so shall you have firm amitie with your neighbours, so shall you have their inland commodities'[7]—good advice not heeded by the eventual English colonists. In 1585 (shortly after Raleigh had obtained his patent from the Crown for the exploration and settlement of northern America) Richard senior wrote of *Inducements to the liking of the voyage intended towards Virginia in 40 and 42 degrees of latitude.*[8] The inducements included the planting of the Christian religion among infidels; enlarging the dominions of the Queen; a future market for woollen clothes; the possible discovery of a North West Passage; exports to England of oil, wines, hops, salt and sugar; and giving an opportunity for young men to emigrate and work in gold or silver mines.[9]

In 1570 Richard junior entered Christ Church College, Oxford, and in 1574 obtained his degree of Bachelor of Arts. According to his own account,[10] he spent a good deal of his time at Oxford collecting information about English exploration and, after obtaining his degree, he lectured in Oxford on geography. In 1578 he was ordained as a priest. From 1583 to 1588 he served as chaplain to the English ambassador to France. There he found that other nations extolled their discoveries, but 'the English of all others for their sluggish security and continual neglect of the like attempts are exceedingly condemned.'[11] He continued to collect accounts of voyages by English sea captains, who were 'stirrers abroad and searchers of the remote part of the world.'[12]

---

[4] ibid, Doc 20.

[5] ibid, Doc 25.

[6] ibid, Doc 23 and see Doc 36 *Notes on the Levant Trade.*

[7] ibid, Doc 18.

[8] ibid, Doc 47.

[9] It was not published until much later, in J Brereton, *A Briefe and True Relation of the Discouerie of the North Part of Virginia* (London, Eliot's Court Press, 1602).

[10] See Preface to *Principall Navigations* above n 1.

[11] ibid.

[12] ibid.

On 25 March 1584, Queen Elizabeth granted Raleigh a patent to discover, search and find out remote and heathen places. In response to optimistic reports from those who, under Raleigh's direction, first tried to settle in America, Richard junior published *A discourse concerning the great necessities and manifold commodyties that are like to growe to this Realme of England by the Westerne discoveries lately attempted, written ... at the request of Mr Walter Raleigh.* It amplified many of the arguments used by his uncle in favour of settling in North America and gave detailed instructions on how to fit out an expedition. On 5 October 1585 he was summoned to present his discourse to the Queen.[13] He received his reward, being made a canon of Bristol Cathedral (sometimes referred to as a prebendary on account of the prebend or income he received as canon). Although favouring the establishment of a colony, the Queen, true to character, offered no financial support. Raleigh was knighted in 1586. Richard junior's appointment to Bristol was probably deliberate because of its connection with trade to the west. In any event it gave him contact with merchants that would prove useful when the Virginia Company was established. An expedition attempted to settle on Roanoke Island, off what is now the coast of North Carolina; Ralph Lane was appointed governor and sent a report extolling the colony to Richard senior in September 1585.[14] Unfortunately, it was wildly overoptimistic and eventually, in 1586, the settlers who survived were rescued by Sir Francis Drake and returned to England arriving at Portsmouth on 22 July. Four days after landing, Drake dined in the Middle Temple, possibly to report to Raleigh.

1588 brought the defeat of the Armada. In 1589, no doubt to exploit the mood of national confidence, Richard junior published the first edition of his *Principal Navigations and Voyages and Discoveries of the English Nation made by Sea or over Land,* addressed to Francis Walsingham. It collected together accounts, in the main by others, of such voyages in an attempt to assert England's right to colonise America. The following year Richard junior was made rector of Wetheringsett in Suffolk. It was no coincidence that those recruited for later expeditions were drawn mainly from the west country and East Anglia.

The Hakluyts were concerned to provide a legal justification for England's claim to settle in America. Chapter 18 of Richard junior's *Discourse on Western Planting* was headed 'that the Queen of England's title to all the west Indies or at least as moche as is from Florida to the Circle articke is more lawful and righte then the Spaniardes or any other Christian Prince.' His argument placed principal reliance on John Cabot's discovery of and claim to Newfoundland in 1497. It was a considerable step to assert on this basis, as he did, title to the greater part of the north eastern coast of North America. To understand why it was made, it is necessary briefly to trace the history of European colonisation. From 1418, the Portuguese gradually explored the west coast of Africa and were granted papal permission to invade, search out, capture, vanquish and

---

[13] See introduction to Taylor n 3 above.
[14] R Hakluyt Jnr n 1 above.

subdue all Saracens and pagans whatsoever and to appropriate the kingdoms or other territories so seized to their own use.[15] The justification for this was set out in the preamble to the Bull *Romanus Pontifex* issued by Pope Nicholas V in January 1455:

> [W]e bestow suitable favours and special graces on those Catholic kings and princes, who like athletes and intrepid champions of the Christian faith … not only restrain the savage excesses of the Saracens and of other infidels, enemies of the Christian name, but also for the defence and increase of the faith vanquish them and their kingdoms and habitation, though situated in the remotest parts unknown to us and subject them to their own temporal dominion.[16]

In other words this was a Christian *jihad*.

When competition arose between the Portuguese and Spanish as to which nation should receive these special favours, Ferdinand and Isabella of Spain persuaded Pope Alexander VI on 4 May 1493 to issue the Bull *Inter Caetera*, dividing the right to annexation of non-Christian territory between the two nations, but giving favour to Spain. The King of Portugal protested at this papal incursion. In the end, however, he entered into the treaty of Tordesillas with Spain in the summer of 1494, accepting the right of annexation by discovery and drawing a line demarcating the spheres of interest of the two kingdoms to a position 370 leagues to the west of the Azores. All lands discovered or to be discovered to the west of this line should belong to Spain and those to the east to Portugal. Having established a fort in Florida in 1565, the Spanish claimed the whole of the east coast of North America.

The English came late to the party. In 1496, John Cabot, a Venetian who had tried but failed to gain sponsorship from the Spanish and Portuguese for a voyage of discovery to the west, came to London. On 5 March 1496 Henry VII by letters patent granted him and his three sons authority to sail 'under our banners and ensigns … to finde whatsoever isles, countries, regions or provinces of the heathen and infidels … which before this time have been unknowen to all Christians.' Once found such territories could be occupied by the Cabots as feudal vassals of the English Crown. They made landfall in and named Newfoundland.

In his *Discourse on Western Planting*[17] Richard junior claimed that America had been discovered by Madock ap Owen Guyneth, Prince of North Wales, in 1170. He went on to assert that Columbus had sought the support of King Henry VII of England; it was only when his brother was captured by pirates on his way back from England that he turned to the Spanish for backing. Most important, however, was his claim that John Cabot's son had recounted how his father had reconnoitred the eastern seaboard from 68 degrees north (which crosses modern Canada) south to Florida. Hakluyt dated this as occurring in

---

[15] See Bull *Romanus Pontifex* January 8 1455 found in FG Davenport (ed), *European Treaties bearing on the History of the United States and its Dependencies to 1648* (Washington, Carnegie Institute of Washington, 1917) 13–26.

[16] ibid.

[17] Ch 18.

1496. Whilst Columbus had arrived in the Bahamas in 1492 he had not reached the mainland of north America until 1498, so Richard argued that Cabot had discovered the coast of north America down to Florida for the English Crown, 'if to have a right to a countrie it sufficeth to have first seene and discovered the same.'[18] It does appear true that Columbus did not reach the mainland of north America until after Cabot's landing in Newfoundland (in itself an island off the coast of north America), but a voyage by the latter along the whole eastern seaboard seems unlikely, given that he returned to England for lack of supplies. There is no other evidence to confirm it.

If argument 'A' failed to convince, Richard produced argument 'B' in *an answer to the Bull of Donation of all the west Indies granted to the kings of Spain by Alexander VI.*[19] He argued that no Pope had lawful authority to make any donation of territory. Christ said his kingdom was not of this world. 'Why then doth the Pope that would be Christes servaunte take upon him the devision of so many kingdoms of the worlde?'

The failure of the Roanoke settlement demonstrated that Raleigh had grossly underestimated the extent of the challenge presented by overseas settlement. Hostility from native inhabitants, difficulty in growing crops in unaccustomed soil, diseases caught from the natives and difficulty in keeping the colony supplied, all contributed to the failure. This was to prove a recurring theme. Raleigh's interest was principally in finding precious metals, such as the Spaniards had found in what is now South America. This remained an objective of those who persisted in the attempt to colonise the New World. It was satirised by Jonson, Chapman and Marston in *Eastwood Hoe* published in 1605. Captain Seagull explains what is to be found in Virginia:

> [G]old is more plentiful there than copper is with us; and for as much red copper as I can bring, I'll have thrice the weight in gold. Why, man, all their chamber pots are pure gold ... and for rubies and diamonds, they go forth on holidays and gather'em by the seas.[20]

The Hakluyts certainly did not ignore the possibility of such riches, but their writings demonstrate a more general patriotic approach. Richard senior, in particular, was interested in extending English trade. Both saw colonies as a cure for unemployment in England and a way of introducing criminals to an industrious life.

Raleigh did not give up on the idea of settlement. Richard Hakluyt senior had recommended that the first settlers should take an artist with them to record what was found. John White was chosen and he painted watercolours of Roanoke and particularly of the native Americans. In 1587, Raleigh organised a second attempt to establish a settlement, naming John White as governor with 12 named assistants to help administer it. Although the site intended for

---

[18] ibid.
[19] Ch 19 of a *Discourse on Planting*.
[20] George Chapman, Ben Jonson, John Marston, *Eastward Hoe* (London, William Aspley, 1605) Act 3 Sc 3; see GA Wilkes (ed), *Complete Plays of Ben Jonson* (Oxford, Oxford University Press, 1951).

settlement was in Chesapeake Bay, the colony in fact established itself on Roanoke. Once again the settlement got into difficulties and at the end of the year White returned to England in search of supplies and further settlers. Unfortunately the Armada intervened and he could not return until 1590, to find no trace of the settlement or settlers.

It was now clear that a more sophisticated approach to colonisation was required. Richard Hakluyt senior died in 1591, but his nephew soon found a new ally amongst the students in the Middle Temple, a near neighbour from Suffolk called Bartholomew Gosnold. The two men became friends and Richard's enthusiasm for exploration seems to have rubbed off on Bartholomew. He gained a place on the Earl of Essex's expedition to the Azores in 1597 and thereafter took part in privateering against the Spanish, gaining a small fortune. In 1602 he received financial backing from the Earl of Southampton for an expedition to reconnoitre and possibly settle on the east coast of America. He sailed from Falmouth in the *Concord* with a complement of 32, including Raleigh's half brother Bartholomew Gilbert. The voyage was intended to leave 20 settlers on American soil, including Gosnold. It arrived initially off the coast of what is now Maine and then explored southwards, naming Cape Cod and Martha's Vineyard (after Gosnold's daughter) on the way. Gilbert was supposed to have provided stores sufficient for settlers to overwinter, but Gosnold found them inadequate and the ship and intended settlers returned to England.

The following year Queen Elizabeth died. Up to the end of her reign, Richard Hakluyt junior had continued to promote overseas exploration. With the accession in 1603 of James I, however, Hakluyt's old ally Walter Raleigh fell out of favour. He was charged with conspiring to place Lady Arabella Stuart on the throne instead of James, and this led to his conviction for treason and subsequent death sentence. He was sent to the Tower and remained there for 13 years, before being released to mount an expedition to discover El Dorado, famed city of Gold, in Guyana. He failed, broke his undertaking not to get involved in action with the Spanish and on his return was executed in 1618.

3

The Virginia Company:
John Popham

B Y 1603 **JOHN** Popham had been Lord Chief Justice of England and Wales
for 20 years.[1] He presided over the trial of the Earl of Essex in 1601 and
one of those who gave evidence against the Earl was a fellow conspira-
tor called Sir Ferdinando Gorges. Gorges had been responsible for fortifying
Plymouth, had erected the fort there and been appointed its governor. He joined
the Essex rebellion and was one of those who, when it was clear there was no
popular support, sought safety in Essex House off the Strand. The Queen sent
Popham to negotiate with them, but they took him hostage. It was Gorges who
freed him, probably hoping to save his own skin. The link between the two men
was to prove vital to western exploration. Gorges did avoid trial, though he was
stripped of his governorship of the fort. On his accession, King James restored
him to it.

Popham was born around 1531 in the English west country in Bridgwater,
Somerset. In 1547 he went to Balliol College, Oxford, and in 1551 was admitted as a student in the Middle Temple and called to the bar in 1557. In 1571
he became both Recorder of Bristol and Member of Parliament for that city.
His daughter, Penelope, married Thomas Hannam, another Middle Templar,
who eventually succeeded Popham as Recorder of Bristol and played a part in
the Virginia Company. Another daughter, Elizabeth, married Richard Champernowne, through whom she became related to Adrian and Humphrey Gilbert and
Walter Raleigh. In 1578 Popham was elevated to the rank of Serjeant at Law
(senior counsel) and in 1579 was appointed Solicitor General. In 1581 he was
Treasurer (head) of the Middle Temple and in the same year became Speaker
of the House of Commons. In 1592 he was appointed Lord Chief Justice of
the Queen's Bench. Professor CM Andrews in his *Colonial Period of American
History* says that Popham

> was largely, if not entirely responsible for the idea of a public plantation as against
> a private venture and had lent the weight of his great influence at Whitehall to the
> securing of the patent, of which he was doubtless the chief author.[2]

---

[1] DW Rice, *The Life and Achievements of Sir John Popham* (NJ, Fairleigh Dickinson University
Press, 2005).
[2] CM Andrews, *Colonial Period of American History* 4 vols (New Haven, Yale University Press,
1934–38) 89.

Some of Popham's motivation was revealed in a letter written in March 1606 by Sir Walter Cope, a member of the royal court, to the King's chief minister, Sir Robert Cecil:

> My Lord Chief Justice, foreseeing in his experience of his place the infinite number of cashired captains and soldiers, poor artisans that would and cannot work and of idle vagrants that may and will not work, whose increase threatens the State, is affectionately bent to the plantation of Virginia in which he has already great pains and means to disburse £500 per annum for 5 years, if the action prosper. He desires for his better expedition two lines from you in particular, or from the herald general, by virtue whereof he may cull the undertakers, gentleman merchants, unto him.[3]

The need for governmental approval was revealed by Popham's first approach to the merchants of the west country. At first the merchants of Bristol were unwilling to take part, unless the King joined the charge; those of Exeter declined to fund the expedition, though those of Plymouth agreed to support it.[4]

The form of the Charter, when it was granted, represented a significant advance on former licences. Up to 1606 grants for exploration were made by letters patent. The Crown had various methods of evidencing its orders. Letters close were for the information of the recipient only; letters patent were open to the general public, as were the more formal charters. The fact that the promoters of the Virginia Company were granted a Charter indicates the importance attached to the grant.

In issuing patents for discovery neither Henry VII nor Elizabeth I offered any financial support, indeed they claimed one fifth of any gold or silver ore recovered by the explorers. Humphrey Gilbert's patent of 1578 and Raleigh's of 1584 were similar in form. Each was addressed to them personally and licensed them to occupy any land not inhabited by Christian people (in other words not occupied by the Spanish); they could repel any others who tried to settle in areas they claimed. They could grant ownership of land in the occupied territories to whomsoever they chose and could make and enforce laws for the colony. Of particular significance for the development of the colonies was the undertaking that settlers and anyone born in a colony had all the rights and privileges of those born in England.

Why did the explorers feel the need to seek and receive such grants? Why not simply discover and occupy new lands and declare themselves rulers? The granting of a royal charter would encourage investment, even if the Crown did not underwrite the expedition. Moreover the feudal system of landholding placed an obligation on the lord to protect his vassal. Cabot's grant expressly referred to him as holding the territory as a vassal of the King. Explorers may have hoped to receive some naval protection from the Crown. Most important from the explorers' viewpoint, however, was the grant of a monopoly to exploit what they discovered. In Tudor times the Crown raised money by granting monopolies to individuals to trade in a particular commodity in return for payment. These

---

[3] Cited in Rice above n 1, 20 and 236.
[4] RA Preston *Gorges of Plymouth Port* (Toronto, University of Toronto Press, 1953).

patents of discovery were in effect granting monopolies to discover and appropriate land overseas, in return for a share in the spoils. This obviously gave the patent holder a huge advantage if the settlement were successful.

After the failure of the Roanoke settlement it was obvious that a patent granting a monopoly to an individual was unlikely to work. The model of a group of merchants banding together and being granted a monopoly of trade with a certain area had already been established.[5] King Henry IV had granted a charter to English merchants in the low countries trading with their English counterparts, giving them financial privileges. In 1505 Henry VII granted a charter to the Merchant Adventurers of London, providing for a company regulated by a governor and 24 assistants. The Adventurers were given a monopoly on the export of cloth. Admission to the company was either by paternity, apprenticeship, purchase or occasionally by gift. By 1603 there were some 200 members. Adventurers were not seeking to settle land (other perhaps than establishing a trading post), but usually ventured their capital on an individual voyage or transaction. In 1555 the charter granted to the Muscovy Company gave it a monopoly of trade with what then amounted to Russia. It is credited with being the first joint stock company, that is members contributed in varying degrees to the company and received profits on a pro rata basis.[6] The Levant Company was given a monopoly of trade with the Middle East in 1580. In 1600 the East India Company (strictly the Governor and Company of Merchants of London trading into the East Indies) was granted a monopoly of trade with Asia.[7] All these were trading rather than settling enterprises.

The charters granted to these companies offered precedents upon which lawyers drafting the Virginia Charter could rely, but now permanent settlement was contemplated by those willing to venture their capital. There was recent experience in the plantations of Ireland.[8] In 1581, when he was Solicitor General, John Popham had drawn up a Charter for the Corporation of Dublin.[9] 'Plantation' came to mean not merely planting trees, but also people to live in a particular area. Dublin became the focal point for organising plantations in Munster. Following the defeat of the Desmond Rebellion, captured lands were allocated to English landlords, who undertook to plant settlers there. John Popham himself sent 70 tenants there. His nephew, George, became the principal administrator of the scheme and also an undertaker, as did Raleigh.[10] The scheme was a failure, both in the short and long term—continued violence from the indigenous Irish made it difficult to attract settlers. George Popham gave up his undertaking

---

[5] See E Lipson, *The Economic History of England—The Age of Mercantilism* (London, Adam and Charles Black, 1959).

[6] See TS Willan, *The Early History of the Russia Company* (Manchester, Manchester University Press, 1968).

[7] See R Brenner, *Merchants and Revolution: Commercial Change, Political Conflict and London's Overseas Traders, 1550–1563* (NJ, Princeton University Press, 1993).

[8] See NP Canny, *Making Ireland British* (Oxford, Oxford University Press, 2001); M Maccarthy-Morough, *The Munster Plantation—English Migration to Southern Ireland 1583–1641* (Oxford, Oxford University Press, 1986).

[9] See Rice above n 1, 73.

[10] ibid, 76 and for the identity of George Popham see ibid, 105.

in 1587, having lost £1200. Nevertheless the seed of an idea was sown, which might prove more profitable in a region currently inhabited by less sophisticated natives.

The First Charter of Virginia was granted by James I on 10 April 1606 and named persons joining in two separate companies to establish a plantation and habitation along the coasts of America. The named members of the first company were Sir Thomas Gates and Sir George Somers, Richard Hakluyt and Edward Maria Wingfield. They were described as '[A]dventurers of and for our cittie of London and all suche others as are or shalbe joined unto them of that Colonie'. Thomas Gates was a west countryman who was knighted for his service in the raid on Cadiz which had 'singed the King of Spain's beard', and had been a lieutenant under Drake's command when the first Roanoke settlers were rescued. Somers was a contemporary of Walter Raleigh, from Dorset in the west country; he had commanded a number of prestigious vessels in the Royal Navy and was to become Admiral of the Virginia Company. Although Wingfield came from the Midlands, his uncle Jacques had an estate near Wetheringsett, where Richard Hakluyt was vicar. His uncle was also Constable of Dublin Castle and one of the undertakers of the Munster settlements; Edward visited Ireland with him. The second Company, described as adventurers of Bristol, Exeter and Plymouth, named in the Charter as members Thomas Hannam, Raleigh Gilbert, William Parker and George Popham. William Parker was a privateer who had gone with Drake to Cadiz and later become Mayor of Plymouth. Raleigh Gilbert was Walter's nephew.

Sites intended for settlement on the east coast of America were targeted. The London Company was to plant between 34 and 40 degrees of latitude and the West Country Company between 38 and 45 degrees. Although the areas stated overlapped, the two settlements were to be at least 100 miles apart. Each company was given the right to exploit the territory for 50 leagues each way along the coast from the first settlement. The 34th parallel crosses the American coast roughly on the boundary between North and South Carolina, near the town of Wilmington, and the 45th crosses roughly on the modern border between the United States and Canada. Thus the areas to be planted could be chosen along most of the eastern seaboard of America, but at a safe distance from Spanish settlements in Florida.

Most important, the settlements were to be established and administered by the companies, subject to a payment of a fifth of the value of gold and silver and a fifteenth part of the value of copper recovered in the colonies to the Crown. Once again there was no provision for the government to supply any capital. The Charter set out how the companies should be organised. There was to be a Council in England and separate Councils in each of the colonies. Each Council should have 13 members. The London Council was to be called the Council of Virginia and its members were to be appointed by the Crown and have 'the superior Managing and Direction, only of and for all Matters that shall or may concern the Government, as well of the said several Colonies'. The local Councils were to 'govern and order all Matters and Causes, which shall arise, grow or happen to or within the same several Colonies, according to such Laws,

Ordinances and instructions as shall be ... given and signed with our Hand ... and pass under the Privy Seal of our Realm'. These provisions were obviously intended in the first place to create an organisation separate from the State, but subject to a measure of control by the government. Although the company had in effect a monopoly over settlement and any profits gained from it, this monopoly was in the hands of a group rather than an individual. Second, they were designed to give a measure of local autonomy. The weakness was that that autonomy was partial.

The status of landholding was changed. The local councils were given power to assign land to individuals 'to be holden of Us, our heirs and Successors as of our Manor in East Greenwich in the County of Kent in free and common socage only'. Socage was a form of feudal landholding, where the service was not military, but agricultural. With time the feudal system weakened and the advantage of socage holding was that land could be more easily inherited and assigned by a simple money payment. The reference to East Greenwich was presumably a reference to precedent, since there might be local variations of socage holding. Socage holding was gradually replaced by fee simple, which curiously was the term used in Raleigh's Charter.

The whole of the Charter indicates the hand of a lawyer. It is a very clearly thought out document. There is no direct evidence as to who actually drafted it, but Sir John Popham was clearly behind the whole venture. He was Solicitor General when Raleigh was granted his patent and would almost certainly have had some knowledge of that. Of those named in the Charter as members of the Bristol Company, George was his nephew, Hannam his son in law, and he himself was connected to Raleigh Gilbert by the marriage of his daughter into the Champernowne family. The Bristol Company's first expedition to settle (as it turned out in what is modern Maine) was led by George Popham and it became known initially as the Popham Colony. By virtue of his presence and authority as Lord Chief Justice in London, John would also be uniquely placed to encourage investment by the City merchants and his west country connections would have offered a similar opportunity. He must at least have had oversight of the drafting.

In October of 1606 the Bristol Company sent two vessels to explore the more northerly coast of America. In the previous year a Captain Weymouth returned to Plymouth, after reconnoitring the coast of what is now Maine, with five native Americans. He gave three to Sir Ferdinando Gorges.[11] It was Gorges, who, on behalf of the Bristol Company, now organised the funding and despatch of a further boat under the command of Challoner. Unfortunately this boat was captured by the Spanish, though Challoner eventually returned to England. Ferdinando later wrote a *Brief Relation of the Discovery and Plantation of New England* in which he described what happened next:

> It pleased the noble lord chief justice, Sir John Popham knight to send out another ship, wherein Captain Thomas Haman [Hannam] went commander and Martine Prinne of

[11] See Preston above n 4, 138.

Bristowe with all necessary supplies. Having found the coasts, havens and harbours answerable to our desires, they returned. Upon which relation the lord chief justice and we all waxed so confident of the business that the year following every man of any worth formerly interested in it was willing to join in the charge for sending over a competent number of people to lay ground for a hopeful plantation. Hereupon, Captain Popham, Captain Rawley Gilbert and others went away with two ships and a hundred landmen, ordnance and other provisions necessary for their sustenance and defence.[12]

One of the tasks allotted to the settlers in this new colony was to seek a North West passage to China.[13] George Popham was chosen as President and remained there whilst others returned to England. The settlers suffered a harsh winter. In February 1607 John Popham died and later in that year George also died. These two events so discouraged the settlers that, when a supply ship arrived in 1608, they decided to return to England. Maine, however, was to feature in the next wave of colonisation.

Meanwhile, by the end of 1606 the London Company had despatched three vessels for Virginia, one of them captained by Gosnold, who was destined to be the first Englishman to die in America. After taking a rather circuitous route they made landfall in America on 26 April 1607; shortly after Edward Wingfield, who was chosen as the first President of the Council in Virginia, picked the site he named Jamestown as the place to set up a fort. The members of the local Council fell out among themselves, deposed Wingfield and in 1608 sent him back to London on the pretext that he was an atheist. The London Council had difficulty securing the attendance of sufficient Councillors at their meetings and it was plain that it was not easy controlling the settlement at a distance. This led the King on 23 May 1609 to issue a new Charter annulling the earlier one.

The 1609 Charter recites that adventurers and planters of the First Colony had already engaged themselves in furthering the business of the plantation and now were humble suitors for a new charter. A grant of the Charter was made to some 650 of them. Some, such as John Smith and Edward Wingfield, had travelled to and settled in Virginia. The bulk, however, seem to be those who had ventured their money to back the Colony. They included members of the aristocracy, knights, merchants and livery companies of the City of London. The length of the list demonstrates a widespread support for the scheme. The title of the new company was to be the 'Tresorer and Companie of Adventurers and Planters of the City of London for the First Collonie in Virginia' and it was to operate as one body or community with one common seal. The area of land to be under the control of the Company was enlarged. Cape Comfort is at the tip of the Virginia Peninsula, bounded by the York and James rivers where they flow into Chesapeake Bay. It had originally been the boundary of the colony, but now that was extended along the coast 200 north and south. Nothing was said of the extent inland, which later led the State of Virginia to claim large tracts of the hinterland.

---

[12] Quoted in JP Baxter, *Sir Ferdinando Gorges and His Province of Maine* (Maine, 1923).
[13] Rice above n 1, 247.

Now there was to be one Council in London and just over 40 were named as members, headed by the Earls of Southampton, Pembroke, Lincoln and Exeter and including the Mayor of London and a prominent city merchant with experience in the East India Company, Sir Thomas Smyth, who was named as the first Treasurer. Future membership of the Council was now to be determined by a majority of the Council assembled, though members had to be presented to one of the high officers of state to swear an oath as a counsellor of the King. The Council was given specific power to appoint governors of the Colony. Anyone inhabiting the Colony and anyone born there were to enjoy all the liberties of an Englishman. In order to exclude Roman Catholics, however, they were obliged to swear the oath of Supremacy.

The new company got off to a bad start when the first Governor, Sir Thomas Gates, was shipwrecked on his way to Virginia and did not arrive until the following year.[14] The settlers suffered from starvation and by the summer of 1610 were about to abandon the colony, when he appeared with fresh reinforcements. By this time it appeared that the colony was a bad investment. Although the company had been granted the right to mine, no precious metals had been found. Although tobacco was grown, its importance as an export had not been properly realised. The settlers were dying. In the autumn of 1610 a new subscription was sought, but only half taken up.[15] By 1612 the adventurers were complaining that only the name of God was more frequently profaned in the streets and markets of London than the name of the Virginia Company.

In 1612 the King granted another new charter. In an attempt to encourage further investors, the power to elect officers and admit new members was transferred from the Council to an Assembly of the whole company. The same assembly was given power to pass laws for the company, creating a measure of democracy within the company in London. In order to alleviate the financial difficulties of the company, it was authorised to hold a lottery. The first was launched in the same month and over the ensuing years lotteries became the company's main and valuable source of income.

---

[14] Generally on the history of the Company and Colony see WF Craven, *The Virginia Company of London, 1606–1624* (Williamsburg VA, Virginia 350th Anniversary Celebration Corporation, 1957).

[15] ibid, 22.

4

Democracy: Edwyn Sandys

IT WAS NOW becoming clear that the new English colony was not providing anything like the yield that the Spanish had achieved from their colonies in South America. Critics of Smyth's administration were led by **Sir Edwyn Sandys,** who had been a member of the London Council since 1609. He favoured increased local government and, when he had the opportunity to put this into effect, he played a significant part in the establishment of the first democratic assembly on American soil and eventually the Virginian legislature.

Edwyn's uncle, Miles Sandys, had been Treasurer of the Middle Temple; Edwyn himself was admitted to the Inn in 1590 and appears to have had rooms there until 1596. Edwyn's father was Archbishop of York and seems to have had no problem with nepotism, because he gave Edwyn leases of valuable lands in his diocese and in due course created him Chancellor of the Diocese, a position which had a legal role. Although he trained as a lawyer, there is no evidence Edwyn practised at the bar. His income from the diocese of York seems to have been sufficient to support him. He was elected to Parliament in 1593 and thereafter his energies were mainly directed to a parliamentary career, in which by 1603 he had become a very influential politician.

James I on his accession created the rank of baronet and distributed the honour widely, including to Edwyn Sandys. The antiquary, Anthony Wood, wrote later in the century that Sandys received his baronetcy 'for some exemplary service which he did that prince upon his first coming into England.'[1] Sandys did not show his gratitude; when James proposed that his two kingdoms should be united, Sandys was a principal opponent of this proposal and largely influential in its defeat. On 19 April 1604 he advised the Commons to proceed with caution before agreeing to a union, since there was no basic unity between the two kingdoms.[2] He questioned whether the House had power to effect union; whether union would invalidate existing laws; and whether the reputation of England would suffer. A week later he summed up the debate. 'There is not any example of any kingdoms which, though they have a united head, which is the Prince, have held the course in the body by union of laws, customs, privileges and styles of honour.' Sandys was supported in the debate by Richard Martin, a fellow Middle Templar, who was to become Secretary of the Virginia Company. It took another century for England and Scotland to be united.

---

[1] TK Rabb, *A Jacobean Gentleman, Sir Edwyn Sandys 1561–1629* (Princeton NJ, Princeton University Press, 2005) 52.
[2] ibid, 78–83.

More important from the point of view of the development of the Virginia Company was Sandys' support of what he called Free Trade.[3] Earlier joint stock companies tended to operate like the old craft guilds. Companies, such as the Muscovy or Levant, were controlled by a small number of merchants anxious to keep their monopoly of a particular trade in as few hands as possible. Sandys had already spoken out against monopolies in the late Elizabethan parliaments. He had been a member of the East India Company, chartered in 1600, which had attracted over 1500 members and this was an example Sandys wished to follow. In 1604 he chaired two committees of the Commons, which drew up a Free Trade Bill. In debate he stated that 'All free subjects are born inheritable as to their land, so also as to the free exercise of their industry, in those trades whereunto they apply themselves'.[4] It was against the natural right and liberty of the subjects of England to restrain trade in the hands of a few. The Bill in due course passed the Commons, but was rejected by the Lords. The long list of adventurers named in the Virginia Charter of 1609 reflected Sandys' view that whosoever wished could invest in the enterprise. In fact the investors were to get little or no return on their investment.

Meanwhile things went from bad to worse in the colony. The colonists found it hard to prosper; no gold or silver was found and the crops they grew at first proved uncommercial. Changing weather conditions in America at times left them unable to feed themselves adequately. At first they established friendly relations with the indigenous inhabitants, but then alienated them so that no local help was available in times of famine. The settlers were decimated by starvation and diseases against which, as Europeans, they had no immunity. By April 1618 only 400 of them remained and the London Company was close to insolvency. The governor at this time, Samuel Argall, was unpopular with the settlers because of his strict enforcement of the *Laws Divine Moral and Martial*,[5] with which the colony was governed.

Sandys' view was that to improve the state of the colony its agriculture had to diversify, more land had to be granted to private ownership and more power invested in the colony rather than London. In 1618 Sandys headed a committee of five, which drafted a description of the officers of the Company and their duties. A new governor, Yeardley, was appointed in place of Argall; his instructions (which became known as the Great Charter of Virginia), were drafted by Sandys on 18 November 1618, and attempted a thorough going reform of the colony.[6] The existing plantations were to be grouped into four cities or boroughs, named Jamestown, Charles, Henrico and Kicoughtan. Provision was to be made for the establishment of a university in Henrico. Land was to be set aside for securing and maintaining cattle. Private land tenure was allowed and

---

[3] ibid, 88–96 and see also TK Rabb, *Enterprise and Empire: Merchant and Gentry Investment in the Expansion of England* (Cambridge MA, Harvard University Press, 1967).

[4] Quoted ibid, 93.

[5] William Strachey, *Laws Divine Moral and Martial* (London, Barre, 1612).

[6] SM Kingsbury, *Records of the Virginia Company 1606-26* (WA, Government Print Office: Library of Congress, 1905) Vol III 98–109; and compare WM Billings, *The Little Parliament* (Virginia, Library of Virginia, 2004) 5–6.

indeed encouraged. Anyone who paid his own passage was to be given 50 acres, with an additional 50 acres for each additional settler he brought with him. The old system of laws was to be replaced. Most importantly, separate commissions authorised the governor to establish a Council in the colony and to convene a General Assembly with 'free power to treat, consult and conclude all emergent occasions concerning the public weal of the said Colony and every part thereof.' Democracy in America was born.

Hostility between Smyth and Sandys continued and in 1619 Sandys effectively managed a coup which replaced Smyth with himself as Treasurer of the Company. On 25 June 1619 Yeardley issued writs to freemen and tenants requiring them in their districts 'by plurality of voices to make election of two sufficient men to meet with him and the Council in a general assembly.' On 30 July, 6 councillors and 22 burgesses met in Jamestown. The new assembly was established on the model of the House of Commons in England. In 1618 Yeardley had married Temperance Flowerdew (or Flowerdieu—he was the second governor she had married). Her cousin, John Pory, went to Virginia as Yeardley's secretary.[7] He had been educated at Cambridge and was widely travelled, having served for a short period as secretary to the English ambassador in Istanbul. He had also served as a Member of Parliament in England from 1605 to 1610. Yeardley appointed him Speaker of the new assembly. A Clerk to the assembly and Sergeant at Arms were sworn and the members swore oaths of supremacy and allegiance.[8]

This assembly mimicked the English House of Commons. Pory kept a careful record of proceedings. They discussed tobacco prices, servants' contracts and relations with the native Americans; on the other hand they referred a dispute about the entitlement of a particular burgess to sit in the assembly to the Council in London. Although Smyth later forced Sandys from the Treasurership, Sandys in effect continued to administer the company under his successor, the Earl of Southampton. For a time the colony prospered. The prospect of owning property in the colony persuaded more settlers to emigrate there. Sandys, however, was wrong about the need to diversify agriculture—eventually what saved the colony was a single crop, tobacco. Once more the colonists bickered amongst themselves; the King cancelled the right to hold a lottery and in 1622 an Indian raid killed a third of the settlers. James had had enough and brought the Charter to an end. The colony was now under direct royal control.[9] What then of the assembly? Neither James I, nor Charles I when he acceded, abolished it, and both used it as a means of communicating with the colonists. By default it survived and became used to wielding local authority. By 1639 the population had increased to 10,000 and the tobacco trade increased in profitability. By 1641 the assembly was no longer simply an adjunct to a London Council, but

---

[7] See WS Powell, *John Pory, the Life and Letters of a Man of Many Parts 1572–1636* (North Carolina, University of North Carolina Press, 1976).

[8] See Billings above n 6, 44.

[9] Billings above n 6, 11.

an effective form of local government.[10] It was destined to grow into the first state legislature. The seed Sandys had planted was of as great importance as the physical planting of men. In 1625 Sandys' supporters drew up a list of achievements in the colony under his authority. These included that the government of the colony was ordered like that in England; the colonists 'had the liberty of a general assembly.'[11] He died in 1629.

Sandys performed one other service to the future United States. In 1617 he met representatives of a nonconformist community who had moved from England to Leiden in Holland in order to practise their faith without persecution.[12] They found life in Holland difficult and became interested in settling in America. He encouraged their ambition, gave them money and was instrumental in the Virginia Company granting them a patent to settle in the Hudson valley. Eventually they did not settle there, but did establish themselves further north in what became known as New England. They were the Pilgrim Fathers and started a chain of settlements based on religious affiliation.

[10] ibid, 12–24.
[11] See Rabb above n 1, 39.
[12] ibid, 331.

5

Religion and Liberty:
Nathaniel Ward

NATHANIEL WARD WAS a barrister and religious minister from Essex in the east of England, who emigrated to Massachusetts in 1633 and in 1638 drafted the first original Charter of Liberties in the New World. He was part of a wave of immigrants seeking freedom of religious worship there. The sixteenth century reformation in England spawned a multiplicity of Protestant faiths—groups such as Adamites, Anabaptists, Barrowists, Bohemianists, Brownists, Diggers, Familists, Fifth Monarchists, Levellers, Philadelphians, Quakers, Sabbatarians and Seekers. Tudor governments, however, attempted to enforce a uniform Anglican faith with increasing severity. In 1563 the Church of England published 39 articles of faith, steering a middle way between the Catholic doctrines of the Roman Church and the extreme protestant doctrines of Calvin in Geneva. The Catholic doctrine of transubstantiation, that the body and blood of Christ were actually present in the sacraments of wine and bread administered in Holy Communion with God, was rejected, though the sacraments were still taken as symbols of a relationship with the Almighty. On the other hand the Calvinist doctrine of predestination—that the just were predestined to enter heaven—was equally rejected. Organisation of the Church was as much an issue as doctrine. The Church of England rejected the authority of the Pope and General Councils of the Catholic Church, but maintained a hierarchy of Archbishops, bishops and clergy—they and only they could baptise, give the sacraments and conduct marriage services. The organisation of the so-called puritan sects ranged from the Presbyterian view that the Church was governed by individual congregations of the Church led by presbyters or elders, to the Quaker view that each individual had a direct route to God.

Acts of Uniformity and Supremacy, passed by Tudor parliaments, required all to conform to the practice of the Church of England and recognise the Sovereign as head of the Anglican Church. The Elizabethan government approved a revised Book of Common Prayer, which it hoped would unite religious belief. The Act of Uniformity of 1559 (replacing earlier similar acts) required religious ministers to follow its text on pain of fine and imprisonment. All subjects were required earnestly and diligently to attend their local church of England, or be fined 12 pence if they failed to do so. Believers who dissented from the doctrines of the Church of England began to look for a new life, where they could practise their beliefs and organise their churches without being penalised.

One such group, known as Brownists from the name of one of their founders, formed in the Midlands in the latter part of the sixteenth century, adopting government by elders rather than vicars. They worshipped secretly in houses in Lincolnshire and came to believe that their religious views required them to separate themselves from the Church of England—hence their other title of Separatists. Their journey to Leiden in 1608 was not a success; they found it difficult to speak Dutch or obtain work and after 10 years decided to look for another home. They approached the Virginia Company for a patent to settle in America and in June 1619 they were given permission by the Company to do so near the mouth of the Hudson River. In August 1620 the *Mayflower* and *Speedwell* sailed from Dartmouth and in November made landfall, some considerable way north of the Hudson River, near modern day Provincetown on Cape Cod. The next month they established a settlement on the west side of Cape Cod Bay, which they named Plymouth.[1] These were the Pilgrim Fathers (though this name became current only at the end of the eighteenth century, the group actually calling themselves the Saints). They were thankful for their safe passage. Leiden had suffered severely in a siege by the Spanish in 1574 and, on the anniversary of the day when it was lifted, held services of Thanksgiving for their deliverance. The Pilgrim Fathers adopted this practice on the anniversary of their landfall.

As the area where they settled was outside that granted by their patent from the Virginia Company, the male passengers decided they were free to organise their own government. Shortly before landing, 41 of them entered into a compact, which, having first expressed loyalty to James I, agreed to combine 'in a civil body politic for our better ordering ... to enact ... such just and equal laws ... as shall be thought most meet and convenient for the general good of the colony.' This was a true social contract. The colony operated without a Charter until in 1692, after a period of turbulent government, it was merged with the Massachusetts Bay Colony under a royal governor.

The Massachusetts Bay Colony was established slightly later than, and separate from, the Plymouth colony. A group consisting largely of Presbyterians settled in Massachusetts Bay to the north of the Plymouth colony, around modern day Boston. In March 1628 they persuaded Charles I to grant a charter to the 'New England Company for the establishment of a plantation in Massachusetts Bay'.[2] This was a joint stock company with a Governor, Council in London and stockholders along the lines of the Virginia Company. On 25 November 1629, at a meeting of the General Council of the Company in London, Nathaniel Ward was elected a member. The Charter (unlike the Virginia Charter whose General Council was required to meet in London) failed to particularise where the Council was to be located or the stockholders to hold their annual meeting. They met in Cambridge, England later in 1629 and agreed that those who wished to

---

[1] See N Philbrick, *Mayflower: A Story of Courage, Community and War* (New York, Viking, 2006); S Morison, *The Story of the Old Colony of New Plymouth* (New York, Knopf, 1955).

[2] See B Labaree, *Colonial Massachusetts, a History* (Millwood NY, Kraus International Publications, 1979); W Hubbard, *A General History of New England, from the Discovery to MDCLXXX* (Boston MA, Massachusetts Historical Society, 1815).

emigrate and settle in America should buy out the shares of those who did not wish to do so. As a result the seat of government of the new company moved to Boston, where it was administered by a General Court. It was the first colony to be governed entirely from its own territory and in due course became the centre of the most virulent opposition to the British government.

Nathaniel Ward (or Warde) was brought up in Haverhill, Suffolk, the son of a prominent puritan minister.[3] He attended Cambridge University, joined Lincoln's Inn in February 1607 and was called to the bar on 17 October 1615. He appears to have practised as a lawyer for a time and also travelled on the continent of Europe. His interest in religion grew, for by 1618 he was chaplain to a group or factory of English merchants in Prussia and in 1628 he became vicar of Stondon Massey in Essex. He maintained his father's puritan faith and practices and, as a result of his preaching, Archbishop Laud censured him in 1631 and in 1633 dismissed him from his post as vicar. This prompted him the next year to emigrate to Ipswich, Massachusetts (Indian name Aggawam), where he was vicar for a time. The 1628 Charter of the Massachusetts Bay Company was a commercial document, which, whilst giving wide terms of governance to the Company, was silent on the administration of justice. The early part of the seventeenth century had seen a renewal of interest in England in the liberties granted by Magna Carta; common lawyers, led by Lord Chief Justice Coke, employed them to argue against the claim made by James I and Charles I to rule by divine right. In 1638 Ward was part of a committee instructed to draw together fundamental laws necessary for the governance of the colony; it seems to have been he who was largely responsible for drafting a *Body of Liberties* setting out around a hundred fundamental laws. It was presented to the General Court in 1641 and, after some amendment, sent to all the towns in the colony. It was first of its kind in America. The *Body of Liberties* reflected the English common law, which Ward had studied in Lincoln's Inn, and the constitutional arguments which were taking place in England when he was a student. It was a forerunner of the English and United States Bills of Rights. The General Court accepted it in preference to a version drafted by John Cotton, which was based on the bible.[4]

Ward's version commenced with a clause clearly derived from Magna Carta:

No man's life shall be taken away, no man's honor or good name shall be stained, no man's person shall be arrested, restrained, banished, dismembered, nor any ways punished, no man shall be deprived of his wife or children, no man's goods or estate shall be taken away from him, nor any way indamaged under color of law or countenance of authority, unless it be by virtue or equity of some express law of the country warranting the same, established by a general court and sufficiently published, or in case of

---

[3] Details of his life may be found in Theodore de la Guard's edn of Ward's *The Simple Cobler* to be found on the Gutenbook Project e book, www.gutenberg.org/files/34974/34974-h/34974-h.htm, released in 2011.

[4] WB Stoebuck, *Reception of English Common Law in the American Colonies* 10 *William and Mary Law Review* 399 and see JK Hosmer (ed), *Winthrop's Journal: History of New England 1630–1649* (New York, Charles Scribner's Sons, 1908).

the defect of a law in any particular case by the word of God. And in capital cases, or in cases concerning dismembering or banishment, according to that word to be judged by the general court.[5]

It went on to guarantee freedom of speech, the right to jury trial and the rule against double jeopardy (that a man could not be tried twice for the same offence). It established capital punishment for a number of offences, amongst them witchcraft (by either sex) and blasphemy. Sentences of imprisonment, however, were limited and powers were given to grant bail. There was provision for speedy trial, whipping as a punishment was limited to 40 stripes and torture forbidden, except in capital cases after conviction where the condemned man might reveal the identity of confederates! No bodily punishments were allowed that were inhumane, barbarous or cruel. Military service could only be required for defensive wars. It also reflected the opposition in Stuart Britain to the granting of monopolies, saying they should be granted only for new inventions that are profitable to the country and for a short time.

The *Body* went on to set out the machinery of government. Freemen had the right to elect their deputies to a general court, which in turn could elect the governor of the colony and other officers and had power to deselect them. It also dealt with the liberties of others who were not freemen. If a man on his death did not leave a competent portion of his estate to his wife, the General Court could grant her relief. A married woman was to be free from bodily correction or stripes by her husband, except when he was defending himself from her assault. Not a total feminist agenda, but at least an advance on English law. Children too had liberties—provision was made for inheritance on intestacy, including by daughters in the absence of sons. Parents could not unreasonably refuse to give their consent to marriage or use unnatural severity towards children. Servants were similarly protected from maiming or disfigurement, had rights against dismissal and if they had served diligently or faithfully for seven years 'shall not be sent away empty.' Christian foreigners who fled tyranny or war were to be entertained or succoured.

It also had an interesting take on slavery: clause 91 provided that 'there shall never be any bond slavery, villeinage, or captivity amongst us unless it be lawful captives taken in just wars and such strangers as willingly sell themselves or are sold to us.' Slaves were known in the colony from early in its history, though not in such numbers as were later imported into the southern colonies. Boston became one of the principal ports trading in slaves between Africa, the West Indies and the southern colonies.

In the Congregationalist tradition, church government was given to individual congregations, who had control of admission and expulsion. Those who were orthodox in judgement and not scandalous in life could establish churches and every church should have freedom of election of all their officers, provided they were able, pious and orthodox. This provision, however, did not involve total religious freedom—if you did not qualify as orthodox you could suffer extreme

---

[5] Stoebuck, ibid.

punishment. Despite having suffered discrimination themselves, the Massachusetts settlers were not prepared to show religious toleration to others.

This is demonstrated in a lengthy pamphlet published by Ward entitled *the Simple Cobler of Aggawam in America*.[6] It is a marvellous example of the extravagance of seventeenth century prose, but its central message is clear—no faith is to be tolerated other than that of the puritans. He wrote of unfriendly reports of New England:

> We have beene reputed a Colluvies of wild Opinionists, swarmed into a remote wilderness to find elbow-roome for our phanatick Doctrines and practises; I trust our diligence past and constant sedulity against such persons and courses, will plead better things for us. I dare take upon me to bee the Herauld of New England so farre as to proclaim to the world, in the name of our Colony, that all Familists, Antinomians, Anabaptists and other Enthusiasts, shall have free Liberty to keep away from us, and such as will come to be gone as fast as they can, the sooner the better.

It went on to lament a Charter in a West Indian island which provided 'free stable room and litter for all kind of consciences, be they never so dirty or jadish.'

Whatever protection the *Body of Liberties* made for women, Ward expected them to act as modest puritans. He had strong views on their dress:

> I honour the woman who can honour herself with her attire ... whatever Christianity or Civility will allow, I can afford with London measure: but when I heare a nugiperous Gentledame inquire what dresse the Queen is in this week: what the nudiustertian fashion of the Court; I mean the very newest with egge to be in it in all haste, whatever it be; I loke at her as the very gizzard of a trifle, the product of a quarter of a cipher, the epitome of nothing, fitter to be kickt if shee were of a kickable substance; then either honour'd or humour'd.

Whatever one thinks of his views, it is difficult not to warm to his style.

Of all the various dissenting sects, the Society of Friends was the most universally unpopular with other religionists.[7] They appeared as a group in the religious tumult which took place in England during the Commonwealth. Their founder, George Fox, started preaching in the mid seventeenth century, urging that every individual had the capacity to form a direct relationship with God, who would shine his inward light on them. In 1653 John Burnyeat described how 'we met together and waited together in silence; it may be not a word in our meetings for months, but everyone that was faithful waited upon the living words in our hearts.'[8] Such was their zeal that when the light shone in them they would tremble or quake—the name Quakers originated as a mocking description of them by others. One explanation given for this phenomenon was that

---

[6] See above n 3.
[7] See JE Calvert, *Quaker Constitutionalism and the Political Thought of John Dickinson* (Cambridge, Cambridge University Press, 2008) and R Moore, *The Light in their Consciences: Faith, Practices and Personalities in Early British Quakerism* (PA, Pennsylvania State University Press, 2000).
[8] Calvert, ibid, 34.

the believer trembled in contemplation of his sins. They held that no hierarchy of priest, elder or congregation was necessary to salvation. This cut across the beliefs of Papists, Anglicans and Presbyterians alike. The light could come to women as well as men—they allowed women to preach and travel alone.

All this was bad enough from the viewpoint of other religions, but matters were made worse by their missionary zeal, interrupting religious services of other believers. Some ran through such services naked to demonstrate the spiritual nakedness of others.[9] They were branded lunatics, heretics and a threat to civil government, being prosecuted for disorderly behaviour. In court they refused to remove their hats or swear an oath on the bible. They nevertheless developed a capacity as barrack-room lawyers, taking technical points during a trial and delaying proceedings whenever they could. Many of them were imprisoned including Fox; in 1669 Penn was imprisoned in the Tower, where he wrote a famous book *No Cross, No Crown*. Fox convinced them that peace was the essence of their belief and their resistance to persecution was to be non-violent.

In 1658 the General Court of Massachusetts passed an Act ordering that any Quaker, who was not an inhabitant, found in the colony was to be whipped and banished on pain of death. An English Quaker called Mary Dyer[10] and three male Quakers were found preaching in the colony and banished. They returned and the men were executed. Mary was sentenced to death, but at the last moment reprieved. She nevertheless insisted on being hanged, which she was. This outraged opinion in England. Charles II forbade the authorities in New England executing Quakers and sent out a royal governor to replace the colonial government.

---

[9] ibid, 49.

[10] R Larson, *Daughters of Light: Quaker Women Preaching and Prophesying in the Colonies and Abroad* (New York, Knopf, 2000).

6

Toleration: Cecil Calvert and William Penn

ECIL CALVERT ESTABLISHED Maryland as a haven for Catholics and William Penn Pennsylvania as one for Quakers. Both colonies practised a religious toleration which Massachusetts had refused. Neither man practised as a lawyer, but both studied in the Inns of Court and the constitutions and legislation of their colonies demonstrate a considerable knowledge of the law.

The Stuart Kings saw the grant of lands in America as a way of rewarding their followers at no cost to themselves. Cecil's father, George, was a covert Catholic, who rose to a high position in the government of James I; after both James and George had died, George's service was rewarded by Charles I granting his son a Charter in 1632, making him proprietor of a large tract of land, which now constitutes Maryland. It was feudal in form, similar to those given since Norman times to Barons in the Marches or borderlands of Wales and in Ireland, making him a vassal of the Crown, but also creating him true and absolute proprietor of the lands, with express power to make laws for its governance himself. Charles II followed this pattern in 1663, when he rewarded eight of those who had helped to restore him to the throne with a proprietorial grant of land in the Carolinas (named after him). In 1664 James, Duke of York (the King's brother, later James II) fitted out an expedition which captured New York from the Dutch and was rewarded by being made proprietor of an area, including modern Manhattan Island, New York State and parts of New Jersey, Delaware and Maine. In 1681 Charles II made the more surprising proprietorial grant of what is now Pennsylvania to William Penn, the reasons for which will appear later.

The Calverts came from a stronghold of Catholicism near Richmond in Yorkshire and in the course of the sixteenth century suffered persecution for their faith.[1] After Oxford, George Calvert studied law in Lincoln's Inn from 1598 to 1601. He then met and was used on missions by Sir Robert Cecil, Queen Elizabeth's and later James I's chief minister. He seems to have hidden his Catholic sympathies, for he rose steadily through the government, being knighted in 1617 and then becoming one of King James's two principal Secretaries of State

---

[1] See JD Krugler, *English and Catholic: the Lords Baltimore in the Seventeenth Century* (Baltimore MD, John Hopkins University Press, 2004); WH Browne, *George Calvert and Cecilius Calvert: Barons Baltimore of Baltimore* (NY, Dodd, Mead, 1890).

in 1619. In 1623 he was given a large estate in County Cork in Ireland, called Baltimore, and created First Baron Baltimore. He soon became unpopular in Parliament for supporting the putative marriage of Charles, Prince of Wales, to the Spanish Infanta and in 1625 he resigned from the government, promptly 'converting' to Catholicism. Thereafter, he devoted himself to establishing a safe place for Catholics to settle in America, in the first instance in Newfoundland, which he visited and found too inclement. After a failed approach for assistance to the Virginians, he approached the King, now Charles I, for a charter to settle in an area to the north of Virginia on the west bank of the Delaware River. Charles was sympathetic, but before a charter could be granted George died; so it was that the Charter was granted to his son. He was named Cecil after his father's sponsor and was admitted in 1633 to Gray's Inn, probably because that Inn had strong links with Robert Cecil's family. The new colony was named Maryland after Queen Henrietta Maria; it was the first colony publicly to adopt religious toleration.

The Charter of Maryland was for settlement between Chesapeake Bay and the Potomac River. Cecil ruled initially as a feudal lord, but the freemen of the colony wanted all the rights of a British citizen and compelled him to accept an Act for the Liberties of the People, enacted in 1638 by the 'Lord Proprietarie; on the advice of the freemen.' All Christian inhabitants of the colony (except slaves) were entitled to the rights and liberties as any natural born subject in England, by virtue of common or statute law. The Act specifically reflected Magna Carta, providing that an inhabitant shall not be imprisoned nor disseised (deprived of his land) nor dispossessed of his freehold goods than according to the laws of the province.

Archbishop Laud's strict enforcement of the Act of Uniformity in England led to the colony receiving not only Catholics, but also members of Protestant sects. This must have produced some friction, for in 1649 the Maryland Toleration Act was passed. Provided they were Christians, all members of the colony were to be treated tolerantly:

> whereas the inforcing of the conscience in matters of Religion hath frequently fallen out to be of dangerous Consequence ... noe person or persons whatsoever within this Province ... professing to believe in Jesus Christ, shall from henceforth be any waies troubled, Molested, discountenanced for in respect of his or her religion.

It also made it an offence, subject to a fine of 10 shillings, to call any inhabitant or person trading of or in the colony 'a heretic, Schismatic, idolator, puritan, Independent, Prespetirian, popish priest, Jesuist, Jesuited papist, Lutheran, Calvinist, Anabaptist, Brownist, Antimonian, Barrowist, Roundhead, Separatist or any other name in a reproachful manner relating to matter of Religion.'[2] It did, however, make blasphemy a capital offence.

In 1654 a group of some 23 Jews arrived in the Dutch Colony of New Amsterdam, fleeing Brazil in fear of persecution.[3] The Dutch governor, Peter Stuyvesant,

---

[2] The inconsistent capitalisation is from the original.
[3] P Johnson, *History of the Jews* (New York, Harper & Row, 1988).

did not want to accept these 'deceitful people', but the Dutch West India Company had Jewish shareholders and forced him to do so. He imposed drastic restrictions on them, but fortunately for them James, Duke of York's expedition soon took control. He allowed the Jews to stay without much restriction. By modern times, the community of 23 had grown to constitute almost a fifth of the population of New York.

The name **William Penn** still resonates in the twenty-first century. His story is, perhaps, the strangest of all the early colonists. He was born in 1644, the son of an Admiral who served the Commonwealth government, but also helped to secure the restoration of Charles II. In 1660 William went up to Oxford. He already had nonconformist sympathies and was first fined and then in the autumn sent down for holding private religious services in his rooms. His father, aghast, beat him and sent him on a tour of the continent, which only served to enforce his beliefs. In February 1665 he enrolled as a student in Lincoln's Inn where he studied law until the autumn of 1666, when he left to sail with his father in a fleet attacking the Dutch. It was in that year he finally became a member of the Society of Friends.

If his legal studies were short, they were at least sufficient to make him a superior barrack-room lawyer and in 1670 he had an unwelcome opportunity to demonstrate his legal acumen. The authorities in the City of London closed the Friends' Meeting House in Gracechurch Street and Penn preached to a gathering of Friends in the street outside, amongst them his fellow Quaker Mead. The two men were arrested and charged that, by agreement between them, Penn had preached to a great concourse and tumult of people to the disturbance of the King's Peace.[4] At their trial they did not have counsel; Penn demanded to have a copy of the indictment, but was refused one. He questioned whether the charge in fact amounted to a criminal offence, but was told it was an offence at common law. He argued that he had not been the cause of any tumult; that was due to those who came to arrest him. Eventually the jury acquitted Mead. By this time Penn's arguments had so enraged the Recorder of London that he ordered Penn be kept in a hole beneath the dock, where prisoners slopped out. Penn shouted from there that as he was charged with a conspiracy with Mead, he too must be acquitted. The Recorder directed the jury to convict him. Their verdict, however, was only that he had preached in Gracechurch Street. The Recorder refused to accept this verdict and locked them up overnight without food or water. Nevertheless, a few days later, the jury acquitted and the Recorder fined them for contempt, ordering they be held in custody until they paid. Penn was also fined and his father, rather to William's annoyance, appears to have paid on his behalf. Thomas Bushell, the foreman of the jury, appealed to Lord Chief Justice Vaughan, who ordered the release of the jurors and so established the inviolability of the jury verdict.[5]

Penn's father died in September 1670, but before he did he extracted a promise from the King and the Duke of York to protect William. Even so it was not

[4] Howell's *State Trials* VI 951.
[5] *Bushell's Case* (1670) 124 ER 1006.

long before he ended up in prison again and so his thoughts turned to establishing a Quaker Community in America. In 1677, with a number of others, he purchased land in what is now New Jersey, where a small Quaker community was established. The Quakers continued to be a thorn in the side of the English government and, when Penn in March 1681 petitioned for a Charter to acquire land in America to establish a safe haven for Quakers, the King acquiesced. A substantial loan from Admiral Penn was still outstanding and the grant may have been recompense for that. The Charter, drafted on the lines of that granted to the Calverts, made Penn the sole proprietor of no less than 45,000 acres north of Maryland and so the largest landlord in the empire other than the King. The territory was named Pennsylvania (Penn Woods) after his father and its principal city became Philadelphia, meaning brotherly love.

The following year Penn issued *Liberties and Frame of Government of Pennsylvania*. There is no evidence who drafted it, but given his power with words and his membership of Lincoln's Inn, it is likely it was Penn himself. He may have had assistance in drafting the Frame from a Quaker lawyer called Thomas Rudyard, who held land in the Quaker colonies in Jersey, but lived in London.[6] Quakers did believe in civil order, indeed that there was a fundamental law emanating from God, thus the Frame begins with a lengthy preamble on the nature of government. God chose man as his deputy on earth, but, as man has erred, law and government are necessary. Government is therefore of divine origin (a claim similar to that made by Kings). It is not merely concerned with punishing wrongdoing. 'They weakly err that think there is no other use of government than correction, which is the coarsest part of it: daily experience teaches us that the care and regulation of many other affairs, more soft and daily necessary, make up much of the greatest part of government.' The Frame goes on to state the general principle behind the Constitution: 'Any government is free to the people under it, where the laws rule and the people are a party to those laws.' It was to be the definition of 'party' that caused trouble. The preamble went on to say that it was not easy to frame a civil government that shall serve all places alike—perhaps conscious that the example of the English constitution was not to be followed altogether. It stressed that while the Frame would guarantee liberties, the freemen of the colony would be free 'by their just obedience.'

The Frame is a remarkably detailed and carefully thought out document and indicates legal learning. It provides that the government of the colony is to be tripartite—a Governor or his deputy, a Provincial Council and a General Assembly. It is silent as to how the Governor is to be appointed—the implication being that either Penn is the Governor or appoints him. The freemen of the colony, subject to a property qualification, are to elect both the members of the Council and the General Assembly. The latter is to have 200 members, chosen by the freemen. They are to meet annually to choose persons of most note for their wisdom, virtue and ability to act as the Provincial Council. There will be 72

---

[6] JR Soderland, *William Penn and the Founding of Pennsylvania—A Documentary History* (Philadelphia PA, University of Pennsylvania Press, 1983).

members of the Council, sitting in rotation; the maximum period anyone may sit is seven years, after which there must be a gap of one year before they can be chosen again 'so all may be fitted for government and have experience of the care and burden of it.'

So far so good, but it is the Governor or his deputy who is to preside at meetings of the Council and have a 'treble voice'. Moreover only the Governor and Council can propose or initiate legislation, though it does not become law until two thirds of the Assembly have approved it. Whilst much of the Frame was democratic, it was in marked contrast to the British Constitution where the House of Commons initiated most legislation and this distinction was to cause friction with the colonists. From correspondence between Penn and Rudyard, it appears that the reason the power of initiating legislation was confined to the Council was that they thought it was more likely that men of substance would be chosen for the Council, hence no doubt the reference in the Frame to their standing in the community. At any rate Penn was cautious about handing over too much power to the freemen of the colony.

The Frame then turns to parts of the laws of England which are to be adopted. The ordinary liberties of England shall be part of the fundamental law of the colony. Elections shall be free and voluntary and anyone receiving a reward for his vote shall lose the right to elect. 'No money or goods shall be raised ... by way of public tax ... but by law.' Courts shall be open and justice shall neither be sold, denied or delayed. All pleadings and process shall be short and in English and in an ordinary and plain character. Trials shall be by jury of 12 as near as maybe of equals of the defendant drawn from the neighbourhood. All prisons are to be free as to fees, food and lodging.

Marriage is to be encouraged, but parents consulted first and the proposed marriage publicised. The marriage shall be solemnised by taking one another as husband and wife before credible witnesses (in other words the intervention of a priest is not required). To prevent fraud, all charters, gifts, conveyances, bills and bonds shall be registered within two months of their making. Births, marriages, burials and wills will be registered and there will also be a register of servants. The estates of capital offenders shall go as to one third to the family of the sufferer and as to two thirds to the family of the offender.

Most importantly the Frame granted religious toleration more widely even than the Maryland Act of Toleration:

> all persons living in this province, who confess and acknowledge the one Almighty and eternal God, to be the Creator ... of the world and that hold themselves obliged in conscience to live peaceably and justly in civil society, shall in no way be molested or prejudiced for their religious persuasion or practice, in matters of faith and worship, nor shall they be compelled, at any time to frequent or maintain any religious worship, place or ministry whatever.[7]

Whilst this was wide enough to include non-Christians, membership of the legislature and holders of public office had to possess faith in Jesus Christ.

---

[7] Clause XXXV.

In 1682 Penn visited the colony and the first General Assembly of the Colony adopted his document with some amendments. Penn wrote to the King urging him 'to improve and thicken his colonys with people not his own.'[8] The religious tolerance of the colony attracted immigrants not only from England, but also Scotland, Ireland and particularly Wales, Germany, France, Holland and Sweden.[9] The Germans developed their own dialect known as German Dutch, which persisted for many decades. Amongst these colonists were Catholics and Jews. The Assembly and Council, however, remained largely in Quaker hands.

Thereafter, the colony suffered from factionalism and also from the fact that Penn himself spent much of his time in England. This was to give an important role to David Lloyd, Speaker of the General Assembly. He was born in Montgomeryshire in north Wales.[10] He had a Quaker uncle called Thomas, who had been imprisoned for his refusal to swear the oath of supremacy on his appointment as sheriff of the county and sailed to Pennsylvania with Penn in the first vessel containing colonists. David Lloyd is said to have studied law in the Inner Temple chambers of George Jeffreys (later to become infamous as the hanging judge suppressing the Monmouth uprising under James II), who also came from north Wales, in his case near Wrexham. It is not entirely clear if David was admitted to an Inn of Court, though given that he ended up as Chief Justice of Pennsylvania it seems probable he was.[11] He was appointed Attorney General of Pennsylvania and supported the colonists in disputes with the British government. In 1700 Lloyd was accused by the vice admiralty judge in Pennsylvania of failing to enforce the Navigation Acts, which protected British trade with the colonies, and of aiding smugglers. The Board of Trade in London demanded his dismissal. Penn, who was always fearful of losing his Charter, removed him from office. This caused great bitterness on Lloyd's part and thereafter he allied himself with the Assembly members and their grievances.

So it was, that on 28 October 1701, when Penn was about to return to London, Lloyd persuaded him to issue a new Charter of Liberties, which Lloyd had drafted and the Assembly had approved.[12] This effectively put the power of government in a unicameral assembly, relegating the Council to part of the executive. The General Assembly was to have power to prepare bills in order to pass them into laws, to impeach criminals and redress grievances and have all other power and privileges of an assembly, according to the rights of the

---

[8] See J Illick, *Colonial Pennsylvania—a History* (NY, Kraus International Publications, 1976) 122.

[9] TC Purvis, Pattern of Ethnic Settlement in Late 18th Century Pennsylvania' (April 1987) 70(2) *The Western Pennsylvania Historical Magazine* 107.

[10] See Dictionary of National Biography (DNB) and BA Konkle, David Lloyd, Penn's Great Lawmaker' *Pennsylvania History: A Journal of Mid-Atlantic* Studies Vol 4 No 3 (Penn State University Press, July 1937) 153.

[11] There is a record of David Lloyd from Merionethshire being admitted to the Inner Temple on 18 April 1670. Merionethshire adjoins Montgomeryshire, but if the date of birth in the DNB is correct he would only have been 14. The DNB does not state the source for his date of birth. Young men did join the Inns of Court at such an early age if they did not go to Oxbridge.

[12] See Konkle n 10 above, 1.

freeborn subjects of England. Legislation was to be in the form 'by the Governor with the consent and approbation of the Freemen of the General Assembly.' The 1701 Charter repeated the liberties granted by the 1681 version. This was now the most democratic constitution in the world. It lasted for 75 years until new constitutions were drawn after the revolution. In May 1729, when Lloyd was Speaker of the Assembly as well as Lord Chief Justice, the Assembly granted an appropriation for the building of the capitol of Pennsylvania. It was to be called the Hall of Liberty and Law and there was to be a portrait of Lloyd hung on its walls.[13]

13 ibid.

7

Representation: James Otis Junior

JAMES OTIS JUNIOR was born in Barnstable on Cape Cod on 25 February 1725. New England, from its early puritan tradition and degree of self government, was the least receptive of all the colonies to British control. Massachusetts was 'always the sulky child, rebellious against things English.'[1] The Otis family were puritans, who emigrated from Glastonbury in Somerset, England to Massachusetts in the 1630s.[2] The son of the original immigrant, John Otis, became a judge and started a family connection to the law, which lasted several generations. This was the tradition that spawned James Otis junior, who led opposition to taxation of the colonies by the British government. The right of the British parliament to tax its colonies became mired in abstruse argument, but at its heart was a simple proposition—'no taxation without representation.' The man credited with the invention of that phrase was James Otis junior, though the idea behind it was already established.[3]

He was a home-grown lawyer. In the early days of the colonies, there were relatively few English trained lawyers there. The Mayflower carried copies of Coke's Law Reports written in the early seventeenth century, but no lawyer. Maine had an English trained lawyer, John Winthrop, as governor. Virginia appears to have had two English trained lawyers in this period, one of whom, the perhaps aptly named Henry Justice, had been transported for theft.[4] There were very few American legal publications and only restricted access to English legal material. Many of the courts were conducted by the legally untrained, who, even when in England, would have had little idea of what the common law was; they probably followed the traditions of the local English manorial courts. In England, practice at the bar was (and still is) preceded by a period as a pupil of a practising barrister. A similar system of apprenticeship grew up in America. The Virginian, George Wythe, who was the first of the Virginian delegates to sign the Declaration of Independence, trained in his uncle's law office and in his turn trained Jefferson, Marshall, Madison and Monroe. In Boston, Jeremiah Gridley trained William Cushing, who became a judge of the Supreme Court. After graduating from Harvard in 1743, Otis joined and trained in Gridley's

---

[1] WB Stoebuck, 'Reception of English Common Law in the American Colonies' (1968) 10 *William and Mary Law Review* 393.

[2] W Tudor, *The Life of James Otis of Massachusetts*, (Boston MA, Wells and Lilly, 1823).

[3] The phrase certainly represented his views, but there is no record of him using the precise phrase.

[4] Stoebuck above n 1, 413.

office.[5] He built a successful career and in 1760 was appointed Advocate General to the Court of Admiralty in Boston.

Successive British governments treated the colonies with neglect,[6] leaving their assemblies to raise local taxes. The only interest of British governments was to secure as much benefit as they could from colonial trade, monopolising it for the mother country and imposing customs dues on items imported into the colonies. This resulted in a good deal of smuggling and those caught in New England with uncustomed goods were tried in the Admiralty Court in Boston; it operated without a jury and was not popular. Between 1651 and 1696 the British parliament passed a succession of Navigation Acts restricting shipping of goods into any part of the British Empire to boats built and owned by citizens of Britain or the Empire. In 1733 it went further and passed the Molasses Act, placing a specific duty for the next 30 years on molasses imported into America from countries that did not form part of the British Empire. America and in particular Boston had a considerable trade in rum, for which molasses were the base; many parts of the Caribbean produced molasses more cheaply than the British colonies. Smuggling now grew exponentially.

The Molasses Act ran out in 1763, shortly after the end of the Seven Years' War between Britain and her allies and France and hers. Part of the war had been fought on American soil and ended in victory for the British. The bulk of north America was now British. Britain, however, was left seriously in debt and in 1760 William Pitt the Elder, who headed the British government, wrote to colonial governors requiring them to enforce the collection of customs dues strictly, adding that if this were done there would be no need for new taxes.[7]

In October of that year, George II died. All official documents bearing his seal had to be renewed within six months with the seal of George III. The Surveyor of Customs in Boston requested renewal of writs of assistance.[8] They enabled customs officers to call for assistance in searching and seizing goods imported or exported illegally. Originally they were issued by the Boston Court of Admiralty, where a customs' officer swore there was a high probability of contraband being found. Gradually they had changed to general writs, which did not name individuals or places, but simply allowed a customs officer to search or seize whenever and wherever he chose. News of the King's death reached Boston in December and 63 Boston merchants joined together to challenge the validity of any new general writs. The collector of customs brought a counter suit—his name was Paxton and the case ever since bears his name. Otis resigned his post as Advocate General to argue the case on behalf of the merchants. Jeremiah Gridley was instructed by the government to support the validity of the writs.

In 1760 a new royal governor, Francis Bernard, had arrived in Massachusetts, determined to make his mark as a colonial administrator. His deputy was Thomas Hutchinson and Bernard appointed him, in preference to Otis' father, to

[5]   ibid, 413.
[6]   See below Ch 9.
[7]   JR Galvin, *Three Men of Boston* (WA, Brassey's Inc, 1997).
[8]   ibid, 27.

sit in the Superior Court of the colony. In February 1761, the validity of general writs of assistance was argued before Hutchinson. Otis addressed the court for five hours. He accepted the legality of special writs which named an individual and place, but argued that general writs were illegal, being contrary to Magna Carta and the rights of man: 'If this commission be legal, a tyrant may in legal manner also control, imprison or murder anyone with the realm.' The reference to a tyrant may have had a special significance, because there was a tradition dating back to classical times that a ruler who acted as a tyrant could be overthrown by his subjects. Before Magna Carta the rebel barons had withdrawn their allegiance from the Crown.[9] Hutchinson adjourned the case in order to obtain a precedent from England. When he reconvened the court in November 1761, he had obtained a general writ from London and upheld the validity of general writs in Boston, dismissing the merchants' claim. Only a few years later, the radical journalist John Wilkes challenged the validity of general search warrants in London and Lord Chief Justice Mansfield ruled them illegal.[10]

Listening to the case in the Boston courthouse was a 26 year old lawyer called John Adams, who was to be one of the main instigators of revolution and the second President of the United States. He recorded Otis' argument and described him as a 'flame of fire.'[11] Adams was inspired and Otis became the darling of the colony.

He soon had another opportunity to test the resolve of the Massachusetts' governor. In 1762 Governor Bernard despatched a sloop (small warship) to sail in protection of the Massachusetts' fishing fleet against possible attacks by the French. The approval of the General Assembly of the colony was necessary before the Governor undertook any expenditure. Bernard had not obtained it,[12] but justified this expenditure as an emergency act. By now Otis had been elected as Speaker of the House of Representatives of Massachusetts and was chosen as head of a committee of the House to investigate the expenditure; they reported that taking the money was as arbitrary as the acts of Louis XIV in France. In 1762 Otis published a pamphlet in vindication of the conduct of the House. This was the first of many pamphlets setting out his attitude to the government of the colony.

> Justice to ourselves and to our constituents oblige us to remonstrate against the method of making or increasing establishments by the Governor and council. It is in effect taking from the house their most darling privilege, the right of originating all Taxes ... it is clear from hence, that without the aid of an Act of the province, the Governor and Council cannot legally take a shilling out of the treasury, let the emergency be what it may.[13]

---

[9]   See AJ Arlidge and I Judge, *Magna Carta Uncovered* (Oxford, Hart Publishing, 2014) ch 5.
[10]   *Money v Leach* 97 ER 1075.
[11]   CF Adams (ed), *Works of John Adams* (Boston MA, Charles C Little and James Brown, 1850) II 522.
[12]   Galvin above n 7, 46.
[13]   The text is to be found in an Appendix to N Allen, *Arsonist: The Most Dangerous Man in America* (Griffins Wharf Productions, 2011)

After the Seven Years' War ended, there were a large number of British troops in America and the government in England, led by George Grenville, was anxious to avoid their mass return. It was decided to keep 10,000 of them in America. Grenville was insistent that the colonists should bear a share of the cost of the war and keeping the troops in America. On the face of it, this was not unreasonable, since the colonies benefited considerably from the British victory. On the other hand the removal of the threat from the French army, also removed the necessity for the maintenance of an army in America.

On 5 April 1764, Parliament in London passed the Sugar Act (replacing the Molasses Act), which placed a duty on the importation of sugar products from outside the Empire, but at one third of that previously placed on molasses. The government calculated that the lower tax rate strictly enforced would produce more income than the old Act had. The preamble, however, stated that revenue from the duties would be used 'towards defraying the expenses of defending, protecting and securing the American colonies.' Previously the colonists had not opposed the British government's claim to be able to regulate trade. The result of the preamble to the Sugar Act was that Americans swiftly suggested that this was not a measure to regulate trade, but a tax. That conclusion was driven home when, during the debate leading to the passage of the Bill, the government stated that it might be necessary to place a stamp duty on formal documents produced in the colonies.

Protests were quick to follow. In May 1764, instructions were drafted in the Annual Meeting of the citizens of Boston to their representatives in the Massachusetts General Assembly:

> We ... expect that you will use your earliest endeavours in the General Assembly ... that will effectually prevent the proceedings against us (new taxes) ... we have reason to hope an application, even for a repeal of the act ... will be successful ... What still heightens our apprehensions is that these unexpected proceedings may be preparatory to new taxations upon us: For if our trade may be taxed, why not our lands? Why not the produce of our lands, and everything we possess ... if taxes are laid upon us in any shape without having legal representation where they are laid, are we not reduc'd from the character of free subject to the miserable state of tributary slaves ... That the trade with the colonies has been of surprising advantage to Great Britain ... is past all doubt. Great Britain is well known to have increased prodigiously both in numbers and wealth since she began to colonize. To the growth of the plantations Britain is in great measure indebted for her present riches and strength.[14]

In late July 1764 the Boston Gazette carried an advertisement stating that a pamphlet entitled *The Rights of the British Colonies asserted and proved*, written by James Otis Esquire, was now available.[15] It was a lengthy document, discussing the views of the English philosopher John Locke and accepting his contention that all men are born equal and free. Otis followed Locke's argument to its logical conclusion—all men were born free, white or black. 'Does it follow that 'tis right to enslave a man because he is black?'

[14]   ibid.
[15]   ibid, Introduction.

Otis also set out in the pamphlet his views on the status of colonies and colonists:

A plantation or colony is a settlement of subjects in a territory disjoined or remote from the mother country, and may be made by private adventurers or the public ... Every British subject born on the continent of America, or in any other of the British dominions, is by the law of God and nature, by the common law and by act of parliament (exclusive of all charters from the Crown) entitled to all the natural, essential and inherent and inseparable rights of our fellow subjects in Great Britain ... These are their (the government's) bounds:

1. To govern by stated laws.
2. Those laws should have no other end ultimately, but the good of the people.
3. Taxes are not to be laid on the people, but by their consent in person, or by deputation
4. Their whole power is not transferable

These are the first principles of law and justice and the great barriers of a free state and of the British constitution in particular.

He dealt with the particular argument that the American colonies should bear some of the cost of maintaining troops there—the colonies could have been invited to pay for a standing army by taxing themselves:

If an army must be kept in America, at the expence of the colonies, it would not seem quite so hard if after the parliament had determined the sum to be raised and apportioned it, to have allowed each colony to assess its quota and raise it as easily to themselves as might be. But to have the whole levied and collected without consent is extraordinary.

This was a constitutional argument, not a revolutionary one. Both the Petition of Right in 1628 and the Bill of Rights in 1689 effectively provided that the consent of the people in Parliament had to be obtained before taxation could be imposed.

A counter blast came from Thomas Whateley, Secretary to the British Treasury.[16] He met the constitutional argument by stating that colonials were *virtually* represented in the British parliament. This was the era of rotten boroughs, before the 1832 Reform Act; towns which had declined to a few inhabitants sent a member to Parliament (usually at the behest of a local land owner), whilst new large cities such as Leeds or Birmingham sent none. Only a very small proportion of the British population were actually entitled to vote. Whateley's argument was that an individual Member of Parliament represented the whole nation, including the colonists. This argument hardly commended itself by the fairness of the system that it relied on. In any event, even the citizens of Leeds and Birmingham had votes in the counties of Yorkshire and Warwickshire and so had members to whom they could turn.

---

[16] J Greene, *Constitutional Origins of the American Revolution* (Cambridge, Cambridge University Press, 2010).

When the Sugar Act was passed, the British government announced they were considering the introduction of a Stamp Act.[17] This was to require that a range of documents were to bear an official stamp, for which those using them had to pay. It was a tax first seen in Holland, which crossed the Channel when it was imposed in Britain under William III and Queen Mary. It proved a successful means of raising money. It was easy to collect—pre-stamped folios were sold by the government to be used in the production of the relevant document, the charge being passed on to the eventual customer. When the Stamp Act was drafted, the selection of items to be taxed in America had no clear rationale. It included levies on land transfers, contracts, licences to act as an attorney (at the high rate of £10), newspapers, pamphlets, playing cards and dice. Grenville and Whateley had no doubt that the British Parliament could tax the colonies in this way, but they gave the colonial governments an opportunity to find an alternative method of raising the monies they required; the colonies did not produce one. The Stamp Act was passed by the British Parliament on 22 March 1765, with an overwhelming majority in both houses.

To many of the American colonists this was a red rag to a bull. This was not an indirect tax arising from a right to regulate trade, but a direct tax on the colonies. In May 1765 the Virginia House of Burgesses[18] drew up a series of Resolves,[19] including:

> That the Taxation of the People by themselves or by Persons chosen by themselves to represent them, who could only know what Taxes the People are able to bear, or the easiest method of raising them, and must themselves be affected by every Tax laid on the People, is the only Security against burdensome Taxation, and the distinguishing characteristik of British Freedom, without which the ancient Constitution cannot exist.[20]

Crucially, the passage of the Stamp Act in London prompted Otis to try to achieve common cause with the other American colonies. His suggestion fell on fertile soil. There had been riots by opponents of the Act in many of the colonies (in Boston Thomas Hutchinson's house was sacked) and a group drawn from across the different colonies formed, calling themselves the Sons of Liberty.[21] The proposal to tax newspapers was ill-judged, inevitably leading to them vociferously condemning the tax. Otis persuaded the House of Representatives in Boston to issue an invitation to all the colonies to send representatives to a meeting to require the repeal of the Act.[22] Representatives of eight of the colonies met in New York in October 1765.[23] Only New Hampshire declined to attend;

---

[17]   Generally see ES Morgan and HM Morgan, *Stamp Act Crisis Prologue to Revolution* (North Carolina, University North Carolina Press, 1995).

[18]   See above Ch 4

[19]   R Middlekauff, *The Glorious Cause* (Oxford, Oxford University Press, 1982); Galvin above n 7, 93.

[20]   Galvin above n 7, 73.

[21]   ibid, 2, 97.

[22]   ibid, 92.

[23]   ibid, 111.

Virginia, North Carolina and Georgia could not send representatives, since their colonial governors refused to convene their assemblies to choose delegates. Otis was one of the Massachusetts' delegation. Governor Bernard persuaded a veteran of the French Wars, Timothy Ruggles, to go as well. He was chosen to chair proceedings, since Otis was thought too much of a firebrand. Congress drew together men of the north eastern colonies with others such as John Dickinson of Pennsylvania and John Rutledge of South Carolina (both members of the Middle Temple) who were to play leading roles in the move for independence. The delegates sent by the various states included businessmen, farmers and soldiers, though about a third were lawyers. On 7 October 1765, they assembled in New York City Hall (now called Federal Hall) and debated there until the 25 October in what they described as a Congress.

On 19 October the Congress adopted *a Declaration of Rights and Grievances*, drafted by the lawyer John Dickinson. It commenced with an expression of loyalty to the King and his government and attachment to the protestant succession in Britain. It then offered its humble opinion on the rights and grievances of the colonial citizens, including the assertion that the people of these colonies are not, and, from their local circumstances, cannot be, represented in the House of Commons in England; that the only representatives of the people of these colonies are persons chosen therein by themselves and that no taxes ever have been or can be constitutionally imposed on them, but by their respective legislatures. The Declaration called for the repeal of the Stamp Act. Copies were sent to the British government.

So far the arguments advanced by the colonists had been constitutional rather than revolutionary. Otis, however, saw the possibility of taking the example of the Congress further. Shortly before Christmas 1765, he adopted the pen name Hampden (after he who had refused to pay Ship Money to Charles I) for a series of articles in the Boston Gazette. There he argued that the American colonies were governed by their charters, not by the British Parliament. The articles spoke of forming a loose union of the American colonies, raising the possibility that America could be the basis of a greater empire than the world had ever seen.[24]

In July 1765 Grenville had been replaced by Lord Rockingham (one of the chief weaknesses of the British Parliament at this time was a swift turnover of administrations).[25] On learning of the degree of opposition in the colonies, Rockingham's administration took fright. There had been threats of boycotts in America against British goods and some British merchants protested about the effect of the Stamp Act on their trade. In February 1766 the Stamp Act was repealed. In debate Pitt the Elder, now in opposition, argued that the British Parliament had no right to tax the colonies. 'Americans are the sons, not the bastards of Englishmen.' The House of Commons, however, also passed a Declaratory Act affirming the British Parliament's right to legislate for the colonies 'in all cases whatsoever.'

---

[24] ibid, 118.
[25] ibid, 122.

Otis's star now waned. He had long held a reputation for volatility and his condition seemed to others to deteriorate.[26] Early in 1769 he announced that, as he was tiring, he would give up his legal practice.[27] On 5 September 1769 he had a serious altercation with a customs collector called John Robinson. He invited Robinson to fight him and in the ensuing struggle Otis received a heavy wound to his head. It may be that this affected his later behaviour or he may have developed some form of mental illness, but from then on he faded from public life.[28] The cause would be taken up by others.

His legal background and wide reading, however, had given his fellow colonists an intellectual basis for their hostility to the British government. That government's constantly changing administrations and frequent shifts of policy and repeal of legislation did them no favours in the eyes of the colonists. Reliance on the distinction between internal and external taxes and their insistence on virtual representation were not intellectually attractive. Otis' arguments were more attractive and certainly consistent. Perhaps his greatest contribution, however, was to draw the independent colonies in America together in protest.

---

[26]   ibid, 185.
[27]   ibid, 173.
[28]   On the Robinson incident see Morgan and Morgan above n 17, 4 and 51 and Galvin above n 7, 183 and 299.

8

The Common Law: William Blackstone

WILLIAM BLACKSTONE WAS a London barrister and Oxford academic. He was a Tory (and eventually a Member of Parliament) and a supporter of the establishment, particularly the monarchy; he expressed the view that the colonies in America were subject to the royal prerogative. He never visited America; yet more than anyone he influenced the development of the law in America. He was the first Professor of English Law at Oxford University, a subject which had never before been taught in the English universities. By 1750, no up to date text of the common law existed. Blackstone first lectured on the subject and then between 1765 and 1769 published his *Commentaries on the Laws of England*,[1] which sold like hot cakes in England and America. Lawyers in America, who wanted English common law to run there, had to find out what that law was; Blackstone gave them the basic material.

He was not an original thinker, but rather a compiler. In 1762 a New York merchant, John Watts, described him thus:

> We have a high character of a Professor at Oxford, who they say has brought that Mysterious Business (the study of law) to Some System, besides the System of Confounding other People and picking their Pockets, which most of the Profession understand pretty well.[2]

Some of his ideas on natural law can be traced to the English philosopher Locke and on separation of powers to the French Montesquieu, but these ideas would have been familiar to American lawyers in any event. Blackstone had his critics. In 1776 Jeremy Bentham published *Fragments of Government* anonymously; it contained a rigorous attack on Blackstone's *Commentaries*, criticising his views on natural law and the social contract. Whatever the status of his views on a particular aspect of law, what he did achieve was a clear, readable and systematic account of the state of English law as he saw it.

---

[1] See W Morrison (ed), *Blackstone's Commentaries on the Laws of England Volumes I–IV* (London, Routledge Cavendish, 2001).
[2] Quoted in P Hamlin, 'Legal Education in Colonial New York' (1939) 64 *New York University Law Quarterly Review*

As a Member of Parliament, Blackstone voted against the repeal of the Sugar Act.[3] The Colonists certainly dissented from his view on the authority of the English government in the colonies:

> [I]f an uninhabited country be discovered and planted by English subjects, all the English law then in being, which are the birthright of every subject, are there in force ... But in conquered or ceded countries, that have already laws of their own, the king may indeed alter and change those laws; but, till he does actually change them, the ancient law of the country remain, unless such as are against the law of God, as in the case of infidel country. Our American colonies are principally of this latter sort being obtained in the last century either by right of conquest and driving out the natives (with what natural justice I shall not at present inquire), or by treaties. And therefore the common law of England, as such, has no allowance or authority there; they being part of the mother country, but distinct though dependent dominions. They are subject, however to the control of parliament ... And, because several of the colonies had claimed a sole and exclusive right of imposing taxes upon themselves, the statute 6 Geo III c 12, expressly declares, that all his majesty's colonies and plantations in America have been, are, and of right ought to be, subordinate to and dependent upon the imperial crown and parliament of Great Britain.[4]

This last is a reference to the Declaratory Act of 1766. Blackstone based his propositions of law on a memorandum of a case in the Privy Council reported by the Master of the Rolls in 1722.[5] This stated that where an uninhabited country is found by the English, the laws of England apply. Where the King of England conquers a country, the conqueror by saving the lives of the people conquered, gains a right and property in such people, in consequence of which he may impose upon them what law he pleases; until such law is given by the conquering prince, the laws and customs of the conquered apply. The precise application of this doctrine to America was not obvious. In the first place, it was the various companies or proprietors who had conquered the land. Further the local population had not been taken prisoner, but allowed to exist to an extent side by side with the planters. It was unrealistic to consider the laws of the native Americans as remaining in place and governing the territory. The first Virginia Charter expressed the hope that the natives would be converted to Christianity, but otherwise was silent about them. The various colonial charters in general gave the planters the same liberties as Englishmen, but did not say the whole of English law ran in the colonies. In other parts of the Empire, such as Australia and British Columbia, land occupied by non-Christian indigenous tribes was treated as terra nullius—land that could be occupied and receive English law.[6] Blackstone's views on colonies did not prevent the American colonists arguing

---

[3] D Nolan, 'Sir William Blackstone and the New Republic: A Study of Intellectual Impact' (1976) 51 *New York University Law Review* 283 at 290.

[4] Morrison above n 1, 79.

[5] *Case 15*, Reports of Cases Argued and Determined in the High Court of Chancery and of Some Special Cases Adjudged in the Court of King's Bench Collected by William Peere Williams 2 P Wms 75; this followed the decision in *Blankard v Galdy* (1693) Salkeld 411.

[6] M Connor, *The Invention of Terra Nullius: Historical and Legal Fictions on the Foundation of Australia* (Sydney, Macleay Press, 2005).

that they were entitled to all the liberties of Englishmen nor that the common law ran in America.

Before Blackstone appeared, the Universities of Oxford and Cambridge taught Civil, that is Roman, law, not the common law of England. Elements of the English legal system go back to Anglo Saxon times. The Normans organised it on a nationwide basis. Their Kings initially presided over cases in the Royal Court and then deputed that role to royal judges, who travelled the length and breadth of the kingdom on Assize—literally a sitting. The Norman rulers spoke French and required that to be the language of the Royal Court and courts, so the early reports of cases were in that language. Gradually, as the dynasty became partly anglicised, this morphed into a special legal language called Law French. The law was not codified—the judges decided case by case, quoting earlier precedents. Because the judges travelled the country it became a law common to all the kingdom. The principal education in the universities was in the classics. About 1540, Henry VIII created Regius Professorships in Civil Law at Oxford and Cambridge, hence students could become Bachelors or Doctors in that discipline. The Professors were required to give a certain number of lectures. As the universities did not teach the common law, fourteenth century barristers in London formed Inns of Court, where they associated collegiately and taught the common law to aspiring barristers. Education was oral, including lectures and moots or mock legal arguments. There followed apprenticeship to a practising barrister, the whole taking seven years.

William was born in 1723, the son of a silk merchant in Cheapside in the City of London. In 1730 a friend of his mother's nominated him for a scholarship to Charterhouse School; the original Carthusian monastery just outside the City walls was dissolved by Henry VIII and in 1611 a school was endowed on the same site.[7] It has now moved out of London, but the original buildings survive near Smithfield meat market. His father died the following year and his mother a few years later. Pembroke College, Oxford, offered two scholarships a year to students at Charterhouse; William was awarded one of these and in 1740, now seventeen, he enrolled to read for a Bachelor of Civil law. All Souls College, Oxford, had been founded by an Archbishop of Canterbury to train canon (or ecclesiastical) lawyers. Henry VIII had forbidden the teaching of canon law and the College was now recognised as a centre for the study of civil law. Its fellowships were not then as prestigious as they have now become, but they were nevertheless highly desirable. William was awarded one in November 1743. He nevertheless had his eyes on the practice of the law, because he was admitted as a student to the Middle Temple in November 1741 and in November 1746 called to the bar. From then on he divided his time between the Temple and University. After William's death his brother in law, Clitherow, wrote a memoir about him and stated that he made his way very slowly at the bar, lacking powerful friends

---

[7] For an account of his life see W Prest, *William Blackstone: Laws and Letters in the Eighteenth Century* (Oxford, Oxford University Press, 2008).

or connections.[8] In 1753 he announced his retirement from practice and in June of that year issued a prospectus for four terms of lectures in Oxford in which he would

> lay down a general and comprehensive plan of the Laws of England; to deduce their History to enforce and illustrate their leading Rules and fundamental Principles; to explain their reason and Utility; and to compare them with the Law of Nature and other Nations; without dwelling too minutely on the Niceties of Practice or the more refined Distinctions of particular cases.[9]

These were private lectures, for which those attending had to pay. Lecturing at the university had declined in quantity and quality, leaving a gap in the market; William received a welcome additional income.

Between 1628 and 1644 the former Lord Chief Justice Edward Coke had published Four Volumes of *Institutes on the Laws of England*. The Restoration Chief Justice, Matthew Hale, had written an *Analysis of the Common Law*, which Blackstone praised for its scientific approach and took as his model. These, however, were old texts and nothing like as extensive as those Blackstone now planned. His lectures proved popular and this led him in November 1756 to publish an improved Plan for further lectures. The prospectus went into great detail, running to 200 pages. This in itself was bought in numbers, running eventually to six editions.[10] Blackstone had become involved with college and university administration, completing the Codrington Library of History and Law in All Souls and reforming the Oxford University Press (including the Clarendon Press which printed his work).

In 1742 an Oxford alumnus had published a book in no less than 23 volumes entitled *A General Abridgement of Law and Equity*. His name was Charles Viner; he had chambers in the Temple, but was never called to the bar. He spent some 50 years compiling all the accounts he could find of English legal cases. His book is both exhaustive and exhausting. It did, however, earn him a good deal of money and when he died in 1756 he left his whole estate, valued at £12,000 to his old university, with instructions that it should be used to establish a Chair of English law. The holder had to be qualified both in civil and common law. The university authorities took some time to recognise such a grubby workaday subject as worthy of academic study and so it was not until October 1758 that Blackstone was elected to be the first Vinerian Professor. News of his inaugural lecture reached the ears of George, Prince of Wales (who was to accede to the throne two years later); he was interested in constitutional law and asked Blackstone to read the lecture to him. William's immediate duties in Oxford prevented this, but he did send an account of the laws to the Prince. Blackstone's monarchism was personal as well as general.

His assumption of the Chair brought him some fame and he decided to exploit this by returning to practice; he took chambers in Inner Temple in the summer

---

[8] Quoted ibid, 71.
[9] ibid, 113.
[10] ibid, 142.

of 1759. This time his practice was more successful, but though he had a steady stream of work, he was not regarded as a leader of the bar. He married in 1761, which meant he had to surrender his Fellowship at All Souls, though he bought a house at Wallingford-on-Thames, some 12 miles from Oxford. In the same year he became a Member of Parliament under the patronage of Lord Bute. At this point the King decided he wished to appoint him King's Counsel, but this would have involved his resigning as a member of parliament and seeking re-election (you can begin to see why others might want to start a new nation). He was instead given a patent which gave him seniority after all King's Counsel, but before all other counsel. His income from lectures began to fall, partly because students who had attended them started selling their notes to other students. He decided to produce a printed edition of his lectures.

In November 1765 the first volume of his *Commentaries on the Laws of England* appeared. 1500 copies were printed and several hundred of them shipped to America.[11] The whole print sold rapidly. Volumes 2, 3 and 4 followed by 1769, with equal success. At the beginning of Volume 1 he acknowledges the influence of the compilation of Roman law in the Institutes prepared on the order of the Emperor Justinian.[12] Volume 1 dealt with Rights of Persons, Volume 2 with Rights of Things (largely property law), Volume 3 with Private Wrongs and Volume 4 with Public Wrongs. At the outset he states that

> the science thus committed to his charge, to be cultivated, methodized, and explained in a course of academical lectures, is that of the laws and constitution of our own country: a species of knowledge, in which the gentlemen of England have been more remarkably deficient than those of all Europe besides.[13]

He addresses himself not just to lawyers, but to a general audience of gentlemen:

> I think it an undeniable position, that a competent knowledge of the laws of that society in which we live, is the proper accomplishment of every gentleman and scholar; an highly useful, I had almost said essential, part of liberal and polite education.[14]

Volume 1 contains some rather grandiose jurisprudence, drawn largely from Locke. Blackstone treats law as of divine origin:

> [W]hen the Supreme Being formed the universe and created matter of nothing, he impressed certain principles upon that matter, from which it can never depart ... Man considered as a creature, must necessarily be subject to the laws of the Creator ... This will of his Maker is called the law of nature ... God has graciously reduced the law of obedience to this one paternal precept, 'that man should pursue his own true and substantial happinesse' ... This law of nature, being coeval with mankind and dictated by God himself, is of course superior in obligation to any other ... in a state of nature we are all equal.[15]

---

[11] ibid, 219; LC Warden, 'The Life of Blackstone' (1938) 1 *Louisiana Law Review*.
[12] Morrison above n 1, Vol 1, 4.
[13] ibid.
[14] ibid, 4.
[15] ibid, 29–32.

Nevertheless it is natural for men to associate together: 'the community should guard the rights of each individual member and ... (in return for this protection) each individual should submit to the laws of the community.' So beneath the overarching law of nature is 'municipal or civil law, that is the rule by which particular districts, municipalities or nations are governed.'[16] It is this municipal law of England which is to be his principal subject.

He deals with the idea of liberty in this way:

> [N]atural liberty consists properly in a power of acting as one thinks fit, without any restraint or control, unless by the law of nature; being a right inherent in us by birth, and one of the gifts of God to man as his creation, when he endowed him with the faculty of free will. But every man, when he enters into society gives up a part of his natural liberty, as the price of a valuable purchase; and in consideration of receiving the advantages of commerce, obliges himself to conform to those laws, which the community has thought proper to establish.[17]

He describes how the life and limbs of an Englishman are protected by provisions which go back to Magna Carta. The rule of law—that government is restricted by legal process—protects both his personal liberty and his property.[18] Most interesting in the context of the build up to the American revolution, were his views on taxation. He cites the history of taxation from Magna Carta to the Bill of Rights. Magna Carta did seek to establish that certain feudal dues could only be imposed with the consent of the counsel of the realm, but these particular provisions were annulled 10 weeks after the King agreed to them. The Petition of Right, presented by Parliament to King Charles I in 1628, requested that 'no man hereafter be compelled to make or yield any gift, loan, benevolence, tax or such like charge without the common consent by Act of Parliament.' Though this was a petition and not a bill, the King was forced to pronounce the words 'soit droit fait comme est desire' (let the law be made as is desired), which normally ushered a bill into force. He then proceeded to ignore it. In due course, the Bill of Rights of 1689 provided that 'the levying money for or to the use of the Crown by pretence of Prerogative without grant of Parliament for longer time or in other manner than the same is or shall be granted is illegal.' From these precedents Blackstone deduced that 'no subject of England can be constrained to pay any aids or taxes, even for the defence of the realm or the support of government, but such as are imposed by his own consent or that of his representatives in parliament.'[19] Later he describes how money bills, though they must be passed by both Houses of Parliament, must be introduced in the House of Commons: 'supplies are raised upon the body of the people; and therefore it is proper that they alone should have the right of taxing themselves.'[20] He did not, however, regard parliamentary democracy as requiring one man one vote. 'As to the qualification of voters—the true reason of requiring any qualification

[16] ibid, 33.
[17] ibid, 72.
[18] ibid, 95 et seq.
[19] ibid, 104.
[20] ibid, 126.

with regard to property in voters, is to exclude such persons who are in so mean a situation that they are esteemed to have no will of their own.'[21]

Also interesting in the context of the later drafting of the Constitution of the United States were his views on the separation of powers:

> Herein indeed consists the excellence of the English government, that all the parts of it form a mutual check upon the other. In the legislature, the people are a check upon the nobility, and the nobility a check upon the people; by the mutual privilege of rejecting what the other has resolved: while the king is a check upon both, which preserves the executive power from encroachment. And his very executive power is again checked and kept within due bounds by the two houses, through the privilege they have of inquiring into, impeaching and punishing the conduct, not indeed of the king, which would destroy his constitutional independence; but, which is more beneficial to the public, of his evil and pernicious counsellors. Thus every branch of our civil polity supports and is supported, regulates and is regulated, by the rest.[22]

These passages deal with the legislature. Later he deals with the independence of the judiciary.[23] He recites the provisions of the Act of Settlement establishing that judges held office during good behaviour and at ascertained salaries, though they could be removed by a resolution of both Houses of Parliament; he goes on:

> In this distinct and separate existence of the judicial power, in a peculiar body of men nominated indeed, but not removable at pleasure by the crown, consists one main preservative of the public liberty, which cannot subsist long in any state unless the administration of common justice be in some degree separated both from the legislative and also from the executive power.[24]

The *Commentaries* went through numerous English editions up to the twentieth century, increasingly annotated to bring them up to date. The prestige of the original was such as to make such editions saleable. The first American edition was published by John Bell of Philadelphia in 1772,[25] with a commentary on the *Commentaries*.[26] Before publication it had achieved 1600 subscribers. 16 of them became signatories of the Declaration of Independence and six were framers of the Constitution. St George Tucker edited a version in 1803 with references to the Constitution and laws of the federal government of the United States and of the Commonwealth of Virginia. He treated the *Commentaries* as a basic text to be developed in an American context. His commentary had a more republican base. Other practising and academic lawyers followed his imprint, the most popular being Judge George Sharswood of Pennsylvania. In due course the length of the notes in these editions exceeded the original text.

Most of the quotations taken above are from volume 1 of the *Commentaries*. The remaining volumes covered the state of English law as Blackstone saw

---

[21] ibid, 127.
[22] ibid, 115.
[23] ibid, 203.
[24] ibid, 203–04.
[25] Warden above n 11.
[26] See M Hoeflich, *American Blackstones* in *Blackstone and his Commentaries: Biography, Law, History* (ed W Prest, Oxford and Portland OR, Hart Publishing, 2009).

it and they provided a template for the development of American law. Rufus Choate, one of the greatest antebellum advocates, had five different editions of Blackstone. John Marshall was Chief Justice of the Supreme Court from 1801 to 1835. He was born in a log cabin on the Virginia frontier. His father had ambitions for him and bought a copy of the *Commentaries* for his son to read. Marshall frequently cited them in his judgments.[27] Marshall was federalist, that is he tended to favour the rights of the federal government over those of the states. Maybe he was influenced in this by Blackstone's views on the importance of the monarchy in the British constitution. As a young man, Abraham Lincoln bought a job lot of books from a passing salesman, which turned out to include a copy of the *Commentaries*; his interest in the law was kindled.[28] He advised law students to start with Blackstone. The *Commentaries* have been cited frequently in American judgments.

Blackstone may be credited with one other contribution to American life. In the *Commentaries* he advocated the teaching of law in universities.

> [A] science, which distinguishes the criterions of right and wrong; which teaches to establish the one, and prevent, punish or redress the other ... which is universal in its use and extent accommodated to each individual, yet comprehending the whole community; that science like this ever have been deemed unnecessary to be studied in an university, is matter of astonishment and concern. Surely, if it were not before an object of academical knowledge, it was high time to make it one.[29]

Despite the appointment of Vinerian professors to lecture on English law, the University of Oxford did not offer a degree in the subject until the 1870s. Cambridge followed Oxford's example and in 1800 the founder of Downing College endowed a Chair in English Law, but it was not until 1858 that a degree course was offered. Law was probably regarded as a practical subject not suitable for degree study. The Americans were quicker off the mark. In 1779 Thomas Jefferson persuaded the governors of the College of William and Mary in Williamsburg, Virginia to found a Chair of Law, the first professor being his old mentor George Wythe. In 1817 a wealthy Antiguan plantation owner, who had emigrated to Boston, endowed a Chair of Law at Harvard University in that city. It struggled at first, but a further endowment provided the Dane professorship in 1827. A practising lawyer in New Haven set up a private law school there, which in 1820 became affiliated to Yale University and in 1824 turned into the Yale School of Law. These and other great law schools in America have had a pre-eminent effect on the development of the common law.

In 1770 Blackstone became a judge of the King's Bench and then the Common Pleas. His judicial reputation was not high.[30] He suffered increasingly from ill health and died in 1780. The influence of his *Commentaries* remains his chief legacy.

---

[27] Warden above n 11, 135, 328.
[28] ibid, 332.
[29] Morrison above n 1, 20.
[30] See Nolan above n 3, 287.

9

Penman of the Revolution:
John Dickinson

THE PEN THAT James Otis had wielded so effectively was taken up by John Dickinson, indeed his nickname was 'penman' of the revolution. In the next phase of the revolution, he managed better than anyone to encapsulate the feelings of the colonists towards Britain. Yet he was a reluctant revolutionary, persisting in the belief that King George III would recognise the validity of the colonists' grievances and right them.

His family owned property in Maryland and in Kent County, Delaware. Although Philadelphia was on the Delaware River, it was a good way upstream and so William Penn asked for and was granted an area to the south on the west bank of the Delaware River, including Kent County, which had easy access to the sea. Penn gave the inhabitants representation in the Pennsylvania Assembly, but later in 1701 he gave them the right to hold their own assembly. Shortly before the Second Continental Congress, this assembly declared Delaware a state independent of Britain. It sent representatives to the Congress and played an instrumental part in the signing of the Declaration of Independence. Nevertheless, it did not have its own Constitution until a slightly later date.[1]

John's forbears were Quakers and settled in Maryland.[2] John was never formally a Quaker, but he was strongly influenced by their beliefs. His father and mother, Samuel and Mary, were members of the Third Haven Meeting of Friends in Maryland. John was born in Maryland in 1732. He had an elder sister Betsy, who became engaged to marry an Anglican.[3] The Friends' Meeting declared the proposed marriage disorderly. Samuel nevertheless gave his consent, left the fellowship of the Meeting and moved his family to his Kent County property. Thereafter he distanced himself from the Quakers. His father's experience affected John. In 1770, he in turn married Mary (Polly) Norris, who came from a prominent Quaker family, but he refused to marry under the care of the Meeting, insisting on a civil ceremony. He wrote to Mary's sister that he did not wish to live by the rules of a private society—'if an Act is not contrary to the laws of virtue or our country, can any rule of a particular society, however positive it may be, make that act improper or dishonourable?'[4] His mother and his

---

[1] See the Delaware Historical Society Website.
[2] See W Murchison, *The Cost of Liberty: The Life of John Dickinson* (NC, ISI Books, 2013) 5.
[3] ibid, 6.
[4] Quoted JE Calvert, *Quaker Constitutionalism and the Political Thought of John Dickinson* (NY, Cambridge University Press, 2008) 190.

wife remained devout Quakers. John Adams is quoted as saying 'if I had such a mother and a wife, I believe I should have shot myself.'[5] As late as 1801, John wrote 'I am not, and probably never shall be, united to any religious society, because each of them as a Society, hold principles which I cannot adopt.'[6]

Despite this, the influence of Quakerism on John was evidenced by his adoption of their plain way of speaking, using 'thee' and 'thou' and his refusal to swear an oath.[7] He was always opposed to slavery—although he had some domestic slaves, he freed them in 1777. He promoted prison reform and education and was opposed to the opening of theatres, all policies dear to Quakers.[8] He also advocated passive resistance to the British government. In his view the colonists had two alternatives—either simply to ignore British legislation which they regarded as unconstitutional and proceed as if it had not been enacted, or impose economic sanctions.[9] Yet the fact that he was not a member of a Quaker meeting also allowed him, once Congress had declared independence, to give it his support both by the pen and the gun.

The other great influence on Dickinson was his love of English common law and the British Constitution, views which sometimes led him into apparently contradictory stances. The number of English trained lawyers in the colonies had increased in the course of the eighteenth century. Between 1760 and the end of the Revolution some 115 Americans were admitted to the English Inns of Court, though these came mainly from the southern states, South Carolina and Virginia accounting for 68 of them.[10] John Moland was an English barrister, who was appointed King's Attorney in Pennsylvania and became leader of the Pennsylvania bar. John Dickinson was apprenticed to him.[11] It was probably his influence that led John, aged 21, to take an eight week voyage to London to enrol as a student in the Middle Temple in 1753. He took chambers in Essex Court, close to Middle Temple Hall.[12] He was enthusiastic about the study of the common law. In those days the common law courts sat in Westminster Hall, which students were encouraged to attend. He wrote a letter to his father:

> Westminster Hall is a school of law where we not only hear what we have read repeated, but disputed and sifted in the most curious and learned maner, nay frequently hear things quite new, have our doubts cleared up and our errors corrected.[13]

In London he met William Penn's son, who obtained an audience for him with George II, whom he described as the greatest and best King on earth.[14] He never

---

[5] Quoted in D McCullogh, 'John Adams' (2001) 117(1) *Political Science Quarterly* 130.

[6] ibid, 191.

[7] ibid.

[8] ibid, 193.

[9] ibid, 209.

[10] C Warren, *History of the American Bar* (Boston MA, Little, Brown, and Company, 1911).

[11] ibid, 8.

[12] RR Logan, *Collection of Dickinson Papers (Collection 383), the Historical Society of Pennsylvania*, Library Company of Philadelphia, Account Book.

[13] Quoted M Flower, *John Dickinson Conservative Revolutionary* (Charlottesville, University of Virginia Press, 1983) 15.

[14] Murchison above n 2, 14.

met George III, but after he succeeded John expressed his 'warmest sentiments of affection and duty to his majesty's person and government.'[15] Even while he was conducting his campaign against the activities of the British government, he wrote: 'Every drop of blood in my heart is British, and that heart is animated with as warm wishes for her prosperity as her truest sons could be.'[16] Whatever the deficiencies of the British constitution, it was more libertarian than its continental counterparts and in the right to petition the Crown contained a mechanism to correct errors in government. Right up to the Declaration of Independence, while he argued the colonists' case against taxation, he continued to support the colonial connection. In notes for a Speech in Congress in 1775 he wrote 'I have never had and now have not any idea of happiness for the Colonies for several ages to come, but in a state of Dependence upon and subordination to her parent state.'[17] If Otis was a firebrand, Dickinson was quite the opposite. There were many shades of opinion among the colonists about the true relationship between the mother country and the colonies and in due course there were many who remained loyal to the Crown. The ineptness of the British government, however, was enough to drive sufficient of them into the revolutionary camp. Dickinson, though the chief apologist for American opposition, was short of revolutionary zeal.

On his return from England to America, John was admitted to the Pennsylvania bar in 1757 and built up a successful law practice in Philadelphia. Despite its distance from the sea, Philadelphia had developed as a hub of the colonies. By the time of the revolution, it had a population of 30,000; over 400 ships a day cleared its port; and it had an efficient mail service.[18] Any young lawyer would want to make his name there. Having first been elected to the Delaware Assembly, in 1762 he was elected to the Pennsylvania Assembly and as their representative went to the Stamp Act Congress organised in 1765. It has already been noted that he drafted the Declaration of Rights and Grievances approved by the Congress.

In July 1766 there was another change of administration in London. The Earl of Rockingham was dismissed and William Pitt the Elder was reappointed in his stead. Pitt still commanded popularity because he had headed the administration that successfully conducted the Seven Years' War. As he had spoken in opposition in favour of the repeal of the Stamp Act, the colonists must have viewed his appointment with optimism, but two factors caused that to be ill-founded. Pitt in his heyday was given the nickname of the Great Commoner. At the start of his new administration, he accepted ennoblement to the House of Lords, as Lord Chatham, and this not only dented his popularity, but also reduced his ability to manage the House of Commons. At the same time his health was deteriorating and the combination of these factors left his administration without effective

---

[15] PL Ford (ed), *The Writings of John Dickinson* (Philadelphia PA, The Historical Society of Pennsylvania, 1895) 234.
[16] ibid, 184.
[17] ibid, 233.
[18] Murchison above n 2, 20–22.

leadership. In August 1766, he appointed the ambitious Charles Townshend as his Chancellor of the Exchequer; he had been President of the Board of Trade and a Lord of the Admiralty. He initiated a series of Acts, which became known as the Townshend Acts, asserting the British government's control over the colonies. Initially he took punitive action against the State of New York for failing to obey the Quartering Act of 1765. Then he introduced a Revenue Bill, which came into force as an Act in June 1767, imposing duties on a variety of products imported into America from Great Britain, including various types of glass, paper, paint and tea. In the preamble, its stated purpose was not only to pay for the security of the colonies, but also to pay for the government and administration of justice in the colonies. Previously governors of colonies and judges in their jurisdiction had been remunerated by colonial governments; paying their salaries would tie them more effectively to the British government. Townshend regarded his Revenue Act as an internal tax regulating trade.[19] The colonists saw it as a direct tax.

On 4 September 1767 Townshend died. On the 30 November the first of a series of publications, which have become known as *Letters from a farmer in Pennsylvania to his Countrymen*, appeared in the Pennsylvania Chronicle and Universal Advertiser.[20] It was dated 5 November, that being the date on which William of Orange landed in 1688 at Torbay in England to commence the so-called Glorious Revolution. In all, 12 letters appeared at weekly intervals. The anonymous author was John Dickinson, who was above all an advocate.

This is illustrated by the opening of the first letter:

> I am a farmer, settled after a variety of fortunes, near the banks of the river Delaware, in the province of Pennsylvania. I received a liberal education and have been engaged in the busy scenes of life, but am now convinced that a man may be as happy without bustle as with it. My farm is small, my servants are few but good. I have a little money in interest. Being master of my time, I spend a good deal of time in a library, which I think the most valuable part of my small estate ... I believe I have acquired a greater share of knowledge of history and the laws and constitution of our country than is generally attained by men of my class ... from infancy I was taught to love humanity and liberty.

The reference to a modest estate in the backwaters of Delaware suggests a small freeholder, similar to the bulk of colonists. Yet he is educated, has time to contemplate in his library, and so acquire a wider knowledge than the average colonist, thus entitling him to speak out. There is no mention that he is a barrister qualified in the Middle Temple. No matter, this is journalism.

In the body of the letters, Dickinson accepts the principle that the British Parliament has legal authority to regulate trade between Great Britain and its

---

[19] On this subject see P Thomas, *The Townshend Duties Crisis: Second Phase of the American Revolution 1767–73* (New York, Oxford University Press,1987).

[20] The texts can be found in a number of sources: they were published in compendium in 1678 in Philadelphia, New York, Boston and London. RE Halsey produced a useful version with commentary in 1903; they can be found in *Empire and Nations* (ed) Forrest McDonald (Prentice-Hall Inc, 1962). I refer for reference solely to the number of the relevant letter in Roman numerals.

colonies, which exist for the good of both.[21] The policy of establishing colonies was that Great Britain should manufacture and supply goods to America and America should supply her with materials. 'America is a country of planters, farmers and fishermen; not of manufacturers. The difficulty of establishing particular manufactures in such a country is almost insuperable.'[22] This two way traffic has produced the wealth, power and glory of Great Britain.[23] He quotes Pitt the Elder in debate in Parliament: 'This ... kingdom has always bound the colonies by her regulation and restrictions in trade, in navigation—in everything except that of taking their money our of their pockets without their consent.'[24] Dickinson underlined that the Revenue Act provided for funding colonial government and justice.[25] This was not regulation of trade, but a levy contrary to the Bill of Rights. For the last 150 years no British government had passed a statute raising revenue from the colonies.

> Hitherto Great Britain has been content with her prosperity. Moderation has been the rule of her conduct. But now a generous and humane people, that so often has protected the liberties of strangers, is inflamed into an attempt to tear a privilege from her own children, which, if executed, must in their opinion sink them into slaves.[26]

As the letters proceed, he deals with reaction to earlier ones: some people tell him that they are fearful of confronting England and others are for arming against her. Dickinson seeks a balance. To take no action is simply to encourage usurpation, which will grow stronger.[27] The authors of the Stamp Act would not have sought to raise a trifling sum, had they not intended to establish a precedent for future use.[28] Passing to the Revenue Act, he writes

> upon the whole for my part I regard the late act as an experiment made of our disposition. It is a bird sent over the water to discover, whether the waves that lately agitated this part of the world have subsided. If this adventurer gets footing here, we shall quickly be convinced that it is not a phoenix, for we shall soon see it is followed by other of the same kind.[29]

On the other hand if recourse is had to the sword, it is highly probable that the punishment will exceed the offence. The dangers of war are too great to risk.

> If once we are separated from our mother country, what new form of government shall we accept or where shall we find another Britain to supply our loss? Torn from the body to which we are united by religion, liberty, laws, affections, relations language and commerce, we must bleed in every vein.[30]

[21] Letter II.
[22] ibid and Letter V.
[23] Letter V.
[24] Letter II.
[25] ibid.
[26] Letter V.
[27] Letter III.
[28] Letter VII.
[29] Letter XI.
[30] Letter III.

He warns that the cause of liberty ought not to be sullied by turbulence and tumult. Redress should be sought by the constitutional method of petition to the local assemblies or the government in London. If this proves ineffectual, however, we should withdraw from Great Britain all the advantages she has been used to receive from the colonies—in other words civil disobedience on the Quaker model.[31] He concludes in Letter XII by warning against dissension between the colonies. United vigilance will lead to safety, negligence will lead to shame and slavery.

Dickinson sent a copy of his letters to James Otis junior in Boston and he persuaded the merchants of Boston to organise a boycott of imports from Britain. The merchants of New York and Philadelphia followed suit, as in the end did merchants of the remaining colonies. From 1768 to 1769 the value of British goods imported into the colonies fell from £2.1 million to £1.3 million.[32] Nevertheless, Boston became the headquarters of new Customs Commissioners appointed to secure what was due. Their intervention was resented and when in May 1768 customs officers seized the sloop Liberty in Boston harbour on suspicion of smuggling, a mob ran them out of town. In July the Boston Gazette published Dickinson's composition *The Liberty Song,* words to music by William Boyce.[33] In January 1770, there was yet another change of administration, when Frederick Lord North was appointed Prime Minister and in the next month he repealed the Revenue Act 1767, with the exception of the duty on tea. In September 1770 the boycott was called off in Philadelphia. Dickinson's policy appeared triumphant.[34] It was in July of that year that he married.

The tax on tea remained an irritant. In 1771 Dickinson was a member of a committee, which drafted a petition to London asking for the repeal of the tax on tea; it received no response. The East India Company now ran into financial difficulties and accumulated large amounts of unsold tea. They were compelled to land their tea in England, where taxes would be imposed. Now, to meet their difficulties, the Tea Act 1773 was passed, allowing them to export directly to the colonies, where the tea would be sold by British agents, tax only being imposed on sale. In November 1773 Dickinson published a letter in a Philadelphia newspaper to his dear friend Rusticus urging 'that no one will receive the Tea, no one will let his stores, nor suffer the vessel that brings it to moor at his wharf.'[35] It was republished in other colonies. In several colonial ports steps were taken to prevent the landing of tea from Britain.

Others were becoming disillusioned with opposition confined to passive resistance. In the summer of 1765 loose groups, who called themselves the Sons of Liberty, began to appear in various cities along the eastern seaboard. They built up contact. In Boston, on 16 December 1773, some of their number, dressed as native Americans, boarded a vessel trying to land tea and tipped the boxes of tea it contained into the harbour. The Boston 'tea party' has given its name to the

---

[31] ibid.
[32] Murchison above n 2, 64.
[33] ibid.
[34] ibid, 67.
[35] Ford above n 15, 451–52.

modern political faction. The British government's reaction in March 1774 significantly increased the possibility of conflict; they passed the so-called Coercive Acts, which closed Boston to merchant shipping, established British military rule in Massachusetts and required the colonists to quarter British troops.

The original thirteen colonies

This was a fateful step, because colonies with very disparate backgrounds came together. Representatives of 12 of the colonies met in the First Continental Congress in Carpenter's Hall in Philadelphia on 5 September 1774. There was division among the delegates between those who wished to declare independence immediately and those, led by Dickinson, who wished to organise a boycott similar to the one that had succeeded in the recent past. The party of moderation won the day and it was agreed to boycott the importation of British goods from December 1774 and ban exports to Britain from September 1775. The ban on exports was delayed to protect the limited economy of the southern States.[36] Most importantly a date was set for a Second Congress on 10 May 1775. This time there would be representatives from Georgia and so every state would be represented.

By the time they met as planned, there was a serious change of mood. Hostilities between the British garrison in Boston and the New England militia had broken out in the suburbs of the city.[37] Men had died. Now there was the possibility

[36] ibid, 182 et seq.
[37] For a detailed account see below ch 10.

of serious armed conflict. The Second Congress recognised the need for a continental army and on 15 June 1775 they appointed George Washington as its commander.[38] Despite all this, it was decided to make one last petition to the King and on 5 July 1775 Congress adopted the so-called *Olive Branch Petition*. Both Thomas Jefferson and Dickinson produced drafts, but it was Dickinson's which was preferred. It was in the form of a humble petition to their Gracious Sovereign and praised former harmonious relations between Britain and her American colonies; it went on to record their alarm at a new system of statutes and regulations adopted for the administration of the colonies which filled their minds with painful fears.

> We shall decline the ungrateful task of describing the irksome variety of artifices by many of your Majesty's Ministers, the delusive pretences, fruitless terrours and unavailing severities, that have from time to time been dealt out by them ... Your Majesty's Ministers, persevering in their measures and proceeding to open hostilities for enforcing them, have compelled us to arm in our own defence ... we therefore beseech your Majesty, that your royal authority and influence may be graciously interposed ... to settle Peace through every part of our Dominions.

It was in the ancient form of applying to the King to redress the actions of his ministers and proposed no specific action.

To underline the seriousness of its opposition, however, on 6 July Congress also published a *Declaration of Causes and Necessity of Taking up Arms*. Jefferson drafted and Dickinson amended it. It concluded: 'We are reduced to the alternative of chusing an unconditional submission to the tyranny of irrational Ministers, or resistance by force. The latter is our choice.'[39]

The *Olive Branch Petition* was handed to the Colonial Secretary in London by William Penn's son, Thomas, on 21 August 1775.[40] The King refused to look at it. Its force was reduced by the interception by the British of a letter from John Adams, in which he said that war was inevitable. On the 23 August, the King issued a Proclamation for Suppressing Rebellion and Sedition in which he declared the American colonies in a state of rebellion. Dickinson's faith in the monarchy had been sorely misplaced. Any hope of Dickinson's pacific policy continuing was ended in January 1776 with the publication of Thomas Paine's *Common Sense*. 18 months earlier Thomas Paine had met Benjamin Franklin in London and been given an introduction to a newspaper in Philadelphia, which he thereafter edited. In his book he caught the new mood of the colonists in the same way that Dickinson had in his *Letters from a Farmer*. Paine wrote: 'Every quiet method for peace hath been ineffectual. Our prayers have been rejected with disdain ... Wherefore since nothing but blows will do, for God's sake let us come to a final separation.'

On 11 May 1776 Virginia called for the Continental Congress to declare independence. This time Jefferson was entrusted to make a draft. It was debated in Congress for several days and Dickinson argued against its publication on

[38] Ford above n 15,110.
[39] ibid, 111.
[40] ibid, 113.

the basis that the colonists were unprepared and should at least wait until alliance could be made with the French.[41] Even on the day before the Declaration was adopted, he argued in Congress against that course. Independence would lead to a multitude of commonwealths, crimes, jealousies, hatreds, wars and devastations.[42] Dickinson was right that many horrors would follow. The enormity of what the colonists attempted is breathtaking. With a militia of a total of just over 14,000 it was taking on a professional army and the most powerful navy in the world. Many colonists would remain loyal to the Crown and some would fight for it—an inbuilt fifth column. The 13 colonies, springing largely from different and deeply held religious convictions seemed unlikely to coalesce into a single army let alone polity. Whatever happened many would lose their property—as Dickinson himself did—or die.

On 3 July 1776 the Pennsylvania delegation voted by 4:3 against a declaration, but were now in a minority in Congress. The next day Dickinson and one other delegate, who had also voted against, absented themselves and Pennsylvania voted again 3:2 in favour. Jefferson's draft, after some amendment, was approved and the Declaration made.

Dickinson was a colonel in the Pennsylvania militia and was immediately ordered to take his battalion to New Jersey, which he did. He was one of a very few members of the Congress to put himself forward for military service. After a short period the Pennsylvania Assembly recalled the battalion and placed others in command. Dickinson left the military without seeing action.[43] During the war that followed, his house in Delaware was destroyed by fire by the British.[44] After the Declaration he was still willing to serve the cause of the colonists. When a committee was formed to draft articles of confederation, Dickinson was a member, but his draft was rejected because it gave too much power to central government.[45] When Pennsylvania elected new delegates to Congress, his name was omitted and he retired to Delaware, of which he became President.

The American Revolution could have been avoided. Had the British government been more politic, Dickinson's middle way might have prevailed. The conflict became mired in abstruse rhetoric. The arguments on both sides had their weaknesses. The distinction that Dickinson and others made between Acts of the British Parliament regulating trade and those regulating other areas was unreal. Legislation from the Molasses Act to the Tea Act did deal with trade in commodities. Dickinson maintained they did not regulate trade, because the proceeds were to be used for purposes other than improving trade. Yet the monies raised by taxes on commodities never appear to have been ring-fenced— they simply went into the general government pot. The tax in the Tea Act was intended to protect the East India Company and so clearly related to trade. The

---

[41] JH Powell 'Speech of John Dickinson Opposing a Declaration of Independence' (1941) 65(4) *Pennsylvania Magazine of History and Biography* 458–81.
[42] See Calvert above n 4.
[43] ibid, 156–57.
[44] ibid, 169.
[45] ibid, 163.

non-lawyer, Benjamin Franklin, saw the weakness in the argument. In a letter to his son in 1768 he wrote:

> It being difficult to draw lines between duties for regulation and those for revenue and, if Parliament is to be the judge, it seems to me that establishing such principles of distinction will amount to little. The more I have thought and read on the subject, the more I find myself confirmed in opinion, that no middle doctrine can well be maintained, I mean not clearly with intelligible arguments.[46]

Had the British government not spelt out in the various statutes their purpose in raising the money, there would probably been much less opposition.

The British government's argument that the colonists were virtually represented in Parliament was even more unattractive, given the undemocratic state of the British electorate. Moreover the successive governments weakened their case by insisting that they had the right to tax the colonies and then, in the face of opposition, backing down in particular instances. By leaving the American colonies largely to govern and tax themselves, the British government had inevitably encouraged a feeling of independence.

One senses that there were agendas which did not depend on the legal arguments deployed. The British government's huge war debt arose in large part from their defence of the American colonies and it seemed wholly reasonable to them to require the colonies to help in clearing that. Had the government asked the local assemblies to contribute, it is possible they would have done so, at least to some extent. The colonists, however, had contributed militiamen to the war at their own expense and, now the French were defeated, they saw little need to maintain a large number of British troops in America—after all the Bill of Rights forbade standing armies in time of peace. There was an ultimate clash between a government (including the King) who regarded the colonies as their possession or dominion and a collection of colonists who had a growing confidence they could prosper without England's help. The very nature of the religious settlement brought diverse men of independent mind together. Yet there must have been many colonists who, like Dickinson, did not want to be severed from Britain; whose confidence in the British constitution was such that they believed to the last that their grievances would be righted. Had British politicians harnessed this body of opinion and behaved more moderately revolution might have been avoided. Curiously, since independence the American public shows a delight in establishing their own ruling dynasties, from the Adamses to the Roosevelts, to the Kennedys and Bushes and in following the fortunes of the British royal family.

---

[46] LW Labaree (ed), *Papers of Benjamin Franklin, Vol 15, January 1 through December 31 1768* (NH and London, Yale University Press, 1970) 111.

10

Revolution: John Adams

IF JOHN DICKINSON was a reluctant revolutionary, **John Adams** was an enthusiastic one. There were times when he doubted the wisdom of going to war with Britain, but he also saw that the possibility of the government in London acceding to the colonists' demands was remote. He was a practising lawyer in Massachusetts, but from the First Continental Congress he gave nearly all his time to the colonial opposition and thereafter to public office. He played a crucial role in persuading the separate colonies to combine against the British government and in particular, in the Second Continental Congress, persuading all 13 to sign the Declaration of Independence. When the Constitution of the United States was drafted, it took a form which he had long advocated, balancing the various sources of power in the state.

John was born in Braintree, Massachusetts in 1735. The first settlers arrived in Braintree in 1625; it lies nine miles from the centre of Boston. It was one of number of colonies established around Massachusetts Bay, containing some 20,000 settlers, among them Henry and Edith Adams from Somerset in England. At that time, Braintree was in Suffolk County, later changed to Norfolk County. John's forbears seem to have come for religious reasons; John and his family were Congregationalists.[1] John's father, also John, married Susanna Boylston, who came from one of the most prominent puritan families in Massachusetts. The family prospered as farmers. In 1761 John's father died in an influenza epidemic and John inherited farmlands and a farmhouse, called Peacefield, which became his home from then on.[2]

In 1751, he enrolled in Harvard University and his horizons widened. President of the University was Edward Holyoke and he expounded the view that ministers or pastors had no right to impose their interpretations of the law of Christ upon their flocks.[3] John retained a curiosity about other forms of worship and culture. He graduated in 1755 and initially worked as a schoolteacher, but in 1758 became apprentice to a lawyer near his home. He had no family connections in the law, but he made them by networking. He went to Boston and met Jeremiah Gridley and James Otis junior. In 1762 Gridley proposed him for admission to the Massachusetts bar, which gave him rights of audience in the Boston Superior Court. He went back to Braintree initially and lost his first case

---

[1] See D McCullough, *John Adams* (New York, Simon & Schuster, 2001).
[2] P Smith, *John Adams* (Garden City NY, Doubleday, 1962) 57.
[3] ibid, 15.

because the form of the writ he used was defective. In 1765 Gridley invited him to join a select club of lawyers who debated the law and studied oratory.

He practised on the Massachusetts' legal circuit, which took him all over the colony, including to Weymouth, where he was welcomed into the family of the local minister, the Reverend Mr Smith, and fell in love with his daughter Abigail. He courted her and on one occasion arrived with a letter requiring her to give the bearer as many kisses and as many hours of her company after six o'clock as he will command. She replied that he already owed her a considerable sum for the kisses he had stolen from her. This was to be the pattern of their relationship—she was no doormat, but an educated woman whom John often consulted on political matters. He married her in October 1761. Unfortunately for her, but fortunately for posterity, he was separated from her for long periods, initially when he had cases away from Braintree and then for months at a time when he attended the Continental Congresses or represented the United States in Europe. These absences led to a touching correspondence between them, which has largely survived, and shows the strength and support each gave the other.[4] Both quote from the classics and she signs herself Portia. There is a point where she says she would like to have a copy of Lord Chesterfield's *Letters*. He replies: 'you would not choose to have them in your library, because they are like Congreve's plays, stained with libertine morals and base principles.'[5] They had four children of whom they were both very fond and supportive.

John's practice grew rapidly and, when Gridley died in 1767 and Otis retired from practice in 1769, he became in effect leader of the Boston bar. In 1765 he had written *A Dissertation on Canon and Feudal law*, which included a passage reflecting his legal philosophy:

> Let us study the law of nature, search into the spirit of the constitution, read the histories of ancient ages ... set before us the conduct of our own British ancestors, who have defended for us the inherent rights of mankind against foreign and domestic tyrants and usurpers.

In October 1765, he drafted instructions to the representatives of Braintree attending the General Court of Massachusetts: 'we should not be subject to any tax imposed by the British parliament, because we are not represented in that assembly.'[6] These instructions were printed in the Massachusetts' Gazette. His cousin Samuel, who was 13 years older, had been active in Boston politics for some time and drafted similar instructions to the representatives of Boston. Samuel was to attend the Continental Congresses and John frequently consulted him. In this instance, the General Court resolved that no tax could be imposed on the American colonies, but by their respective legislatures. They sent a letter to General Assemblies of other colonies asserting colonial rights. The royal

---

[4] The correspondence is to be found in editions of the *Familiar Letters*; the Massachusetts Historical Society have placed them online; this is the version I have used, giving the letters simply their date.

[5] 5 April 1776.

[6] CF Adams (ed), *Works of John Adams* (MA, Little, Brown and Company, 1850) III 466.

Governor of Massachusetts directed their Assembly to rescind it, but by a vote of 92 to 17 they refused to do so. Paul Revere, a Boston silversmith and Son of Liberty, made a silver bowl dedicated to the 92.[7]

One of the main grievances of the colonists was that the Boston Admiralty Court tried cases by judge alone without a jury. John Hancock, the Boston merchant whose sloop was taken by the British, was the son of the minister in Braintree and a friend since boyhood of John. Hancock was charged in the Admiralty Court in effect with smuggling and retained Adams to defend him; he drew out the proceedings to such a length that in the end the prosecution withdrew the charges. This was not the only case related to the coming Revolution in which Adams appeared.[8] In 1769, Henry Panton, a lieutenant on HMS Rose, boarded an American merchant vessel, the Pitt Packet, in American waters and tried to impress some of the sailors into the British Navy. The Navy did have established powers to impress men into its service, but in this instance some of the sailors resisted and Michael Corbet killed Henry by stabbing him in the neck with a harpoon. Four of the sailors were indicted for murder. Otis was retained for their defence, with Adams as his junior, but when the trial began Otis said he was too ill to conduct it and Adams took over. He found an English statute which forbade impressments in American waters and argued that the actions of the lieutenant were illegal and the American sailors entitled to resist in self defence.[9] After a lengthy adjournment the court acquitted all four.

On 5 March 1770 the 'Boston Massacre' occurred.[10] When, in January of that year, the citizens of Boston resisted payment of duties on the importation of tea, the British government instructed customs collectors to enforce payment and sent two regiments of soldiers to protect them. When a mob collected outside the Customs House, soldiers led by Captain Preston were sent to deal with them. As the mob pressed upon them, some of the soldiers panicked and fired, killing three and wounding others. Captain Preston and some of the soldiers were indicted for murder. He sent a message to John Adams asking him to act in his defence. Adams was mindful of the cab rank rule at the English bar, that, if a case is within his expertise and consonant with his standing, an advocate is bound to defend anyone who asks for his service, whatever his personal opinion of the offender. When he received the message, Adams declared that 'if he thinks he cannot get a fair trial without my assistance, he shall have it without hesitation.'[11] He mounted a vigorous defence, describing the violent hostility of the mob and quoting Blackstone, who stressed the importance of ensuring the acquittal of the innocent. Of the six defendants, four (including Captain

---

[7] See Smith above n 2, 95.

[8] ibid, 102.

[9] ibid, 104 et seq and see JR Vile, *Great American Lawyer* (CA, CO and Ox, ABC-CLIO, 2001) I.

[10] ibid, 124.

[11] RJ Taylor (ed), *Papers of John Adams* (MA and London, Belknap Press of Harvard University Press, 1977) III 291–94.

Preston) were acquitted altogether and two convicted of manslaughter, but sentenced only to branding of the thumb. Adams's reputation as a man of principle was clearly established.

The closure of Boston harbour, following the Boston Tea Party, demonstrated that individual colonies could not withstand such pressure from the British government and Adams was one of those instrumental in the summoning of the First Continental Congress—he was chosen as a representative of Massachusetts. He was also a delegate to the Second Congress up to March 1781. During these periods of absence, John entrusted his letters to Abigail to friends, who were travelling from Philadelphia to Boston, but some of these fell into the hands of the British and after 10 October 1775 it can be seen that he is circumspect about what he divulges.

The distress Abigail and he suffered can be seen in the following extracts, not taken in chronological order. On a personal level, both expressed devotion to each other. Whilst each of them is upset by the prolonged absences, both are clear that it is their duty to accept them. For instance, on 7 October 1775 John writes:

> I would cheerfully retire from public life forever, renounce all Chance for Profits or Honours from the public, nay I would cheerfully contribute my little Property to obtain Peace and Liberty—But all these must go and my life too before I can surrender the Right of my Country to a free constitution.

On 7 May 1776 Abigail writes that

> all domestic pleasures and injoyments are absorbed in the great and important duty you owe your country … a people may let a king fall, yet still remain a people, but if a king let his people slip from him, he is no longer a king. And as this is certainly our case, why not proclaim to the World in decisive terms, your own importance.

Nevertheless, John complains that it is very painful to be 400 miles from his family and friends, when he knows they are afflicted.[12] Although he admires his fellow delegates, he seems to end up very much on his own.

> It used to be some Comfort to me that I had a servant and some horses—they composed a sort of family for me. But now there is not one creature here that I seem to have any kind of relationship with.[13]

In July 1775 he complains of the suffocating heat in Philadelphia and 'that there is more epicurism (sic) and debauchery here than in Boston.'[14] His rather dour puritanism was not attractive to all his colleagues. He makes constant complaints of the tediousness of the proceedings in Congress and its committees. On 3 December 1776 he describes his day. Congress sits in seven committees and as a whole. Committees sit from 7 to 10 am and 6 to 10 pm; it sits as a whole from

---

[12] 18 October 1776.
[13] 22 May 1776.
[14] 17 July 1775.

10 am to 4 or 5 pm. Many of the delegates like the sound of their own voices. John writes on 29 September 1774:

> [T]he Art of Address of Ambassadors from a dozen belligerent powers of Europe, nay of a Conclave of Cardinals at the election of a Pope, or of the Princes of Germany at the Choice of an Emperor would not exceed the Specimens we have here.

Four days after the Congress formally commences he complains that 'I am wearied to death with the life I lead. The Business of the Congress is tedious, beyond Expression.'[15]

Meanwhile Abigail found she had to run the farm as well as carry out domestic activities. The departure of many local men to the war had resulted in the price of labour escalating.[16] On 3 June 1776, she reports that the cost of living has doubled since the same time last year. There is a shortage of pins.[17] There is no coffee, sugar or pepper, only huckleberries.[18] She deals with outbreaks of dysentery,[19] mumps,[20] even smallpox and her own jaundice and rheumatism.[21]

The delegates to the First Congress arrived in dribs and drabs through August and September 1774. At first John is impressed by their quality:

> There is in the Congress a Collection of the greatest Men upon this Continent in Point of Abilities, Virtues, and Fortunes. The Magnanimity and public spirit, which I see here, makes me blush for the sordid venal herd, which I have seen in our own Province.[22]

It is not long, however, before he sees the difficulty of achieving a consensus between 13 colonies, each with a very distinct background. Shortly before the Congress convenes he writes that 'fifty gentlemen meeting together, all Strangers, are not acquainted with Each others language, Ideas, Views, Designs. They are, therefore, jealous of each other—fearfull, timid, skittish.'[23] On the 16 September 1774 those who had arrived discussed a motion to open the Congress with a prayer, but there was opposition from the representatives of New York and South Carolina, because the delegates were so divided in religious sentiments 'some Episcopalians, some Quakers, some Anabaptists, some Presbyterians and some Congregationalists, so that we could not join in the same act of worship.'[24] Samuel Adams, however, persuaded Congress to accept a prayer from a minister in Philadelphia, who was a gentleman of piety and virtue and a friend to America. It was going to be increasingly necessary to rely on delegates being willing to compromise.

To judge by his letters, John, although a provincial lawyer of note, had had little contact before the Congress with the other colonies. Wherever he goes he

---

[15] 9 October 1774.
[16] 14 May 1776.
[17] 16 June 1775.
[18] 5 July 1775.
[19] 8 Sept 1775.
[20] 7 August 1776.
[21] 17 Nov 1775.
[22] 8 September 1774.
[23] 25 September 1774.
[24] 16 September 1774.

shows curiosity about men, places and religious practices. He reports attending services of other denominations, finding some sympathy for Episcopalians 'though they are slaves to the Domination of the Priesthood.'[25] A Catholic service appals him because of what he describes as its superstition. Eventually he finds a preacher in Philadelphia whose principles, prayers and sermons more nearly resemble those of the New England Clergy.[26] He entrusts one letter to Abigail to the hands of a Quaker, Stephen Collins, who is not stiff or rigid and opens his house to everyone.[27] He talks with admiration of a Philosophical Society in Philadelphia.[28] He notes the differences between New England and the southern states. In the former, landholding is in relatively small parcels, whereas in South Carolina 'the Gentry are very rich and the common People very poor. The Inequality of Property gives an Aristocratical Turn to all their processes.'[29] This difference was to lead to a compromise on the wording of the Declaration of Independence where the draft dealt with slavery.

On their arrival in Philadelphia in early September 1774, the delegates were shown the sights and there was much entertaining. Both John and Samuel Adams were appointed to a committee to determine the rights of the colonies.[30] They were influential in persuading Congress to agree to a Declaration of Rights and Grievances[31] and boycott British goods. At the end of October 1774 Adams returned to Boston and there published pamphlets under the pseudonym Novanglus setting out the colonists' position, insisting that the American colonists (which he estimated at 600,000) owed allegiance to the King, but were a separate realm, just as Scotland and Ireland. They had been allowed to govern themselves for 150 years, impose their own taxes and control their internal affairs; the English parliament could regulate their trade, but no more than that.[32]

In September 1774 the English General Gage, seeing the main revolutionary threat in Boston, had withdrawn garrisons from other cities, such as Philadelphia and New York, to concentrate them there. On 19 April 1775 a strong party from the British garrison in Boston was sent to search for arms and gunpowder in nearby Lexington and Concord; the patriots were forewarned. In America local communities formed militia; over the past century these had fought off attacks from native Americans and fought at the side of British troops against the French. They were battle-hardened and had learnt from the native Americans how to fight guerrilla warfare in a terrain with which they were familiar. What they lacked was the discipline of a regular army, gunpowder and cannons, but they were prepared to take on the British regulars if necessary.

---

[25] 9 October 1774.
[26] 11 June 1775.
[27] 4 July 1775.
[28] 4 August 1778.
[29] 14 April 1776.
[30] Smith above n 2, 172.
[31] ibid, 182 et seq.
[32] ibid, 189.

After an initial skirmish at Lexington, where the first shots were fired, a more serious battle took place at Concord; as the British retreated they were harried back to Boston. The patriots laid siege to Boston. The British sent parties out to fortify the hilltops surrounding the city and this led the patriots to confront them on Bunker Hill on the 13 June. The British held on to this strategic point, but in so doing suffered considerable losses. It was now clear that the British intended to use force to put down what they saw as rebellion. It was equally clear that whilst the American militia could not defeat the British army in an open battle, they could still inflict considerable casualties, which made the British generals cautious. The American army then surrounded Boston, so that the only clear access to it was from the sea. From then on John becomes fearful for Abigail's safety. On the 2 May 1775 he tells her in case of real danger to flee to the woods. On 7 May 1775 she reports that 'the distresses of the Inhabitants of Boston are beyond the power of language to describe.'

Two days after the battle of Bunker Hill, Congress chose Colonel Washington as general of a Continental Army and he chose Adams' former clerk, William Tudor, as his aide de camp. To establish the beginnings of an army, Congress resolved that 10 companies of riflemen should be despatched from the southern states to support the militia in Massachusetts.[33] In Congress, whilst the Massachusetts' delegation considered there had been a complete breakdown of communication with Britain, some states remained unwilling to go so far as to declare independence. Virginia offered the greatest support, but the middle states of New York, Pennsylvania, Maryland, Delaware and New Jersey felt it was too early; some of their delegations had no instructions from their state assemblies to support independence. The change of opinion was gradual.[34] Adams, who was clear that the British government would offer no compromise, found an ally in a young delegate from Virginia, called Thomas Jefferson, who sought out Adams; the two formed a close alliance.[35]

Adams formed a less enthusiastic view of some of the other delegates. Unfortunately at the end of July 1775, the British intercepted a letter from him to James Warren in Boston, in which he complained that a 'certain piddling genius, whose fame has been trumpeted loudly, has given a silly cast to our doings.'[36] It was published by the British and Dickinson rightly took this as a reference to himself. In his diary for 16 September 1775 Adams wrote:

Walking to the Statehouse this morning, I met Mr Dickinson on foot in Chestnut Street. We met and passed near enough to touch elbows. He past without moving his head or hat. He past hastily by. The Cause of his offence is the letter no doubt which Gage had printed in Draper's Paper.[37]

[33] ibid, 201.

[34] P Maier, *American Scripture: Making the Declaration of Independence* (NY, Knopf, 1997).

[35] As to authorship see JP Boyd, *The Disputed Authorship of the Declaration on the Causes and Necessity of Taking up Arms, 1775* (1950) 74(1) *Pennsylvania Magazine of History and Biography.*

[36] Adams above n 6, 88; 26 July 1775.

[37] LH Butterfield (ed), *Diary and Autobiography of John Adams* (Cambridge MA, Belknap Press of Harvard University Press, 1961).

The previous day he had complained in his diary that

> there is a remarkable lack of judgment in some of our members ... Much time is indiscriminately expended. Points of little Consequence are stated and debated warmly ... Rutledge is a very uncouth and ungraceful speaker ... His brother John dodges his head too, rather disagreeably and both of them Spout out their language in a rough and rapid torrent, but without much force or effect ... Mr Dickinson's Air and Gate and Actions are not much more elegant.[38]

On 24 September, he records Dr Rush's complaint that Dickinson was blundering and warped by the Quaker Interest.

When the *Olive Branch Petition* was sent to the King, Adams wrote in his diary that the petition would be 'received graciously, but we can expect no success from it.' In fact it was not received graciously at all. This together with the passage of the Prohibitory Act in August 1775, declaring a blockade of all American ports, fatally weakened the moderate case.[39] Moreover, for the first time, there were signs that the patriots might have a way to defeat the British. On 16 March 1776 Abigail reported the good news that they had taken Dorchester Hill, overlooking Boston, thus allowing them to threaten the city with heavy artillery they had captured and then the great news that the British ships were leaving Boston—ever since 17 March is named 'evacuation day' in Boston. Adams's hand was immeasurably strengthened. On 17 May 1776, he writes that 'Great Britain has at last driven America to the last step, a compleat separation from her, a total absolute Independence not only of her Parliament, but of her Crown.'

On 31 March 1776, Abigail had written a famous letter to John, often quoted in part, but worth repeating as a whole:

> I long to hear that you have declared an independency—and by the way in the new Code of Laws which I suppose it will be necessary for you to make I desire you would Remember the Ladies, and be more generous and favourable to them than your ancestors. Do not put such unlimited power into the hands of Husbands. Remember all men would be tyrants if they could, if particular care and attention is not paid to the Ladies we are determined to foment a Rebellion and will not hold ourselves bound by any Laws in which we have no voice or Representation. That your sex are naturally Tyrannical is a Truth so thoroughly established as to admit of no dispute, but such of you as wish to be happy willingly give up the harsh title of Master for more tender and endearing one Friend. Why then, not put it out of the power of the vicious and Lawless to use us with cruelty and indignity. Men of all Ages abhor customs which treat us only as the vassals of your Sex. Regard us then as Beings placed by providence under your protection and in imitation of the Supreme Being make us of that power only for our happiness.

On 14 April, he replied with what can only be described as male condescension:

> As to your extraordinary Code of Laws, I cannot but laugh. We have been told that our Struggle has loosened the bands of Government every where. That Children and

---

[38] The Rutledges were delegates from South Carolina.
[39] Above ch 7.

Apprentices were disobedient—that schools and Colledges were grown turbulent— that Indians slighted their Guardians and Negroes grew insolent to their Masters. But your letter was the first intimation that another Tribe more numerous and powerfull than all the rest were grown discontented—this is rather too coarse a compliment but you are so saucy, I wont blot it out. Depend upon it, We know better than to repeal out Masculine systems. Altho they are in full Force, you know they are little more than Theory. We do not exert our Power in its full Latitude. We are obliged to go fair and softly and in Practice you know We are subjects. We have only the name of Masters and rather than give up this, which would compleatly subject Us to the Despotism of the Petticoat, I hope General Washington and all our brave Heroes would fight.

Abigail did not surrender. On 7 May, she replied:

I cannot say that I think you are very generous to the Ladies, for whilst you are pro-claiming peace and good will to Men, Emancipating all Nations, you insist upon retaining absolute power over Wives. But you must remember that Arbitrary power is like most other things which are very hateful, very liable to be broken and notwith-standing all your writs, Laws and Maxims we have it in our power not only to free ourselves, but to subdue our Master and without violence throw both your natural and legal authority at our feet.

Her plea had no effect.

On 15 May 1776, the Virginia Convention at Williamsburg resolved that their representatives should instruct Congress to declare independence.[40] Their delegate to the Congress, Richard Henry, produced a draft resolution:

That these United Colonies are, and of right ought to be free and independent States, that they are absolved from all allegiance to the British Crown, and all political connec-tion between them and the State of Great Britain is, and ought to be, totally absolved.

The middle states still did not have authorisation to vote for such a resolution, so a vote on it was postponed for three weeks. In anticipation that it might pass Congress, however, a committee of five was appointed on 10 June to prepare a draft Declaration of Independence. The members of the Committee included both those in favour of immediate independence and those at that time against it. Adams was appointed, no doubt as he had taken the lead on independence; now aged 40, he was an experienced lawyer and politician. Although Dickinson had led the way previously on behalf of Pennsylvania, its representative was now the 70 year old Benjamin Franklin.[41] He was born in Boston, but moved to Philadelphia where he established the Pennsylvania Gazette. He was famed as a scientist, his studies included population growth, ocean currents, a wave theory of light, meteorology, cooling and electricity—he remains most famous for sug-gesting that lightning consisted of electricity. From 1757 he had been in England advancing the interests of Pennsylvania and he arrived back in America not long before the revolution as a man of great fame, whose adherence to the colonists'

---

[40] JP Boyd, *The Declaration of Independence, The Evolution of the Text* (Library of Congress/ Thomas Jefferson Memorial Foundation, 1999).
[41] ES Gaustad, *Benjamin Franklin* (Oxford, Oxford University Press, 2006).

cause gave it great weight. He was not, however, a lawyer and by this time his health was not good. As a result, he did not play a large part in the drafting of the declaration. In any event the Pennsylvania Assembly and its delegation to the Congress were not yet committed to independence.

Connecticut's representative on the committee was the taciturn but influential Roger Sherman. He was opposed to the immediate declaration of independence and argued against it in Convention, even after the draft declaration was produced. Unsurprisingly, he does not seem to have had a great hand in the wording of the Declaration. New York was represented by Robert Livingston; in the summer of 1776 he was only 29 and had been admitted to the New York Bar only six years before. In any event, New York was not yet ready to declare independence. The final member of the committee was Thomas Jefferson.

It seems clear that the committee initially asked Adams to draft a declaration, but he insisted this should be done by Jefferson. In his autobiography Adams gives his reasons: Jefferson was from a southern state and in any event 'I had been so obnoxious for my early and constant zeal in promoting the measure that any draft of mine would undergo a more Severe Scrutiny and Criticism.'[42] Adams wrote that at the time of the Declaration, Jefferson had been a member of Congress for about a year, but had attended only a small part of the time. 'I never heard him utter three sentences together.'[43] Much later in a letter to James Madison dated 22 August 1822, Adams wrote:[44] 'Mr Jefferson came into Congress in June 1775 and brought with him a reputation for literature, science and a happy talent for composition. Writings of his were handed round, remarkable for the peculiar felicity of expression.'[45] When Adams and Jefferson came to write their autobiographies in the 1820s they accorded themselves slightly different roles in the drafting process, Adams giving himself a greater role in amending the original than Jefferson would allow.[46]

The final draft was sent to Congress on 27 June 1766. On 2 July, Congress constituted itself a Committee of the whole Congress and discussed the draft for three days. Some important amendments were made, which will be considered when Jefferson is assessed. Suffice it to say here that the tie that was broken was expressed to be to the King and not to the people of England and their Parliament and that a passage which attacked shipments of slaves was removed.[47]

On 1 July, an initial vote was taken with nine states voting in favour of the declaration and two, Pennsylvania and South Carolina, voting against. There were only two delegates from the three counties now called Delaware,[48] who

---

[42] Boyd above n 40, 20.

[43] Butterfield above note 37, 335.

[44] Reproduced in Boyd, above n 40, 29–30.

[45] Probably *A Summary View of the rights of British America*, which Jefferson handed to another Virginian delegate, Randolph Peyton Boyd, above n 40, 15.

[46] ibid, 29–30 and see Butterfield above n 37, III 336; Letter J Adams to Timothy Pickering 6 August 1822 *Works of John Adams* II 512; PL Ford (ed), *Writings of Thomas Jefferson* (New York, GP Putnam's Sons, 1893-99) Letter 10 August 1822 X 267; PL Ford (ed), *Autobiography of Thomas Jefferson* (New York and London, GP Putnam's Sons, 1914; Paper Back Penn 2005).

[47] Below Ch 11, and generally see Boyd above n 41.

[48] Above Ch 9.

were split. The New York delegates did not have authority from their assembly to vote for independence. By 2 July a third Delaware delegate had arrived and provided a majority within their delegation in favour. The South Carolina delegates had received fresh instructions in favour. New York delegates still lacked instruction. The real stumbling block was Pennsylvania, without which the declaration would have lacked all substance. The general mood of the Congress was now in favour of a Declaration, and Dickinson bowed to this; the next day he and fellow delegate, Robert Morris, absented themselves leaving the remainder of the Pennsylvania delegates to vote in favour. The final vote was 12 in favour with New York abstaining; a week later they adopted the resolution. It was a triumph of negotiation in which no doubt Adams played a great part.[49]

Whilst these constitutional manoeuvres took place, there was still a war to be won. Adams was appointed chairman of the Board of War and much of his time was taken up with trying to improve the discipline of and supplies to the army. On 3 July 1776, General Howe (who had replaced Gage) attacked New York, arriving on Staten Island and then decisively defeating Washington's Continental Army on Brooklyn Heights on 27 August. Washington retreated, but preserved the larger part of his army. On 9 September Adams, Franklin and Edward Rutledge went to meet Howe on Staten Island. They were sent as a committee of Congress, but he would only meet them as private gentlemen. He offered merely that Parliament would redress their grievances. The three men demanded that Britain recognise the independent states in America, but returned to Philadelphia empty handed. The British then launched a two-pronged attack with General Burgoyne leading an army from Canada and General Howe attacking Philadelphia. In September 1777 Philadelphia was taken and Congress fled to York. In October, however, the Continental Army defeated Burgoyne at the Battle of Saratoga and Howe was replaced by General Clinton, who withdrew the British garrison in Philadelphia to protect New York. An uneasy stalemate settled.

Once the American states had declared themselves independent, the next matter of concern was what recognition any new American government would receive from the various European states. Adams served on the Committee of Congress regularising relations between the United States and overseas powers. The necessity to achieve this was certainly as important as the wording of the Declaration of Independence—the American Revolutionaries needed at least some financial backing from outside their country. The French royal government made substantial loans to them and early in 1778 Adams was asked to join Benjamin Franklin and Arthur Lee in Paris as one of three Commissioners of the United States to France. He arrived there on 1 April, along with his 10 year old son John Quincy, for whom he arranged education. He found his mission difficult: he did not speak French, as Franklin could, and the other two Commissioners were often at loggerheads. Franklin was feted by the French, and lived what Adams thought a libertine life. Gradually as John's French improved, his

---

[49] See Boyd above n 40 and LH Butterfield (ed) *Diary and Autobiography of John Adams* (MA, Belknap Press of Harvard University Press, 1961).

natural curiosity led him to the theatre and art and he came to admire French civilisation.[50] He wrote to Richard Lee that 'he must be of a strange disposition who cannot be happy at Paris, where he may have the choice of all the pleasures, amusements and studies which human life affords.'[51] He nevertheless found the feuding between the other Commissioners made the mission impractical and requested that Franklin be appointed sole Commissioner in his place. Adams returned to New England in June 1779, but by the autumn of that year he was back in Paris. By this time the British were defeated and he was one of three ministers plenipotentiary with authority to enter into treaties with Britain and other European powers. The negotiations, in which he played a prominent part, were lengthy and eventually resulted in the Treaty of Paris on 3 September 1783 (in fact three separate treaties with Great Britain, France and Spain).[52] The Commissioners had negotiated separately with the representatives of the British government. It was Adams' draft which was the basis of the eventual treaty with Britain. The British government relinquished all authority over territories in America. The 13 American states were recognised as sovereign nations. There were two particular sticking points in negotiations. First the British negotiators demanded that property taken from those loyal to the Crown during the Revolution should be restored to them or they should have compensation. In the end Congress agreed to recommend to the individual states that they provide restitution to those whose property had been confiscated. This was included in the Treaty, but in practice little was restored. Second, the United States wanted to retain fishing rights off Newfoundland and in the Gulf of St Lawrence, which they were granted. The Treaty in general was very favourable to the United States; the British government foresaw the possibility of successful trade with the new States and in practice this developed in favour of Britain.

Thereafter Adams was appointed a Minister Plenipotentiary to negotiate commercial treaties on behalf of the government of the United States. He moved to London and in July 1784 arranged for Abigail and his daughter Nabby to join him in London (John Quincy and Charles were already with him). Abigail fell in love with London life.[53] In February 1785, he was appointed the first American Ambassador to the Court of St James (in other words Great Britain). He presented his credentials to King George III, expressing his wish to restore the confidence and affection between people 'who though separated by the ocean and under different governments, have the same language, a similar religion and kindred blood.'[54] The King replied that he was the last to consent to the separation; it having been made, he would be the first to meet the representatives of the United States as an independent power. In practice Adams received a cool reception from the British government and in the end, at his request, he was withdrawn on 20 February 1788 and the post left open.

[50] Smith above n 2, 349.
[51] ibid, 422.
[52] ibid, 540 et seq.
[53] ibid, 584 et seq.
[54] ibid, 628–29.

When the Constitutional Convention met in September 1787, Adams was in England and did not participate directly. He learnt from friends in America that the Articles of Confederation, lacking a real central government, were proving increasingly ineffective. He made his views known to those who did attend the Convention. In 1787 he published a series of letters (the first dated October 1786) under the title *A defence of the Constitutions of the various States of America* and followed this in 1790 with *Davila* (named after an Italian historian), all of which set out his views on constitutional government. Despite the Revolution, he still saw the English constitution as a model. He was in favour of a strong executive and indeed suggested that the highest executive posts should be hereditary; this led to charges that he was a monarchist.[55] He denied that, but added in a letter to Benjamin Rush on 5 July 1789,[56] 'I deny that there is or was in Europe a more free republic than England or that any liberty on earth ever equalled English liberty, notwithstanding the defects in their Constitution.' He firmly believed in the separation of powers.[57] Every democratic state should have a popular assembly responsive to the people, but there was a danger that the rich, well-born and the able would acquire undue influence. The remedy was to place those men whose talents were recognised in a separate chamber, where they could be checked by the popular assembly; bicameral legislatures provided essential checks and balances. In a letter to a friend called Van der Kemp, he warned that the single assembly adopted in the French constitution would lead to domination by demagogues.[58] Paine in his pamphlet, *the Rights of Man*, advocated such a single chamber legislature. In 1791 Jefferson republished Paine's pamphlet, with a forward by himself calling on all to rally round the standard of *the Rights of Man*. Adams viewed this as an attack on himself. The views of the two men became increasingly opposed. When Robespierre and the Jacobins seized power in France, under the banner of the Committee of Public Safety, and the Terror commenced, Adams must have thought his view fully confirmed.

He was not, however, a populist. When John Sullivan, a member of the Massachusetts' General Court, sought his views on electoral franchise, Adams replied that power always follows property; in every society those who are wholly destitute of property are also too little acquainted with public affairs to form a right judgement.[59] The qualifications for franchise and office-holding in the Massachusetts Constitution reflected this view, as did his description of an upper chamber as one of talent. Adams was very familiar with the work of European philosophers and in particular the English empiricists; the great John Locke himself wrote that the basis of power is property. We shall see that when the Constitution of the United States came into force, it adopted some, but not all of Adams's ideas.

---

[55] ibid, 723.
[56] Boston Public Library, quoted Smith above note 2, 755.
[57] ibid, 693.
[58] Historical Society of Pennsylvania, cited Smith above n 2, 785–86.
[59] Cited Smith above n 2, 258.

Adams was out of the country for the most part of 10 years and only resumed a role in domestic affairs on his return. He was to hold high office under the new Constitution. He was appointed President of the Senate and served as Vice President to Washington from 1789. In the elections of 1796 Adams defeated Jefferson for the Presidency by 71 votes to 68 in the Electoral College. Jefferson was elected Vice President.

In the course of Adams' administration, loose political groupings began to appear. He was seen as leading a federalist faction, while Jefferson led the anti-federalists. The federalists favoured a strong central government, whilst the anti-federalists favoured strong state rights. Antagonism grew between Adams and Jefferson and this was exacerbated when war between Great Britain and France resumed, leading to incidents between American and French vessels. Adams wished to remain neutral and sent Commissioners to Paris to regularise relations. In the end he became aghast by what he saw as a bullying attitude by the republican French government. Their price for a new agreement was a large payment to their government and bribes to individual ministers. Matters ended with a simple treaty ending any alliance between the two nations. Jefferson continued to favour links with the republican government of France. The gulf between him and Adams was widening.

In 1800 the electoral position was reversed and Jefferson won in the Electoral College by 73 votes to 65. Among his last acts as President was to appoint pro-federalist John Marshall to be Chief Justice. At the end of his term as President, Adams retired to Braintree where he continued to express his political views in newspapers. Time healed his division with Jefferson and, after Abigail's death in 1818, they resumed their friendship and regularly corresponded. John died in 1826. His eldest son, John Quincy, became the sixth President of the United States. Over the preceding decades, the provincial lawyer had become the prime mover for independence and an international lawyer and diplomatist.

11

Independence: Thomas Jefferson

WHEN **THOMAS JEFFERSON** was chosen as one of the committee of five to produce a draft declaration of independence, he was only 33 and had been admitted to the Virginian bar for just nine years. Adams's choice of him as draftsman arose partly from the fact that Jefferson was a Virginian and so would be acceptable to the southern states.[1] Whilst Adams came from and reflected the views of a stern puritan colony, Virginia had a more commercial background. Unlike their northern counterparts, the original Virginian settlers had not rejected church government in England and the Anglican Church became the established church in that State, with membership of it essential for office-holding in the colony. Thomas was brought up an Anglican. By the mid-eighteenth century it was the largest and by far the most populous colony—Thomas calculated the total population at about 285,000 whites, 260,000 slaves and half a million native Indians,[2] figures roughly corresponding with those in the 1790 census.

Jefferson's father, Peter, was self-educated, but took one of the avenues open to young men of ambition, but without means—surveying. The early Virginian settlements were along the coast or rivers; the Virginia Charter did not set any inland boundary and those who acquired untried territory needed it surveyed. Virginia sub-divided into two broad regions—the tidewater country close to Chesapeake Bay, or one of the rivers which flowed from it, and the area called the Piedmont (foot of the mountain) leading up to the Blue Ridge Mountain range (the eastern edge of the Appalachians). The tidewater country had the most fertile soil and it was here that the prosperous tobacco plantations were established. Tobacco required rich soil and a large labour force—hence the importation of African slaves. The Piedmont had poorer soil and more difficult access to the sea and, therefore, supported less commercial crops and animals. The tidewater plantations were owned by rich families, who had formed what Adams regarded as a new aristocracy. Their daughters were a prize for ambitious young men.

In the north east of the colony was an area of undeveloped land known as the northern neck, between the Rappahannock and Potomac rivers. It was part of another proprietorial grant by Charles II of no less than five million acres to the Culpepper family and by 1750 encompassed about a quarter of Virginia. The Culpeppers married into the Fairfax family, descendants of the English Civil War

---

[1] See above ch 10.
[2] T Jefferson, *Notes on the State of Virginia* (London, John Stockdale, 1787).

general, and Lord Fairfax came to live in Virginia. He needed surveyors to map his territory: Peter Jefferson (Thomas's father) became one; George Washington, who had a family connection to Lord Fairfax, became another; and Thomas Marshall (father of John, the most important Chief Justice of the United States) yet another. A remarkable number of prominent revolutionaries came from this north eastern corner of the state, including George Mason and Henry Madison. Surveyors were able to spot land in which they themselves could invest and both Jefferson and Washington inherited modest estates from their fathers. Washington married a rich widow who owned some 18,000 acres of plantation and many slaves and he soon became established as one of the social elite. Peter Jefferson also married well to Jane Randolph, a member of one of the most powerful families in the State. Thomas was their third child born on 13 April 1743. The Randolphs invited Peter to manage a large plantation at Tuckahoe on the James River near Richmond and the whole family moved with him.

Tuckahoe was on the outskirts of Richmond, where the newly established college of William and Mary was situated; Thomas enrolled there in 1760. He first studied mathematics, ethics and rhetoric with Dr Small. Before Small returned to Europe in 1762, he introduced Thomas to George Wythe. Long after Wythe's death, Thomas made notes for the biographer John Sanderson, saying of Wythe, 'no man left behind him a character more venerated, devoted as he was to the natural and equal rights of man.'[3] Thomas studied under Wythe for five years,[4] a longer period than normal for those intending to be lawyers. He became familiar with Lord Chief Justice Coke's rather selective view of English constitutional history, that there was a fundamental law dating from Anglo Saxon times to which everyone including the King was subject. He would also have become familiar with Coke's assertion in the Petition of Right in 1628 that subjects of the English Crown could not be taxed without the consent of Parliament. Like other revolutionaries, his initial claim was to his rights as an Englishmen; independence was not his starting point.

Under Wythe's tutelage, Jefferson read much more widely than mere law and continued to do so for the rest of his life. In 1815 he sold his library of around 10,000 books to the United States Government to form the basis of the Library of Congress.[5] In particular he studied philosophers, including the British empiricists—scientists such as Bacon and Newton, who believed that human knowledge was achieved by study of evidence, not revelation—and then Locke and Hume, who together with their French counterparts Voltaire and Montesquieu, applied the same test to all human knowledge, including government. This was the Age of Reason—a description coined by Thomas Paine in a series of pamphlets first published in 1795, but applicable to the era of revolution—according to which all beliefs, however long held, had to be subjected

[3] 18 Aug 1820 Library of Congress, cited RB Bernstein, *Thomas Jefferson* (Oxford, Oxford University Press, 2005) 71.

[4] Bernstein, ibid 7.

[5] ES Gaustad, *Sworn on the Altar of God, A Religious Biography of Thomas Jefferson* (MI, William B Eerdmans Publishing Co, 1996) 19.

to reason. Jefferson saw himself as a child of this new Enlightenment. In 1787 he wrote advice to his nephew, Peter Carr, who was about to attend university: 'Fix reason firmly in her seat, and call to her tribunal every fact, every opinion. Question with boldness even the existence of God, because if there be one he must deserve more the homage of reason than of blindfolded fear.'[6] Jefferson was not a great public speaker and found the realities of political power uncongenial; he was happiest in his library reading or drafting documents.[7]

Though brought up an Anglican, he shifted his religious views. He did not make this change public and so his position has to be deduced from private documents.[8] He kept a Commonplace Book in which he noted passages from authors that captured his interest. The most quoted author was Henry St John, Viscount Bolingbroke, essayist, politician and a friend of Pope and Swift. Though an Anglican and Tory, he made a rational critique of Christianity, concluding that the deity revealed by the Bible could not be explained by reason.[9] It was not rational to suppose that the God of the whole universe should reveal himself only to one small nation in the Eastern Mediterranean, nor was it for him to send his only son to be sacrificed by man to expiate his sins. This led Jefferson to examine his own views on religion. Much later he wrote to a correspondent called Ezra Stiles Ely: 'You say you are a Calvinist. I am not. I am of a sect by myself, as far as I know.'[10] His thought became most closely allied to the principles of Deism or the Unitarian Church. He believed in a benevolent Deity—in his first inaugural address as President he acknowledged 'an adoring and overwhelming providence.' He did not, however, believe in the doctrine of the Trinity or miracles; most importantly he regarded Jesus Christ as a supreme moral teacher, but not a God. He did believe, however, in an afterlife, which many Deists did not.

Jefferson's erudition gave the Revolution an intellectual base. He recognised a concept of natural law dating back to classical times, when philosophers defined a law, which was higher than any law local to a particular country. In his *Rhetoric* Aristotle wrote: 'universal law is the law of nature. For there really is, as everyone to some extent divines, a natural justice and injustice that is binding on all men, even on those who have no association or covenant with each other.'[11] Cicero in *De Legibus* saw both justice and law as deriving from what nature has given to man.[12] Happiness was a proper goal of law.[13] Jefferson recorded

---

[6] Online Library of Liberty, *Works of Thomas Jefferson* II 217.

[7] See eg Bernstein above n 3, 47.

[8] C Sanford, *The Religious Life of Thomas Jefferson* (Charlottesville VA, University of Virginia Press, 1988); ER Sheridan, *Jefferson and Religion* (University of North Carolina Press, 2001); Gaustad above n 5.

[9] Gaustad above n 5, 22.

[10] Letter of 25 June 1819, replicated by Encyclopedia of Virginia (encyclopediavirginia.org, published 2012).

[11] Aristotle, *Rhetoric*, WR Roberts (translation) (NY, Modern Library, 1954) Book I Ch 13.

[12] Cicero, *Marcus Tuillius Cicero on the Law*, D Fott (translation) (NY, Cornell University Press, 2014), Book I ss 16–18.

[13] ibid, book II s 11.

some of Cicero's writings in his Commonplace Book.[14] These ideas seeped into early and medieval Christian thought—in the thirteenth century Thomas Aquinas saw natural law as the rational creature's participation in eternal law.[15] The traditional view was that such a law emanated from God and so had authority to overrule domestic law. Under the thinking of the Enlightenment, God came to be replaced by reason as the source of such a law.[16] The American Revolutionaries muddled along between both ideas—as noted, Jefferson while lauding reason did recognise a benevolent Deity. Of course, the existence of a higher law may be of great advantage if you want to start a revolution.

Most pertinently in the context of the American Revolution, the idea of an overriding natural law had entered English common law. In *Calvin's case*[17] Coke stated that the law of nature is that which God at the time of creation of the nature of man infused into his heart. The Court of King's Bench went on to hold that the law of nature was part of the common law of England and was immutable. In 1610, in *Dr Bonham's Case*[18] Coke stated that in many cases the common law will control Acts of Parliament, and 'sometimes adjudge them to be utterly void: for when an Act of Parliament is against common right and reson, or repugnant or impossible to be performed, the common law will control it and adjudge such Act to be void.' Coke was engaged in fierce resistance to the claims of James I to a divine right to rule and was looking to the common law as a weapon to achieve this, but these observations could now be turned to advantage by the American revolutionaries.

Overlade on these medieval ideas were the arguments of the European Enlightenment, typified in John Locke's *Treatises on Government*, published in England in 1690 and in the United States in 1773.[19] They reflected political events in England in the summer of 1688, when William of Orange and his wife Mary effectively made a compact with the English Parliament to take the English throne, subject to a promise to abide by a Declaration of Rights. In his second treatise *Concerning the True Original Extent and End of Civil Government* Locke expounded his ideas of constitutional government:

> To understand political power aright, and dirive its original, we must consider what estate all men are naturaly in, and that is a state of perfect freedom to order their actions and dispose of their possessions and persons as they think fit, within the bounds of the law of Nature, without asking leave or depending upon the will of any other man. A state of equality, wherein all the power and jurisdiction is reciprocal, not one having more than another, there being nothing more evident than that creatures of the same species and rank, promiscuously born to all the same advantages of Nature, and use of

[14] DL Wilson (ed), *Jefferson's Literary Commonplace Book* (NJ, Princeton University Press, 1989) 161.

[15] *Summa Theologica* I—11 90 et seq.

[16] See RS Barker, 'Natural Law and the United States Constitution' (2012) 66 *The Review of Metaphysics* 105–30.

[17] 7 Co Rep 1a, 77 ER 377.

[18] 8 Co Rep 113b; 77 ER 638.

[19] JR Milton, *John Locke* (Oxford, Oxford University Press, 2004).

the same faculties, should also be equal one amongst another, without subordination or subjection ...[20]

> But though this be a state of liberty, it is not a state of licence ... The state of Nature has a law of Nature to govern it, which obliges every one, and reason, which is that law, teaches all mankind, who will but consult it, that being all equal and independent, no one ought to harm another in his life health, liberty or possessions.[21]

Practicality nevertheless requires human government, which derives from a compact between the governed and the governor. All men remain in a state of nature

> till by their own consents, they make themselves members of some politic society ...[22]

> It is evident that absolute monarchy ... is indeed inconsistent with civil society ... the end of civil society being to avoid and remedy those inconveniences of the state of Nature which necessarily follow from every man's being judge in his own case, by setting up a known authority to which everyone of that society may appeal upon any injury received, or controversy that may arise.[23]

Such an authority requires funding: 'Government cannot be supported without great charge and it is fit for everyone who enjoys his share of the protection should pay out of his estate his proportion for the maintenance of it. But still it must be with his own consent.'[24]

Perhaps most important, a bad government may be overthrown.

> Wherever law ends, tyranny begins, if the law be transgressed to another's harm, and whosoever in authority exceeds the power given him by the law and makes use of the force he has under his command, to compass that upon the subject, which the law allows not, ceases in that to be a magistrate, and, acting without authority, may be opposed as any other man, who by force invades the right of another.[25]

Here was a gospel of Reason fit for a Revolution.

In his *Essay on Human Understanding* Locke defined the aim of human organisation as 'the highest perfection of intellectual nature lies in a careful and constant pursuit of true and solid happinesse.'[26] In the early eighteenth century in Europe, there developed a quasi-scientific interest in the pursuit of happiness.[27] The Marquis de Chastellux, who came to America as an envoy from the French royal government and corresponded with Jefferson, wrote in 1772 that the purpose of government was to create the greatest happiness for the greatest number of individuals. Now the Revolutionaries had a golden opportunity to put these ideas into effect.

---

[20] S 4.
[21] S 6.
[22] S 15.
[23] S 90.
[24] S 140.
[25] S 202.
[26] Bk 2 Ch 1, 51.
[27] G Willis, *Inventing America: Jefferson's Declaration of Independence* (Lon, Athlone, 1980 149–64.

Based on an examination of Jefferson's papers, Willis in *Inventing America* argues,[28] that he was not greatly acquainted with the *Treatises on Government*. In fact the first draft of the famous preamble to the *Declaration of Independence* was penned by George Mason, so if there is a link it might be found there. Given his education, however, it is likely that Jefferson read the English version of the *Treatise*; publication in America shortly before the Declaration of Independence meant that Locke's ideas must have been current.

Having obtained a broad general background to current intellectual thought, the young Jefferson approached a career in the law. In 1767 George Wythe proposed him for admission to the Virginia bar; he practised successfully,[29] but was soon drawn to politics. In May 1769, he was elected a member of the Virginia General Assembly, shortly before the royal governor dissolved it.[30] Members repaired to the Raleigh tavern and formed themselves into a voluntary convention and drew up articles of association against the use of any merchandise imported from Britain. They set up a Committee of Correspondence to make common cause with Massachusetts and the other States. Those two states passed simultaneous resolutions adopting common cause and messengers from each to the other passed en route. The axis of revolution was formed.

By November 1774 Jefferson was sufficiently prosperous from his practice and landed interests to give up the bar and concentrate on politics.[31] He produced draft instructions for the Virginian delegates to the First Continental Congress, arguing that the relationship between the colonies and Great Britain was the same as the British government had with Scotland, Ireland and Hanover—having the same Chief Executive, ie the King, but otherwise no political connection. Only Wythe agreed with this and the Virginia Convention took the same position as Dickinson, that the British government could regulate trade with the colonies, but no more. Jefferson attacked this surrender, saying that there was no support for the supposed right to regulate trade between Great Britain and colonies in any principle of colonisation or reason.[32] He published these propositions in *A Summary View of the Rights of British America*. Some copies reached England and resulted in the British Parliament issuing a bill of attainder against him.

From John Adams' comment that at the time of the Declaration of Independence Jefferson had been a member of Congress for about a year, it would appear that he attended the First Continental Congress, but took little part in it—Adams said he had not uttered more than three words. He was chosen as a delegate for Virginia to the Second Continental Congress in case another, Peyton Randolph, who was Speaker of the Virginian House of Burgesses, was called away

---

[28]   ibid, Ch 16.

[29]   For details of his legal career see FL Dewey, *Thomas Jefferson: Lawyer* (Charlottesville VA, University of Virginia Press, 1986).

[30]   PL Ford (ed), *Autobiography of Thomas Jefferson* (Philadelphia, University of Pennsylvania Press, 2005) 10.

[31]   ibid, 13–18.

[32]   ibid, 13–14.

to deal with business in Virginia, which he was. On his arrival in Philadelphia, Jefferson argued against Dickinson's claim that a Declaration of Independence was premature, urging that a declaration of independence was necessary before any European powers, such as France or Spain, would recognise the new state and trade with it.[33] His fellows in Virginia were already taking steps to this end. A Declaration of Rights was adopted by the Virginia Convention on 12 June 1776 (of which George Mason was the main author) and the Constitution of the State of Virginia adopted on 29 June (of which James Madison was the main author). Neither Mason nor Madison were practising lawyers, though Madison had spent two years independently reading legal texts. Away in Philadelphia, Jefferson became frustrated at the terms in which the Virginian documents were drafted.[34] Mason's draft of the Virginian Declaration of Rights was in Jefferson's view too general and required a more specific justification for revolution. No foreign state would recognise an independent government of the United States, unless its rejection of British rule could be justified. The most obvious ally would be the royal French government, but even though the French government looked on the English as sworn enemies, a French king would not have wanted to support rebels unless they had a clear case.

Jefferson drafted an important preface to a proposed American Declaration of Independence (which largely found its way into the final version), reciting that 'the history of his present majesty is a history of unremitting injuries and usurpations ... all of which have the indirect object of the establishment of an absolute tyranny over these states.' It went on to list 24 acts of usurpation committed by King George III. Having set out a factual account of the tyranny of the British government, Jefferson borrowed from Mason's text. Mason's draft Virginian Declaration contained these words:

> All men are born equally free and independent, and have certain inherent natural rights of which they cannot by any Compact, deprive or divest their Posterity; among which are the Enjoyment of Life and Liberty, with the means of acquiring and possessing property and pursuing and obtaining Happiness and Safety.

Jefferson's reads:

> We hold these truths to be sacred and undeniable; that all men are created equal and independent, that from that equal creation they derive rights inherent and inalienable, among which are the preservation of life, and liberty and the pursuit of happiness; that to secure these ends, governments are instituted among men, deriving their just powers from the consent of the governed; that whenever any form of government shall become destructive of these ends, it is the right of the people to abolish it.

In turn Congress amended Jefferson's wording to 'we hold these truths to be self-evident, that all men are created equal, that they are endowed by their Creator

---

[33] ibid, 26.

[34] The texts of these documents are to be found on the Avalon Project Website, the Library of Congress website and, in the case of Mason's draft Virginian Declaration of Rights, the Gunston Hall website. There is a useful analysis in JP Boyd (ed), *The Declaration of Independence. The Evolution of the Text* (Library of Congress/Thomas Jefferson Memorial Foundation, 1999).

with certain inalienable rights.' The reference to truth being self-evident harks back to the axioms of Aristotle, but the origin of the rights is now clearly divine. Tellingly John Adams pointed out that these rights were not self-evident—all men were not born in equality of condition or accomplishments; to treat all men as equals would lead to anarchy,[35] but the self-evident truth made its way into the final text.

They became even less self-evident by the excision of a passage that Jefferson had inserted on slavery. Amongst George III's acts of tyranny Jefferson asserted that

> he has waged cruel war against human nature itself, violating its most sacred rights of life and liberty in the persons of a distant people, who never offended him, captivating and carrying them into slavery in another hemisphere, or to incur miserable death in their transportation ... warfare of the Christian king of Great Britain, determined to keep open a market where MEN should be bought or sold.

Jefferson wrote later that the condemnation of the slave trade was struck out in complaisance with South Carolina and Georgia, 'who have never attempted to restrain the importation of slaves and who still wished to continue it.'[36] They were amongst the smallest of the new states in terms of population and the fact that they won the day on the issue of slavery, shows the importance attached above everything to unanimity between the 13 states. The immediate effect, however, was to belie the voice of reason declaring all men equal. The failure to deal with the issue of slavery was (as the postponement of difficult issues often is) storing up trouble for the future. No one seems to have given any thought to Abigail Adams' plea on behalf of women.

Despite the boldness of his condemnation of slavery, Jefferson's personal connection to slavery was complex. In 1776 he prepared a draft constitution for Virginia, which provided that 'no person hereafter coming into this county shall be held within the same in slavery under any pretext whatever.' In 1778, slave importation, whether by sea or land, was banned in the state of Virginia. This, though a major step in principle, had no effect on the existing slave population, who by now were sufficiently numerous to fulfil the needs of the plantations. Nevertheless, Jefferson was part of a committee set up by the Virginian General Assembly to revise the common law and make it applicable to conditions in Virginia. They prepared a bill for consideration by the Assembly, which proposed the emancipation of all slaves born after the passing of the Bill into an Act. They were to be brought up at public expense to tillage, arts or sciences, until they achieved adulthood and then be colonized to such place as the circumstances of the time should render most proper.

---

[35] In his *Defence of the Constitutions of the Government of the United States of America*, (NY, De Capo Press Reprint Edition, 1971).
[36] See Boyd above n 34, 35–36.

In his *Notes on Virginia* Jefferson stated his own view of the difficulties which stood in the way of absorbing former slaves into everyday life, wherever they chose to live:

> Deep rooted prejudices entertained by the whites, ten thousand recollections by the blacks of injuries they have sustained, new provocation; the real distinctions which nature has made and many other circumstances will divide us into parties and produce convulsions, which will probably never end but in the extermination of the one or the other race.

He went on to enumerate the real distinctions nature had made between black and white people, concluding by advancing 'the suspicion that the blacks ... are inferior to the whites in the endowments both of body and mind.'[37] He went on to give a quasi-scientific description of the two races, considering the appearance of the blacks more monotonous and their smell (because their kidneys absorb less) disagreeable:

> They are at least as brave and more adventuresome, but this may perhaps proceed from a want of forethought, which prevents them seeing danger until it be present ... They are more ardent after their female, but love seems with them to be more an eager desire, than a tender delicate mixture of sentiment or reason ... In general their existence appears to participate more of sensation than reflection ... in reason much inferior, as I think one could scarcely be found capable of tracing and comprehending the investigations of Euclid ... in music they are more generally gifted than the whites with accurate ears for tune and time.

Despite his condemnation of the slave trade, Jefferson had slaves of his own and, although he does seem to have treated them humanely, he freed very few of them. When his father died in 1757, Thomas inherited a plantation and slaves and in 1783 when his father in law, John Wayles, died Thomas's wife inherited more slaves, who in law now belonged to her husband.[38] As a result, the Jeffersons owned over 200 slaves and, when he became President in 1800, Thomas took some to the White House. Amongst the slaves inherited from Wayles was a woman called Betty Hemmings, with whom Wythe had had a sexual relationship and fathered a child called Sally. In 1787 when Jefferson was appointed United States Minister to the Royal Court in France, he arranged for one of his daughters to join him there. She went accompanied by Sally, then aged 14; Adams was 44 and seven years a widower. Her brother was also there and Jefferson paid each of them wages. In 1789 Sally and Jefferson returned to the United States. Once there, she had six children, four of whom survived into adulthood. A great deal of academic time and energy has been devoted to establishing whether the six children born by Sally Hemmings were fathered by Jefferson.[39] No relationship

---

[37] In answer to Query XIV.

[38] Bernstein above n 3, 15.

[39] See eg JE Lewis and PS Onuf (eds), *Sally Hemmings and Thomas Jefferson: History, Memory, and Civic Culture* (Charlottesville VA, University Press of Virginia, 1999); A Gordon-Reed, *The Hemingses of Monticello* (New York, WW Norton & Company, 2008); H Wiencek, *Master of the Mountain: Thomas Jefferson and his Slaves* (NY, Farrar, Straus and Giroux, 2012); P Finkelman, *Slavery and the Founders: Race and Liberty in the Age of Jefferson* (NY, Routledge, 2014).

between her and any other member of his household is recorded in the estates farm book. The preponderance of evidence (including some DNA) indicates they were his children and on his death they were effectively freed.

The dichotomy between his views and practice on slavery continued into his Presidency. He gave financial support to the French government to suppress the Haitian slave revolution. Yet in his Presidential address to Congress in 1806, he proposed legislation to abolish the slave trade 'which the morality, the reputation and best of our country have long been eager to prescribe.' In the next year, Congress passed an Act which prohibited the importation of slaves, which took effect early in 1808 (the British Parliament had already outlawed the trade in 1807). Perhaps Jefferson summed up his attitude to slavery in a letter to former Senator, John Holmes, on 22 April 1820:

> [T]here is no man on earth who would sacrifice more than I would to relieve us from this heavy reproach ... we have the wolf by the ear and we can neither hold him, nor safely let him go. Justice is in one scale and self-preservation in the other.[40]

Flawed it may be, but the Declaration of Independence came to represent the spirit of Revolution. The first Constitution (the Articles of Confederation) proved a failure and it took until 1787 to prepare the final draft of the eventual Constitution of the United States; it took even longer for the Bill of Rights to be attached to it. So it was that the Declaration of Independence became the talisman of Revolution and the fame of its principal author assured.

The work of the Committee to revise the laws of Virginia completed its work with a report in June 1779, appending 125 draft Bills, which demonstrated a very liberal approach. For instance, one proposed abolishing the death penalty for all crimes except Treason and Murder. A further Bill entitled *for Establishing Religious Freedom* provided that the government of Virginia could not control an individual's beliefs between him and his God. Both of these Bills with some amendments passed into Virginian law. Another far seeing proposition was *a Bill for the More General Diffusion of Knowledge*, which provided for a system of public education giving primary education to all males and gradually promoting the more able first to county schools and then to university. This was not put into effect.

From 1779 to 1781 Jefferson served as Governor of Virginia, but found this too burdensome and tried to return to private life. In 1785, however, he was appointed Minister of the United States to the royal government in France and as a result, much to his regret, was not in America to influence the drafting of the Constitution of the United States.[41] He did, however, correspond on the topic with Madison, who played a large part in determining its form. Jefferson was pressed into being President Washington's first Secretary of State for Foreign Affairs, an office which proved diminished by the fact that Washington liked

---

[40] See JC Miller, *The Wolf by the Ears: Thomas Jefferson and Slavery* (Charlottesville VA, University of Virginia Press, 1991).
[41] Bernstein above n 3, 71.

to conduct foreign affairs himself.[42] At the same time Washington appointed Alexander Hamilton Treasury Secretary[43] and his federalist views created great enmity with Jefferson. The Federalists tended to come from the coastal areas where trade predominated, the anti-Federalists from more rural areas—farmers, large and small, wanted to go about their business without government interference. Initially Jefferson did show some inclination to adopt middle ground. When Hamilton proposed the establishment of a National Bank, Jefferson is said to have drawn off Madison's opposition by obtaining Hamilton's agreement to the siting of the new national capital on the River Potomac, which bordered Virginia.[44] The peace did not last long. It may be that Washington chose Hamilton, the most convinced Federalist, and the anti-Federalist Jefferson, as part of his administration in an attempt to draw together different strands of opinion, but in the end he had to rebuke their feuding. In due course, the hostility between the two men came into the open, perhaps fuelled on Hamilton's side by the fact that Jefferson had not fought in the Revolutionary War and on Jefferson's by Hamilton's inferior social background. It was exacerbated by the fact that Hamilton still saw the British as natural allies and trading parties of the United States, whereas Jefferson supported alliance with France, particularly when it became a Republic. When France and England became opponents in actual armed hostilities in Europe, the quarrel deepened. In December 1793 Jefferson resigned as Secretary of State. The Jay Treaty with the British government in 1794 increased Jefferson's pessimism about the course the government was taking and he encouraged those who agreed with his views to gather in his support. In 1796, he denounced Federalists as an 'Anglican monarchical and aristocratical party ... whose avowed object is to draw over us the substance, as they have already done the forms, of British government ... timid men who prefer the calm of despotism to the boisterous sea of liberty.'[45]

In the Presidential elections of 1796 Jefferson came second and became Vice President. He soon became exasperated by President Adams's moderate policies, particularly by his attempts to remain neutral in the Franco-British war. His role as Vice President limited his influence. The rift between Adams and Jefferson widened to the point that they would not correspond. Though weary of political infighting, Jefferson stood again for presidential office and was chosen President in 1800. He said in his inaugural address:

> We are all republicans, we are all federalist. If there be any among us who would wish to dissolve the Union or to change its republican form, let them stand undisturbed as monuments of the safety with which errors of opinion may be tolerated where reason is left free to combat it.[46]

He served as President for two terms.

[42] ibid, 85.
[43] Below Ch 14.
[44] Below Ch 14.
[45] Letter of 24 April 1796, recorded in *The Works of Thomas Jefferson*, vol 8 (Correspondence 1793–1798) (ed) PL Ford, published online at Online Library of Liberty (http://oll.libertyfund.org/titles/jefferson-the-works-vol-8-correspondence-1793-1798).
[46] ibid, 493.

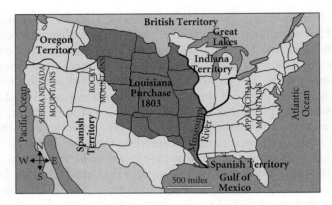

Map showing extent of the Louisiana Purchase

Perhaps the most notable act of his Presidency was the Louisiana Purchase. France claimed an enormous tract of land largely inland from the English seaboard colonies, still evidenced by names such as Quebec, Montreal, St Louis and Baton Rouge. The Napoleonic government in France absorbed Spanish territories around the Missouri and Mississippi valleys, including the port they then named New Orleans. The territory was only sparsely populated by the French (in 1719 prisoners in France were released on condition that they married prostitutes and settled in Louisiana). Jefferson sent Livingston to Paris to negotiate the purchase of the port. Fortunately for him, Napoleon saw these territories as a drain on his finances and offered to sell the whole of the Louisiana territory for 15 million dollars, which amounted to a price of four cents an acre. The way was free for the United States to develop westwards. Jefferson despatched an expedition led by Merewether, Lewis and Clarke to explore the western part of America and search for a Northwest Passage. They reached the Pacific, found that there was no such passage, but that the American continent was a thing of wonders.

Political dissension continued; his own party split and as early as 1803 he looked forward finally to relinquishing public life. In retirement he devoted much time to redesigning his house built on the Palladian model at Monticello, though his greatest project was the establishment of the University of Virginia in Charlottesville. It was a non-sectarian institution with the avowed aim of forming the statesmen, legislators and judges on whom posterity would depend. The death of Abigail Adams brought John and Jefferson together again and they resumed correspondence. They both died on 4 July 1826.

12

Constitution: John Rutledge

I N THE SUMMER of 1787, 11 years after the Declaration of Independence, 55 delegates from the States of the Union arrived in Philadelphia to take part in a Convention, whose purpose was to draw up a Constitution uniting the 13 now independent states of America. Over half of the delegates were lawyers. William Pierce, a delegate from Georgia, wrote pen sketches of his fellows[1] and lavished particular praise on James Wilson a lawyer from Pennsylvania: he ranked 'among the foremost in legal and political knowledge … Government seems to have been his peculiar study … no man is more clear, copious and comprehensive than Mr Wilson.' He also praised the widely read James Madison.[2] He was less complimentary about **John Rutledge**, who was

> one of those characters who was highly mounted at the commencement of the late revolution—his reputation in the first Congress gave him a distinguished rank among American worthies … This Gentleman is much famed in his own state as an orator, but in my opinion he is too rapid in his public speaking to be nominated an agreeable orator.

In fact, Rutledge was very successful as a lawyer in his home state of South Carolina; he argued the southern interest including the preservation of the slave trade. He had to be able to take back to South Carolina a draft that would be ratified and the continuance of slavery was essential to that. There was a good deal of horse trading between the various interests. More particularly his drafting skills were put to good use as chairman of the Committee of Detail, which reduced the many resolutions of the Convention to a generally acceptable written version.

The Rutledge family moved to Ireland as Anglican settlers after Oliver Cromwell subdued the Irish. John's uncle, Andrew, studied at Trinity College Dublin and by 1731 had emigrated to Carolina, establishing a successful law practice.[3] He married a rich widow through whom he acquired a plantation and slaves.

---

[1] See M Farrand (ed), *The Records of the Federal Convention of 1787,* (NH, Yale University Press, 1911) Vol III 87.

[2] Below ch 12.

[3] J Haw, *John and Edward Rutledge of South Carolina* (Athens GA,University of Georgia Press, 1997) 1 et seq; see also R Barry, *Mr Rutledge of South Carolina* (Salem, Duell, Sloan & Pearce, 1942) and R Beeman, *Plain Honest Men: The Making of the American Constitution,* (New York, Random House, 2009).

Not long after his brother John, who was a doctor, followed him and swiftly married Andrew's 14 year old step-daughter, Sarah. He gave up medicine for life as a planter. The couple had seven children, John junior being born in 1739 and his younger brother, Edward, 10 years later. John junior trained in his uncle's law practice. John senior died in 1750 and Andrew in 1755, leaving his estate to John junior, including over 100 slaves.

The Carolinas were originally proprietorial colonies. The eight aristocrats, who had assisted in the Restoration of Charles II, were granted part of Virginia: there was method in Charles's madness—the new colony was intended as a bulwark against the Spanish in Florida. John Locke played a considerable part in drafting a Constitution for the colony which received royal approval in 1669.[4] Its express object, stated in the preamble, was to avoid erecting a numerous democracy—in other words popular suffrage. It gave the colony the status of an autonomous county palatine, similar to that held by the Bishop of Durham. Locke's Constitution divided the colony into counties each governed by a landgrave and the landgraves were made an hereditary aristocracy. As John Adams noted, this aristocratic tradition persisted into the eighteenth century, with influence in the colony largely controlled by rich plantation owners, such as John Rutledge; in the Convention John opposed popular suffrage.[5] More sympathetically, article 97 of the Carolina Constitution provided for religious toleration for Jews and dissenters and even native Americans. Any body of at least seven persons sharing the same religious beliefs could form a church.

The northern and southern parts of the colony developed separate interests; in 1729, the Lords Proprietors sold their interests to the Crown and two royal Colonies of North and South Carolina were created. In 1732 a further royal colony, called Georgia, was established to the south of South Carolina, initially to accommodate the worthy poor of England. North Carolina largely served the procurement needs of the British Navy and shipping; South Carolina became prosperous from the production of rice and indigo for dye. These were labour intensive crops and the labour came from the importation of slaves from West Africa. From the early sixteenth century, the Spanish, and from the early seventeenth century, the Dutch, had transported slaves from West Africa to the New World. In 1660 Charles II chartered a company of Merchant Adventurers to trade with Africa, which became the Royal Africa Company; it began exporting slaves to the West Indies and also to North America. Article 110 of the 1669 Constitution of Carolina gave every freeman in the Colony power over his negro slaves. By 1730 there were about 10,000 white inhabitants and 20,000 black slave inhabitants of South Carolina;[6] the census of 1790 recorded a white population in South Carolina of 140,000 and a slave population of 109,000. The principal port of Charlestown (later Charleston) became very prosperous exporting rice and importing slaves.

---

[4] V Hseuh, 'Giving Orders: Theory and Practice in the Fundamental Constitution of Carolina' (2002) 63(3) *Journal of History of Ideas* 425–46.
[5] Above Ch 10.
[6] Haw above n 3, 21.

In 1756 John went to London. At this time about a third of those who qualified as lawyers in the southern states did so after admission to a London Inn
of Court, particularly the Middle Temple.[7] John was admitted to that Inn on
11 October 1754, though he did not take his place there until 1756. He studied
diligently, but did sample the pleasures of London life. He wrote to a friend
'I know nothing more entertaining and likely to give you a graceful manner of
speaking than seeing a good play well acted. Garrick is inimitable.'[8] He was
called to the English bar in February 1760 and admitted to the South Carolina
bar in January 1761. In November 1761, acting on behalf of a young woman
who sued a rich merchant for breach of promise of marriage, he obtained the
huge sum of £2500 damages and a fee of 100 guineas. It was his first case and
made his name. Earlier that year he was elected to the Commons House in the
South Carolina Assembly. His legal practice grew and between 1761 and 1774
he handled more cases in the Court of Common Pleas of the colony than any
other advocate, including some without fee for poor clients. In 1763 he married
Elizabeth Grimke from a prosperous family of German settlers, built a substantial house in Charleston and in due course had 10 children by her.

In 1765 he was chosen as one of a committee in South Carolina to oppose the
Stamp Act, persuading the courts in the colony to act without stamped paper.
He was one of three delegates from the colony to the Stamp Act Congress,
where, though the youngest member, he played a part in drafting a memorial
to the House of Lords requesting repeal of the Act.[9] In 1767 trouble brewed in
Charleston when customs officers seized vessels; John acted for ship owners trying to recover their vessels and on one occasion for a customs officer, who could
find no other lawyer to represent him.[10]

John's younger brother, Edward, was called to the English bar in the Middle
Temple in 1772 and admitted to the South Carolina bar in 1773. Both brothers
played a prominent role during the Revolution and subsequent conventions—it
has already been noted that Edward was one of three envoys on behalf of the
Confederation to General Howe, seeking an accommodation.[11] Both attended
the First Continental Congress and John was elected to a committee to state
the rights and grievances of the colonists. At this time he wanted to maintain
the possibility of reconciliation with Britain. When some delegates argued that
under natural law the colonists could establish whatever government they chose,
John supported the position that the British Parliament was entitled to regulate
trade with the colonies.[12] When the question of a boycott on exports of goods
to Britain arose, John argued the cause of South Carolina: manufactured goods

---

[7] HP Canady, *Gentlemen of the Bar, Lawyers in Colonial Southern Carolina* (New York,
Garland, 1987) 170–71 and 187–88; JGR Hamilton, 'Southern Members of the Inns of Court'
(1933) 10 *North Carolina Historical Review* 274.
  [8] Rev J Adams, *Laws of Success and Failure in Life: An Address* (1833) cited Haw above n 3, 10.
  [9] Haw above n 3, 29 et seq.
  [10] ibid, 43.
  [11] Above Ch 10.
  [12] Haw above n 3, 63.

from the northern colonies were exported all over the world, so that their trade could continue even with a ban on exports to Britain; rice and indigo from South Carolina were exported almost entirely to Britain, so that trade would be unfairly hit. As a result Congress resolved that the policy of non-importation of goods from Britain should commence at once, but non-exportation to the British Empire should not commence until September 1775; John also succeeded in achieving an exemption in the case of rice.

He helped to draw up a Constitution for South Carolina, which came into force on 26 March 1776,[13] effectively declaring South Carolina independent of Britain. On that date, he was elected President and Commander-in-Chief of South Carolina. He had been chosen as a delegate to the Second Continental Congress, but his fresh responsibilities caused him to withdraw. He was swiftly faced with a crisis—in the spring of 1776 the British decided on a new tactic to attack the underbelly of the colonies in Carolina and then march north.[14] There were a good many loyalists in the state and General Clinton set sail for Charleston, believing they would join him. Troops from the American Continental Army, under the command of General John Lee arrived shortly before the British men of war. There was a fort on Sullivan's Island at the entrance to Charleston harbour; Lee considered its fortifications insufficient to withstand an attack by the heavy guns of the British and ordered its evacuation, but John countermanded him. Perhaps accidentally, he was proved right. The British started to fire on the fort on the 28 June 1776, but the fortifications consisted of soft Palmetto[15] logs and sand, which simply absorbed the British cannon balls, whilst patriot guns inflicted considerable damage on the British ships, forcing them to withdraw.

As a result of his duties in South Carolina, John was not present in Philadelphia during the debates leading to the Declaration of Independence, but his brother Edward was. Initially he argued against a declaration, on tactical grounds that it would reveal the colonists' intentions before they were ready to resist British retaliation; in the end, however, he was the youngest delegate to sign at the age of 26.[16]

The South Carolina Constitution of 1776 specifically stated it was temporary and a new one was drafted, coming into force on 19 March 1778. It provided for a bicameral legislature and an executive. The earlier version had granted suffrage to white men with taxable land. The 1778 version required that they must own 50 acres of such land. Only those who recognised a Protestant God could vote or hold office. Even this suffrage was too large for Rutledge and he resigned. When, however, a military threat to Georgia became apparent, he was elected Governor of South Carolina (the office of Governor had replaced that of President).

---

[13] ibid, 80.
[14] ibid, 85 et seq.
[15] Palmetto trees are small palms.
[16] ibid, 92.

In 1780 the British, having taken Georgia, threatened Charleston, General Clinton sailing south with a large contingent of redcoats.[17] When a force of the Continental Army arrived to oppose them, under the command of a General Lincoln, the general advised evacuating Charleston to save the army. Maybe over-emboldened by his earlier success, John ordered Lincoln to defend the city; by May 1781 it was surrounded by the British and Lincoln was forced to surrender.[18] Clinton's forces soon overran South Carolina causing great damage and loss of life; John advised the militia to lay down their arms and fled first to one of his plantations (which the British later sacked) and then further north to Philadelphia. Edward, who by this time had returned to South Carolina, was arrested and imprisoned in St Augustine, Georgia, though he was released later under an exchange of prisoners.[19] In Philadelphia John found that General Washington, who had previously been slow to send adequate reinforcements, planned to rescue South Carolina with assistance from the French government. A section of the Continental Army marched south and eventually confined the British to an area round Charleston. Meanwhile, the British General Cornwallis was surrounded in Yorktown, Virginia by Continental forces and a French naval force and in October 1781 surrendered with 8000 British troops. Eventually in December 1782 the British evacuated Charleston. The War of Independence was over. The patriots had won. South Carolina had suffered more than most: 18 per cent of battlefield deaths and 31 per cent of the wounded occurred there.[20] The economic welfare of both the state and its governor had suffered heavily and he remained in debt for much of the rest of his life. From now on John was bitterly anti-British.

In September 1786 a convention of state representatives met in Annapolis, the capital of Maryland, to consider general trade. They reported back that there were important defects in the system of federal government created by the Articles of Confederation that were 'so serious as to render the situation of the United States delicate and critical.'[21] The problem was that, when the Articles were drawn up, the individual states saw themselves as a loose confederation still maintaining their individual sovereignty. The second clause stated that 'each state retains its sovereignty, freedom and independence and every Power, Jurisdiction and right which is not by this confederation expressly delegated to the United States in Congress Assembled.' To be valid, decisions of Congress had to be supported by a vote of two-thirds of the states.[22] Although the size and wealth of the states varied considerably, each had one vote. Whilst only Congress had the right to declare war or make peace, charges for the defence and general welfare of the United States were to be funded and collected by

---

[17] ibid, 118.

[18] ibid, 132.

[19] ibid, 143.

[20] ibid, 175.

[21] M Farrand, *The Framing of the Constitution of the United States* (New Haven CT, Yale University Press, 1913).

[22] US Constitution, Article VIII.

the individual states; Congress had no procedure for enforcing the collection of taxes.[23] There was no specific provision for a true executive; there was a committee appointed by Congress with the power, when Congress was not sitting, to manage the affairs of the United States; this Committee had a president, but there was no federal president. Congress had the power to appoint courts for trying piracy and felony on the High Seas and determining prize claims, but other than that no power to create federal courts. By the time of the Annapolis Convention, it was clear to all the states that a stronger central government was required; there was still a good deal of dissension, however, on how strong that government should be.

The Constitutional Convention was summoned by Congress and assembled in Philadelphia in May 1787. John Rutledge—by now having taken an appointment as a judge of the Chancery court in Charleston—was one of the South Carolina delegates. At the time of the earlier debates on the Articles of Confederation, the attitude of the South Carolina delegation had been that confederation should be on the basis of equality between states however disparate their population and wealth; they should delegate only as much sovereignty to central government as was absolutely necessary for the safety of their state.[24] The progress of the war had shown, however, that the Carolinas were very dependent on the northern states for military protection and now the combined weight of the 13 states was needed to combat British trade restrictions—the Carolinas had a severe adverse balance of trade.[25] There had been a subtle change of mood, which probably matched that of many delegates from other states; as the debate proceeded over the coming months, the desire for unanimity increased. On the 8 June, James Wilson urged that

> if we establish a national Government, the States must submit themselves as individuals—the lawful Government must be supreme ... we are one in name, let us be one in truth or fact—unless this power is vested in the General Government the States will be used by foreign powers as engines against the whole.[26]

Nevertheless, the South Carolina delegates hoped to achieve two main objectives. The first was weight in the deliberations of Congress—they were a wealthy state, but in terms of population ranked only ninth amongst the 13 states; when representation on the basis of population alone was proposed they objected. Their second objective was to prevent any limitation on the slave trade.[27]

When the Convention first sat there was not only concern, but also a sense of excitement. James Wilson said:

> After a lapse of six thousand years since the creation of the world, America now presents the first instance of a people assembled to weigh deliberately and peaceably upon the form of government by which they will bind themselves and their posterity.[28]

[23] ibid.
[24] Haw above n 3, 106.
[25] ibid, 192.
[26] Farrand above n 21, 192.
[27] ibid, 202.
[28] JB McMaster and FD Stone, *Pennsylvania and the Federal Constitution* 222 cited Farrand above n 21, 62.

Over the years since the revolution, John Rutledge had become friendly with
Wilson and initially Wilson gave him accommodation in his house in Philadelphia. After a while, John moved to the Indian Tavern, where many of the principal players, including Mason, Madison and Hamilton, lodged. There must have
been a good deal of talk outside the convention and deals done. The Convention
decided at the outset to keep its deliberations secret, in order to avoid popular
pressure. It was resolved that no copy of any official record should leave the
Convention. In fact the Secretary's notes, which constituted the formal record,
consisted of no more than resolutions proposed and the votes recorded. James
Madison, however, realising the great importance of what passed, made detailed
notes of the debates as well as the voting.[29] Secrecy only stimulated a rumour
mill outside the Convention. There was a fear that some delegates would favour
a monarchical Constitution and word spread that the Bishop of Osnabruck,
George III's second son, was to be invited to become King of America.[30] When
Alexander Hamilton argued in Convention that the British Constitution was the
best in the world, he was accused of being monarchical.[31] At one stage, Peyton
Randolph of Virginia proposed a three man executive to avoid too much con-
centration of power in one man.[32] John Rutledge argued for a sole President and
this argument won the day.[33]

The debates were mainly occupied with issues about the nature of the legislature and election to it, the power to tax and the basis of taxation and the powers
of the President and his relationship with the legislature. These were big issues
and there were widely divergent views; behind them lay the wish of states, such as
Virginia and Pennsylvania, which were larger in terms of population and wealth,
to have a voice that reflected their importance, whilst the smaller states, such as
New Jersey, New York, Connecticut, Delaware and the Carolinas did not want
to be overwhelmed by the larger.[34] Carolina had a relatively small white population, but considerable wealth. There were also east-west issues. Some states had
borders adjacent to unclaimed western lands, others were distant from them, so
delegates wanted to guard against their states losing power when the colonies
spread westward. Georgia, with a small population and wealth, but already
owning large tracts of virtually unsettled western land, on occasion sided with
the larger states, anticipating that it might become one. Although arguments of
principle were deployed, the process was essentially political, each state jostling
to preserve its position. Virginia took the initiative and presented a plan, largely
drafted by Madison, as a basis for debate. In general form it was followed by
the eventual constitution. The representatives of the smaller states felt it was too
favourable to the larger states and New Jersey produced an alternative plan.

A system separating the various powers of government and allowing them to
check and balance one another was taken as read—the views of Montesquieu

[29] Farrand above n 1.
[30] Farrand above n 21, 173 and see 162.
[31] ibid, 87.
[32] ibid, 77.
[33] Farrand above n 1, Vol I 65, 69, 230.
[34] Farrand above n 21, 85.

were gospel—but the details of how this should be achieved were hotly debated. The eventual Constitution was said to speak in the name of the People, but how were they to be involved? Hamilton proposed that the executive and two Houses of the legislature should be elected directly by the people.[35] The Convention thought this too radical. Two problems were raised: given differences in population and wealth, how could the individual states be fairly represented in both branches and should the second branch be popularly elected? In tune with the high property qualification for suffrage in their own state, the South Carolina delegation argued that both Houses should be elected by the state legislatures to guard against populism—the populace at large were not well fitted to judge the worth of the candidates.[36] Although the Convention rejected this proposal, it was eventually agreed that the second House should consist of two delegates from each state, chosen by the state legislatures.[37] This gave the smaller states a strong voice in the second House and meant, so they thought, that 'worthy' persons were more likely to be elected. The name chosen for this second House, taken from Republican Rome, was the Senate: it derives from *senex* meaning old—an assembly of elders.

The first House was to be that of Representatives, elected by the people. John Rutledge, supported by another South Carolinian delegate Pierce Butler, argued that representation should reflect both population and wealth, since property was the principal object of society.[38] The argument on this point became so heated that Benjamin Franklin, chairing the proceedings, pointed out that delegates were sent to consult not contend.[39] When it looked as if the argument on this issue was not going to reach a conclusion, he suggested that a committee be formed with one delegate from each state to seek a compromise.[40] This was finally achieved after a resolution put forward by Gouverneur[41] Morris from New York linking representation to taxation: 'representatives and direct taxes shall be apportioned among the several states ... which shall be achieved by adding to the whole number of free persons ... three fifths of all other persons (excluding Indians).' These other persons would be black slaves. This formula avoided any specific criterion of wealth, whilst indirectly recognising it. It was the so called three-fifths or Connecticut Compromise (the representatives of that State having played a leading role in brokering it). If States such as South Carolina wanted to have greater representation in relation to their slave holdings, they would have to pay for it with higher taxes. It effectively found its way into the eventual Constitution as part of Article I, according to which enumeration of the population of the colonies was to take place within three years (hence the census of 1790) and in the meantime the various states would be represented

---

[35] ibid, 87.
[36] Haw above n 3, 204.
[37] Farrand above n 1, I 130–32 and 156.
[38] ibid, 196, 206–07.
[39] ibid, 197.
[40] ibid.
[41] This was a first name, not a title.

by numbers varying from one for Delaware to 10 for Virginia. South Carolina had five. The three-fifths compromise was not an original idea. A similar formula had been put forward in Congress in 1783.[42]

That still left the question of the relative powers of the two branches. Section 8 of Article I of the eventual Constitution gave the Congress power (not found in the Articles of Confederation) to lay and collect taxes for the common defence and general welfare of the United States; section 7 provided that all bills for raising revenue should originate in the House of Representatives, but the Senate might propose or concur in amendments as on other bills. The lack of a popular vote for the second branch was balanced by this greater power in the House of Representatives.

The method of electing and period of office of the President were also the subject of much debate. The period of office was eventually set at four years and the method of election in effect a popular vote at one remove. Hamilton had suggested that the President should be chosen by electors chosen by the people. In fact, this idea of an Electoral College was adopted. Section 1 of Article II provided that 'each state shall appoint, in such manner as the Legislature thereof may direct, a number of electors equal to the whole number of Senators and Representatives to which the State may be entitled in Congress.' These electors were to vote by ballot for two persons (one of whom should not be an inhabitant of the State inhabited by the electors). These votes were to be counted and the candidate with the largest number of votes elected President. The person with the next greatest number of votes would be Vice President. It was open to the state legislatures to have the electors themselves elected by popular vote or some other method if they chose. The President was to be not merely head of the Executive, but also Commander in Chief of the armed forces, including the militia, when they were called into the service of the United States. He was given power to make treaties with other nations, subject to two thirds of each branch of the legislature ratifying. He could appoint judges and public ministers (the nature of their role being left to his discretion). Otherwise his powers were left at large.

There was discussion on the desirability of power to veto legislation passed by Congress or state legislatures. The Virginia Plan provided for a council of revision of laws consisting of the President and judges with powers to veto legislation passed by Congress and for Congress to declare laws of state legislatures unconstitutional.[43] John Rutledge successfully opposed the inclusion of such clauses; he felt it would be wrong for judges to rule on the constitutionality of laws until the point was raised before them in a specific case.[44] He favoured the view that the Supreme Court should have power to declare laws unconstitutional in such cases.[45] The eventual Constitution in section 6 of Article I gave the President power to raise objections to legislation passed by both branches; they

[42] Farrand above n 1, 104.
[43] Farrand above n 21, 209.
[44] Farrand above n 1, II 22–24.
[45] Haw above n 3, 208; Farrand above n 1, II, 22, 24, 28.

would then reconsider and amend if they thought necessary; if the bill was then passed by a two thirds majority of both houses, it became law. No provision was made for the Supreme Court to declare laws unconstitutional, though they did later assume that power.[46] The problem of whether there could be federal courts other than the Supreme Court was in effect postponed in Article III section 1 of the Constitution, which gave Congress power to establish lower tier Federal courts.

The slave trade did not occupy much time in debate, but the question of its continuance was raised and a further compromise reached. On 21 August, Luther Martin of Maryland proposed that prohibition of or tax upon the importation of slaves should be allowed. He said that the three-fifths clause would encourage importation of more slaves, that those parts of the union which opposed such importation were forced now to protect it and that slavery was inconsistent with the principles of the Revolution and dishonourable to the American character.[47] John Rutledge replied that religion and humanity had nothing to do with this question. 'Interest alone is the governing principle with Nations ... If the Northern States will consult their interest, they will not oppose the increase of slaves, which will increase the commodities of which they will become the carriers.'[48] Another South Carolina delegate, General Pinkney, said bluntly that South Carolina would not approve the Constitution if it prohibited slavery. An uneasy compromise was reached in Section 9 of Article I: the migration or importation of such persons as any of the states now existing shall think proper to admit, shall not be prohibited by the Congress prior to 1808, but a tax or duty may be imposed on such importation, not exceeding 10 dollars for each person.

By the end of the Convention, Rutledge had lost some battles and won others, but there was enough there for him to be confident that his state legislature would ratify. He was asked to chair the Committee of Detail and got down to the business of drawing the various resolutions into a coherent and clear whole. Other members, such as Wilson and Randolph, played a large part in this process, but the original documents show Rutledge's handwriting recording the various amendments. It seems to have been the Committee of Detail which produced the ringing preamble:

> We the people of the United States, in Order to form a more perfect Union, establish justice, insure domestic Tranquility, provide for the common defense, promote the general Welfare, and secure the Blessings of Liberty to ourselves and our Posterity, do ordain and establish the Constitution of the United States of America.

The Draft Constitution by its own terms required at least nine states to ratify it before it became law. George Washington as President of the Convention signed it at the end of the Convention. Only 39 of the 55 delegates signed, but all went back to their state legislatures to consider ratification. By the end of December 1787 Delaware, Pennsylvania, New Jersey, Georgia and Connecticut had ratified.

---

[46] Below Ch 15.
[47] Farrand above n 1, II 364.
[48] ibid, 373.

Other states, particularly Massachusetts, held back but eventually ratified without conditions, but in the confidence that the addition of a Bill of Rights would be considered; South Carolina and Maryland followed. The ninth state to sign was New Hampshire on 21 June 1788.

For 18 months between 1789 and 1791 John served as Associate Justice of the Supreme Court. He resigned to become Chief Justice of the Court of Common Pleas in South Carolina. In 1795 he agreed with Washington to accept nomination for Chief Justice of the Supreme Court.[49] Soon after he made an intemperate speech criticising the Jay Treaty with Britain and in December the Senate rejected his nomination. He had by now lost his wife and mother and he became so depressed that on 26 December he tried to drown himself in a river; some slaves spotted him and dragged him to safety. He died on 18 July 1800.

John Rutledge was but one cog in the machinery that made the Constitution, the acceptance or rejection of his arguments demonstrates the course of the debate and, perhaps most importantly the willingness to compromise. There was no section specifically setting out the liberties which the colonists had originally claimed were theirs by right. The question whether there should be such a section of the Constitution was to be the subject of the next phase of the Revolution.

---

[49] Haw above n 3, 243 et seq.

13

Bill of Rights: Roger Sherman and James Madison

T HE TWO GREAT issues which occupied the Constitutional Convention were first how much sovereignty should federated states surrender to a central government and second how should human rights be protected in a federated state? At opposite ends of the spectrum were **Roger Sherman** and **James Madison,** the first a supporter of the power of individual states of the Union and leaving the protection of liberty to the good sense of the new government, the latter a proponent of strong central government and a specific Bill of Rights. Sherman had no university degree, but was a practising lawyer for many years. Madison studied at the university of New Jersey and read about law as part of his general studies;[1] though he never qualified as a lawyer, his subsequent drafting showed he had imbibed a good deal of what he studied. He played a central role in the decision to amend the Constitution to protect human rights. Both men are set on a par in this chapter. Jack Rakove in his Pulitzer Prize winning *Original Meanings* wrote:

> America had more Shermans in its politics than Madisons, and arguably too few of either, but it was the rivalry between competing goals and political styles that jointly gave the great Convention much of its drama and fascination and also permitted its achievement.[2]

The individual states in America had passed their own Bills of Rights, largely modelled on their English predecessor. There was a perfectly respectable view, to which Sherman adhered, that nothing further was required. When it became clear that the Convention was going to vote in favour of a Bill of Rights, Sherman agreed to serve on a committee of six, including Madison, to draft a final text of rights. Madison produced an initial draft. In 1987 James Hutson, head of the manuscript division in the Library of Congress, discovered a manuscript in Sherman's hand setting out an alternative draft to Madison's. The final draft was different to both, but the two alternatives demonstrate that neither man alone determined the text.

Following the discovery of Sherman's version of a Bill of Rights in the Library of Congress, DS Gerber published a comparison of Sherman and Madison's

---

[1] R Ketcham, *James Madison: A Biography* (Charlottesville VA, University Press of Virginia, 1990), 56

[2] J Rakove, *Original Meanings: Politics and Ideas in the Making of the Constitution,* (New York, Knopf, 1996).

drafts with the final version.[3] By way of example, three forms of Amendment One are set out:

> Madison: 'The civil rights of none shall be abridged on account of religious belief or worship, nor shall any national religion be established.'

> Sherman: 'The people have certain natural rights which are retained in society, such are the rights of conscience in matters of religion.'

> Bill of Rights: 'Congress shall make no law regarding an establishment of religion or prohibiting the free exercise thereof or abridging the freedom of speech or the press or the right of the people peaceably to assemble and to petition the government for a redress of grievances.'

It may be noted that Sherman's version reflects his view that civil rights already exist; for him natural law was the law of God. The eventual text prevents, as did Madison's draft, an established church such as the Anglican one, but it also extends its reach to cover subjects, such as freedom of expression, which extend beyond a religious context.

The backgrounds and personalities of the Sherman and Madison were totally different. In 1776 Sherman was 55. He was born and brought up in the Boston area.[4] His family originally came from Dedham (later Constable country) in Suffolk, England and emigrated to Massachusetts about 1636. They were Congregationalists and two of his brothers were ministers of that faith. He did not go to university, though the local minister who taught him had been to Harvard. He worked first as a cobbler and then as a surveyor. At the age of 22 he moved from Massachusetts to Connecticut, borrowed money and bought 250 acres of land. A local lawyer encouraged him to study the English common law and in 1754, at the age of 33, he was admitted to the Connecticut bar and practised successfully until, in 1766, he was made a judge of the Connecticut Court of Common Pleas. He had 15 children by two wives.

Connecticut was a small state; it was conservative, both socially and religiously. Much of its character was formed from the time when Thomas Hooker established a congregational church there.[5] He had been educated at Emmanuel College, Cambridge when it was a hotbed of Calvinist revisionism. Once a minister in Chelmsford (near Dedham) in England, his charismatic preaching drew the attention of Archbishop Laud's agents, who tried to arrest him. He fled in the early 1630s to Holland and then to Massachusetts. In 1636 he moved with a number of parishioners to Hartford, Connecticut and then to New Haven on the coast. He came of a generation committed to Calvinism and fiercely protective of their liberty.

---

[3] SD Gerber, 'Roger Sherman and the Bill of Rights' (1996) 28 *Journal of the Northeastern Political Science Association Polity* 521–40.

[4] See RS Boardman, *Roger Sherman: Signer and Statesman*, (Oxford, H Milford and Oxford University Press, 1938); and C Collier, *Roger Sherman's Connecticut: Yankee Politics and the American Revolution* (Middleton, Wesleyan University Press, 1971).

[5] Dictionary of National Biography.

In due course Roger Sherman also moved to New Haven, a prosperous port, dealing with the West Indies. He set up a general store next to Yale College. The College had been established in 1701 by an Act of the General Assembly of Connecticut for young people to be educated to fit them for public life in the church and civil state. It was named Yale in 1718 after a benefactor from Wales called Elihu Yale, who (perhaps ironically) had made a fortune through the British East India Company. Sherman's stock rose sufficiently that by 1765 he was appointed Treasurer of the College and granted an honorary Master's Degree.

He had been elected to the Connecticut General Assembly, but when delegates were picked to attend the First Continental Congress he was chosen only after two others had turned the invitation down.[6] He served in both Congresses and in the Constitutional Convention, spending over 1500 days on their business and in due course was the only man to sign all of the principal documents they produced—the Declaration of Independence, the Articles of Association, the Articles of Confederation, the Constitution and the Bill of Rights. He played a part in drafting a number of key documents in the course of the Continental Congresses, in particular he was on the committee that approved the final draft of the Declaration of Independence and on another which drafted the Articles of Confederacy—all this while he served on the Board of War.

As his background might suggest, he was not an easy man to work with, but he gained great respect from his associates. William Pierce, in his pen pictures of the delegates,[7] described him thus:

> [A]wkward, un-meaning and unaccountably strange in his manner. But in his train of thinking there is something regular deep and comprehensive, yet the oddity of his address, the vulgarisms that accompany his public speaking and that strange New England cant, which through his public as well as private speaking, make everything that is connected to him grotesque and laughable—and yet he deserves infinite praise—no man has a better heart or clearer head.

Perhaps there was an element of snobbery here over Roger's lack of education. He preferred experience to philosophy and above all was guided by his small state and puritan background. He was an opponent of slavery.

James Madison was a much younger man, being 25 at the time of the Declaration of Independence. He came from the largest state, Virginia, and a rich slave owning background; he was well educated and showed little public interest in religion.[8] His father was one of the largest plantation and slave owners in the state. From 1769 he studied at the College of New Jersey under a Scottish Presbyterian minister, James Witherspoon. He had recently been invited to come from Edinburgh University to become President of the College and brought with him the views of the Scottish Enlightenment, placing particular importance on studying moral philosophy. At a lower level, knowledge of the law was part

---

[6] Boardman above n 4, 26.
[7] See above ch 12, n 1.
[8] See J Rakove *James Madison and the Creation of the American Republic* (New York. Foresman/Little Brown, 1990); L Cheney, *James Madison, a Life Reconsidered* (New York, Viking, 2014)

of the education of a gentleman. In due course, Witherspoon was chosen as a delegate from New Jersey to the Continental Congress and signed the Declaration of Independence. Madison graduated in 1771. Although educated at a Presbyterian institution, he showed little evidence of religious leanings in later life.[9] Madison did not attend Congress until 1780 and so he was not a signatory to the Declaration of Independence. Through their involvement in Virginian politics, Madison and Jefferson became lifelong friends.[10] At Jefferson's suggestion Madison collected treatises on republican government, the Law of Nations and the political history of the New World.[11] In 1787 (whilst Jefferson was still in Paris) Madison, now 36, was one of seven Virginian delegates to the Constitutional Convention. By now a proponent of a strong central government, he drafted the Virginia Plan, which formed the basis of debate.[12] William Pierce in his pen sketches of delegates to the Convention waxed eloquently about Madison's role in debate:

> [E]very Person acknowledges his greatness ... he blends together the profound politician with the scholar. In the management of every great question he evidently took the lead in the Convention ... he always comes forward the best informed in debate.[13]

Both men played considerable roles in the debates in the Constitutional Convention. Sherman first argued that the representation in the House of Representatives should be according to the number of free inhabitants.[14] When this was not accepted he was instrumental in gaining acceptance of the three-fifths compromise.[15] He argued successfully that Congress' powers should be explicitly defined. Along with Gouverneur Morris and Luther Martin he opposed the continuance of the slave trade, but in the end made the crucial compromise that enabled all the states to sign. On 22 August, Madison recorded Sherman as saying that

> he disapproved of the slave trade, yet as the States were now possessed of the right to import slaves, as the public good did not require it to be taken from them and as it was expedient to have as few objections as possible to the proposed scheme of Government, he thought it best to leave the matter as we found it.

He observed that the abolition of slavery seemed in any event to be occurring in the United States and that 'the good sense of the several States would probably by degrees complete it.'[16]

He also thought that human freedoms were too important to depend upon paper protections. 'The only security that you can have for all your important

---

[9] JH Hutson, *Forgotten Features of the Founding, The Recovery of Religious Themes in the Early American Republic* (Lanham MD, Lexington Books, 2003).

[10] I Brant, *James Madison* (Indianapolis, Bobbs-Merrill, 1941) Vol I 272–76.

[11] JP Boyd (ed) *Papers of Thomas Jefferson* Vol VIII 111 (Princeton NJ, Princeton University Press, 1953).

[12] Above Ch 11.

[13] M Farrand (ed), *Records of the Federal Convention* of 1787 (New Haven, Yale University Press, 1911) III 87 et seq.

[14] ibid, 98 et seq.

[15] Above Ch 11.

[16] Farrand above n 13, 102.

rights must be in the nature of your government.' The Convention, in order to press on with ratification of the Constitution, adjourned inviting ratification by the states without a bill of rights. The ratification debates both in the press and in state conventions proved stormy; specific requests for the addition of a bill of rights came from New York, Virginia and Massachusetts. Ratification by nine states being completed and the Constitution taking effect on 21 June 1788, the House of Representatives met for the first time on 1 April 1789. The ratification process did not fully conclude until 1790 when North Carolina and Rhode Island ratified. It had revealed a groundswell in favour of a Bill of Rights and Madison was swift to take this up.

He had been elected to the new House of Representatives on a promise to introduce one and, in a famous speech on 8 June 1789, he produced 9 amendments.[17] He was able to point to the fears expressed in the state ratification conventions that a federal government would override state Bills of Rights:

> It will be a desirable thing to extinguish from the bosom of every member of the community any apprehension that there are those among his countrymen who wish to deprive them of the liberty for which they have valiantly fought and honourably bled.

He put forward the adoption of the amendments as a means of reconciling Federalist and Anti-Federalist views of the Constitution. Sherman objected to any amendment: he argued that as Congress could only exercise the powers given to it by the Constitution, it had no ability to invade human rights; further the Constitution should be tried out as it stood, before attempting to amend it. Others, such as Alexander Hamilton, also argued against a Bill of Rights.

To heal this rift the House appointed a Select Committee of one member from each state to determine whether there should be amendments—Sherman represented Connecticut and Madison Virginia.[18] As the debate proceeded in Committee it became inevitable that some amendment was going to be approved and Sherman devoted his energies to defining what it would be. The principal issue on which he did succeed was the form of amendment. Madison's amendments were sprinkled through the existing document, amending a number of existing clauses; Sherman insisted that they should be set out as separate amendments, so it was clear that that was what they were. 'We cannot incorporate these amendments in the body of the Constitution. It would be mixing brass, iron and clay.' But for this intervention no one would now be claiming the Fifth Amendment.

Article V of the United States Constitution allowed amendment of the Constitution by a two-thirds vote of both Houses; to take effect any amendments so proposed had to be ratified by three-quarters of the state legislatures. Madison's eventual 20 amendments were reduced to 12 (themselves amended) of which 10 were ratified. It is these first 10 amendments to the Constitution that are now known as the American Bill of Rights. They were binding on the federal government; it was only after the passage of the Fourteenth Amendment, guaranteeing due process, that the Supreme Court held most of them were binding on states.

---

[17] *Annals of Congress, House of Representatives*, 1st Congress, 1st Session 451 et seq: these records are available from the Library of Congress' American Memory website at memory.loc.gov.
[18] Farrand above n 13, 135 et seq.

The American Bill of Rights was obviously inspired by its English counter-part. The English version was part of the so-called Glorious Revolution of 1688. Protestant Charles II had been succeeded in 1685 by his openly Catholic brother, James II. He set about trying to improve the lot of Catholics, in particular by suspending or dispensing with laws which prevented them holding public office. James had raised an army to put down a rebellion by the Duke of Monmouth, but after the rebellion he kept the army in being and quartered troops with civilians. He also tried to disarm Protestant opponents. A group of aristocrats invited William of Orange (the Dutch Stadtholder) to invade England; when he did so James fled into exile. On 13 February 1688, both Houses of Parliament, stated to be acting on behalf of the people of England, set out various grievances created by James' conduct. They then rehearsed various rights they claimed for the subjects of the Crown in England and William invited the counties and cities of England to send representatives to declare these rights in Parliament. This assembled on 2 January 1689 and declared 13 basic rights. They then declared William and his wife Mary joint sovereign, on their undertaking that the rights and liberties of Englishmen would be preserved. These liberties did not cover all those to which the British felt themselves entitled. Some depended on Magna Carta, as interpreted in the courts; the details of due process depended on the common law.

It has been noted earlier in this chapter that the **First Amendment** to the United States Constitution goes beyond merely guaranteeing freedom of worship and preventing an established church, adding protection of freedom of speech and peaceful assembly. This probably owes much to the history of religious persecution in Britain, as demonstrated in the trial of William Penn in 1670, which involved all of these elements.[19] Most state constitutions already guaranteed freedom of worship and had passed legislation separating Church from State—by 1790 North Carolina, Maryland, Delaware, New Jersey, Virginia, Georgia and New Hampshire had all done so.[20] The issue was complicated, however, by the fact that under some state legislation provision was made for taxation to support a church or churches. This applied particularly in Massachusetts, where it was used to support congregational churches. Once the Church of England had been disestablished, its former practitioners were named Episcopalians because of their continued adoption of the hierarchy of bishops. What the First Amendment sought to ensure was that Congress (as distinct from the States) could not interfere with disestablishment or freedom of worship. It has been used more widely, for instance to limit the powers of local education authorities. Thus, in *McCollum v Board of Education* in 1948, school lessons on religion were offered in schools in the Champaign District of Illinois.[21] Clergy from some four religions conducted them. A woman, who was an atheist and whose son attended one such school, objected that this was in breach of the First Amendment. The Supreme Court agreed that the use of publicly funded

---

[19] Above Ch 5.
[20] See CH Esbeck, 'Dissent and Disestablishment: The Church-State Settlement in the Early American Republic' (2004) *Brigham Young University Law Review* 1385.
[21] 333 US 203.

property to conduct the classes did create a breach. Similarly in *Engel v Vitale* in 1962 a local board of education had composed a prayer, which it recommended for use in schools.[22] A Jewish parent objected and the action of the board was declared in breach of the First Amendment. 'The First Amendment rests upon the premise that both religion and government can best work to achieve their lofty aims, if each is free from the other within its respective sphere.'

The **Second Amendment** has its source in the English Bill of Rights, which provided that the 'raising or keeping a standing army within the Kingdom in time of Peace unless it be with Consent of Parliament is against Law.' The United States Constitution and Bill of Rights contains no provision forbidding a standing army in time of peace; the Federalists favoured and anti-Federalists opposed one. The compromise is found in section 8 of Article I of the Constitution, which empowers Congress to declare war and to raise and support armies, but no appropriation of money to that use is to be for a longer term than two years.

As important, the English Bill of Rights also provided that 'Subjects which are Protestants may have arms for their defence suitable to their Conditions and as allowed by law.' William Blackstone in his *Commentaries* stated that Catholics convicted of not attending service in the Church of England suffered certain penalties, including that they were not permitted to bear arms. The inhabitants of the colonies were used to defending themselves against native Americans, the French and the British. The Second Amendment specifically provided that 'a well regulated Militia being necessary to the security of a free State, the right of the people to keep and bear Arms shall not be infringed.'

This has proved one of the most controversial amendments. Consideration of its effect culminated in the opinion of the Supreme Court in *The District of Columbia v Heller* in 2008.[23] A police officer, authorised to carry a handgun while on duty in the Federal Judicial Centre, applied for a registration certificate for a handgun, which he wished to keep at home. The District of Columbia had passed a law requiring that registration of a firearm in the home be subject to licence and that, if licensed, it be kept with a trigger lock mechanism to restrict its use. The police officer contended that this provision breached his constitutional right to bear arms. The Supreme Court agreed holding that the right to bear arms was not limited to use in the militia or military defence. The written brief on behalf of the District of Columbia argued that the Second Amendment was limited by its wording and historical background to militia service and possession of firearms outwith was illegal. Justice Scalia delivered the majority judgment, rejecting this argument. It is not possible in a work of this generality to do justice (or injustice) to its detailed reasoning, but some broad points may be made. The Court pointed out that the amendment consisted of two halves, one prefatory, referring to the importance of a militia, and the other declaring a right; it did not follow that the prefatory clause limited the declared right; it merely explained the immediate background which had led to the declaration. Moreover the declaration provided that the right to bear arms should not be infringed; this implied that it was referring to an existing right and not creating a

[22] 370 US 421.
[23] 554 US 570.

new one. This was consistent with the position in British law from which it was derived, which implied that for Protestants there was such a right at common law (it is at least questionable whether there was a specific right to bear arms in English law before the English Bill of Rights). The judgment concluded:

> We are aware of the problem handgun violence in this country, and we take seriously the concerns raised by the many *amici*[24] who believe that prohibition of hand gun ownership is a solution ... the enshrinement of constitutional rights necessarily takes certain policy choices off the table. These include the absolute prohibition of handguns ... what is not debateable is that it is not the role of the Court to pronounce the Second Amendment extinct.

The **Third Amendment** reflected the unease felt in England under James II about quartering a standing army on civilians. The Amendment stated that 'no soldier shall in time of peace be quartered in any house, without the consent of the Owner, nor in time of war but in a manner to be prescribed by law.'

A number of the Amendments in the United States Bill of Rights may be grouped under the heading of 'due process' and traced back to Magna Carta, sealed by King John in June 1215, which provided that freemen could not be deprived of their lives, liberties or possessions without trial by their peers or according to the law of the land.[25] The clause was widened by statutes in the 1340s and 50s in the reign of Edward III, which extended the protection to all men of whatever condition and in 1354 added the words 'without due process'. It is a useful phrase to catch all procedural rights in litigation.

One of the initial sparks which lit the tinder of revolution in America was the use of general warrants, which did not specify a suspect or an offence, by the Admiralty Court in Boston. It has already been noted that James Otis junior failed in his opposition to such warrants and that subsequently in England, in *Wilkes v Wood*[26] (1763) and *Entick v Carrington*[27] (1765) the English courts of Common Pleas and King's Bench condemned the use of general search warrants as illegal. The **Fourth Amendment** provides that:

> The right of the people to be secure in their persons, houses, papers and effects against unreasonable searches and seizures, shall not be violated and no Warrants shall issue, but upon probable cause supported by Oath of affirmation, and particularly describing the place to be searched and the persons or things to be searched.

The first time the phrase 'due process' appeared in America was in the New York Bill of Rights in 1787. It did not appear in Madison's draft for federal rights, but was added at the suggestion of the New York representatives, in the **Fifth Amendment** reading:

> No person shall be held to answer for a capital or otherwise infamous crime, unless on presentment or indictment of a Grand Jury ... nor shall any person be subject for the

---

[24] The Supreme Court allows parties who are not a party to litigation under consideration to submit briefs as friends of the court.
[25] Generally see A Arlidge and I Judge, *Magna Carta Uncovered* (Oxford, Hart Publishing, 2014).
[26] 98 ER 489.
[27] 19 Howells's State Trials 1029; 95 ER 807.

same offence to be twice put in jeopardy of life and limb; nor shall be compelled in any criminal case to be a witness against himself, nor be deprived of life liberty or property without due process of law; nor shall private property be taken for public use, without just compensation.

Like other provisions in the American Bill this amalgamates several different rights.

Trial by peers in Magna Carta did not mean jury trial—it meant trial by one's social equals, in the case of barons by barons in the King's Council. Jury trial developed, as the result of a separate contemporaneous event, when Pope Innocent II forbade priests taking part in trial by ordeal.[28] With the passage of time, however, Magna Carta came to be seen as the origin of jury trial. In the United States Constitution section 2 of Article III provided for jury trial in all criminal cases in the state where the crime was alleged to have been committed. The **Sixth Amendment** reinforced this by providing that 'in all criminal prosecutions the accused shall enjoy the right to a speedy and public trial by an impartial jury.' The **Seventh Amendment** extended such protection to civil cases providing that

in suits at common law where the value in controversy shall exceed twenty dollars, the right of trial by jury shall be preserved and no fact tried by a jury shall be otherwise re-examined in any Court of the United States, than according to common law.

The **Fifth Amendment** also contained provisions which reflected English procedural law. The rule against 'double jeopardy' went back to the twelfth century in England—an accused, who had been tried for an offence to verdict and was indicted again for the same offence, could plead in law French 'autrefois acquit or convict'—formerly acquitted or convicted. If the plea was successful the second trial could not proceed. So the Fifth Amendment provided that no person 'shall be subject for the same offence to be twice put in jeopardy of life or limb.' Likewise, under the Tudors and the Stuarts, the Star Chamber (trying certain criminal offences) and the Ecclesiastical Commission (trying religious offences) effectively compelled accused to answer questions, by imposing harsh sentences, such as loss of an ear or whipping, on those who refused. Many of those who emigrated to America had suffered under Archbishop Laud's pursuit of dissenters through these prerogative courts. During the English Commonwealth the right to silence was established and this was reflected in the requirement of the Fifth Amendment that no person 'shall be compelled in any criminal cause to be a witness against himself.' In England in the late seventeenth century, an accused was given other procedural protections which are reflected in the Sixth Amendment, under which he is entitled to be informed of the nature and cause of the accusation against him and to be confronted by witnesses against him. He was also entitled to have compulsory process for obtaining witnesses in his favour and to have Counsel for his defence. Article X of the English Bill of Rights provided that 'excessive bail shall not be required nor excessive fines imposed, nor cruel and unusual punishments inflicted.' This was repeated virtually verbatim in the **Eighth Amendment**.

---

[28] Arlidge and Judge above n 25.

The fact that the United States' Bill of Rights provided for specific rights did not mean that English common law was redundant. Where American legislation is silent, reference may be made to English common law. For example, the Seventh Amendment is silent as to the number of jurors required in a civil cause. In *Colgrove v Battin*[29] in 1973 the Supreme Court held that a six man jury in a civil case, being consonant with earlier English practice, was lawful.

One disadvantage of defining specific rights is that it may imply that other potential rights are invalid. This was catered for by the **Ninth Amendment,** which provided 'the enumeration in the Constitution of rights shall not be construed to deny or disparage others retained by the people.'

Enshrining human rights in a written constitution may have the psychological effect of causing resistance to amending them, whether advantageous or disadvantageous. In the British Parliament amendments are made by simple majority. This has caused a wide divergence in practice between American and English law. Thus the rule against double jeopardy (subject to some safeguards) has been abolished in England. The right to jury trial in civil cases has been effectively removed (though the court may order one in some defamation cases). The right to silence has been abridged so that adverse inferences may be drawn from an accused's failure to answer questions when interviewed on arrest and at trial.

The first Ten Amendments to the Constitution were ratified in December 1791. Roger Sherman, who had played a part in Connecticut's ratification, died in 1793. James Madison went on to be the fourth President of the United States.

[29] 413 US 149.

14

Nationhood: Alexander Hamilton

O F ALL HIS contemporaries, **Alexander Hamilton** had the most spectacu-
lar rise from obscurity and the most abrupt fall.[1] At the age of 15 he was
a penniless illegitimate orphan on the Danish island of St Croix in the
Caribbean; within 20 years he had risen to be the first man to head the Treasury
Department of the United States; about 15 years on he died in an unnecessary
duel with a political opponent. He was always an outsider in revolutionary politics; unlike his fellow Revolutionaries, he had no strong loyalty to a particular
state and no overtly expressed religious allegiance. On 8 January 1780, he wrote
to his friend, John Laurens, that he was 'a stranger in this country. I have no
property, no connection. If I have talents and integrity… they are justly deemed
very spurious titles in these enlightened days.'[2] Perhaps it was this very independence that gave him a clear-sighted view of what the United States required.

He was essentially a pragmatic man. Experience taught him the necessity, if
the United States were to be prosperous and recognised internationally, of a
strong central government supported by a National Bank, and this set him at
odds with the anti-federalist lobby. He also saw that Britain, a still hated enemy,
was culturally and economically a more natural partner for the United States
than revolutionary France. To his contemporaries he was divisive—throughout
his life he had an almost paranoid desire to argue unpopular causes. He was a
particular opponent of slavery. On 14 March 1779, he wrote to John Jay (of
New York, later first Chief Justice of the United States):

> The contempt we have been taught to entertain for blacks makes us fancy many things
> that are founded neither in reason or experience and our unwillingness to part with
> property of so valuable a kind will furnish a thousand reasons and arguments to show
> the impracticability or pernicious tendency of a scheme which requires such a sacrifice.[3]

---

[1] There are a large number of biographies of Hamilton. JE Cooke, *Alexander Hamilton*
(New York, Charles Scribner's Sons, 1983) is concise and includes most of the important information and an academic commentary of his life; F McDonald, *Alexander Hamilton* (New York, WW
Norton & Co, 1979) gives a longer, but also perceptive account; R Chernow, *Alexander Hamilton*
(New York, Penguin Books Ltd, 2004) is a lengthy and exhaustive account of all aspects of his life.
[2] H Syrett (ed), *Papers of Alexander Hamilton* (New York, Columbia University Press, 1962)
255; an online version is found on the Founding Fathers website (founders.archives.gov).
[3] Syrett above n 2, Vol 2, 1779–81, 17 et seq; From Alexander Hamilton to John Jay, [14 March
1779], *Founders Online*, National Archives.

His mother, of mixed English and French descent, met the younger son of a Scottish laird, James Hamilton, on the Caribbean island of St Kitts.[4] Their child, Alexander, was actually born in Charlestown in the nearby colony of Nevis. His mother had fled an abusive husband in St Croix, to whom she was still married, so that Alexander was illegitimate. His birth is not recorded and is of uncertain date, he claimed it was in 1757, but some documentary evidence suggests it was 1755.[5] The ages given in this account are based on 1755. In 1765 Hamilton and his parents moved to St Croix, in what is now the British Virgin Islands. James's attempts to make his fortune failed and not long after he deserted his family. Alexander's mother opened a store to supply goods imported from New York to planters on St Croix, but in 1768 she died of a fever. Her brother-in-law became Alexander's guardian, but two years later he committed suicide.

At this point luck, which had not so far blessed him, took a turn in Alexander's favour. His mother had been supplied with goods by a Dutch firm in New York, called Beekman and Cruger (later Kortright and Cruger). They had recently established a branch in St Croix run by a son of the family, Nicholas Cruger. In 1769 Alexander obtained a job as a clerk to Nicholas.[6] He did not enjoy the work at first—in November 1769 he wrote, 'I contemn the grov'ling and condition of a clerk or the like, to which my fortune condemns me and would willingly risk my life, though not my character, to exalt my station ... I wish there was a war.'[7] As yet there was not and Alexander had to be content with voracious reading. In 1771 Nicholas Cruger fell ill and returned to New York, leaving Alexander in charge of the business, which he conducted very efficiently. On 31 August 1772, a hurricane struck St Croix causing enormous destruction and Alexander wrote an account of it, which was published in the *Royal Danish American Gazette*. Such was the astonishment at this precocity, that a group of local merchants established a fund, under the management of Kortright and Cruger, to educate him in America. A minister he had met in St Croix recommended him to a Presbyterian academy in Elizabeth, New Jersey, where he studied for six months. He then applied to join the College of New Jersey, asking its principal, Dr Witherspoon, if he could be allowed to advance with as much rapidity as his exertions would allow him to do.[8] His request was refused, so he went to New York and enrolled in the Anglican and Royalist stronghold of King's College (later University of Columbia). Here he began to study law, reading Coke and Blackstone. Near King's was an area called the Fields, which had become a meeting place for patriots, and on 6 July 1774 he joined and addressed such a meeting in support of the patriot cause.[9] When fighting broke out at Lexington and Concord in 1776 he joined a New York militia.[10] He nevertheless admired

[4] Chernow above n 1, 8 et seq.
[5] ibid.
[6] ibid, 30 et seq.
[7] Syrett above n 2, Vol 1, 1768–78, 4 et seq; From Alexander Hamilton to Edward Stevens, 11 November 1769, *Founders Online*, National Archives.
[8] Chernow above n 1, 51.
[9] ibid, 55.
[10] ibid, 62.

the loyalist principal of King's College, Myles Cooper, and when a patriot mob raided the college, he held them at bay by a rousing address, allowing Cooper to escape from the rear of the building. Seeing war approaching, he studied the science of artillery. Congress authorised the establishment of an artillery company to defend New York and on 14 March 1776 Hamilton joined it as a Captain of Artillery. When the British army left Boston and attacked New York, the artillery company played a part in the unsuccessful defence of Brooklyn Heights and the defeat at White Plains, after which the British took New York and remained in occupation for seven years.[11] In early 1777, however, his company crossed the Delaware River with Washington and took part in the surprise attack on a section of the British army at Trenton, taking a large number of prisoners. Washington was sufficiently impressed to invite Hamilton to become one of his half dozen aides de camp, a post he took up on 11 March 1777.[12] Though he proved of great value to Washington, Hamilton chafed at the duties of an aide de camp, finding he was turned down for command posts because Washington found him indispensable and for diplomatic missions because Congress did not know him well enough. Eventually Washington did agree to give him command of three battalions and he saw action in the successful assault on Yorktown.[13]

Hamilton's experience in the army led him to the view that the government of the United States was a shambles. Supplies to the army were erratic and insufficient, largely because they were dependent upon contributions from individual States and insufficiently coordinated. On 3 September 1780 he wrote to an older colleague in New York, Irish American lawyer John Duane, setting out his views on government and stating that the Articles of Confederation were not fit for war or peace and a new Constitution was required. The fundamental defect at present was want of power in Congress:

> [There is] an excess of the spirit of liberty which has made the particular states show a jealousy of all power not in their own hands; and their jealousy has led them to exercise a right of judging in the last resort of the measures recommended by Congress, and of acting according to their own opinions of their propriety or necessity.[14]

Congress should have considered themselves vested with full power to preserve the republic from harm. 'Providing of supplies is the pivot of everything ... There are four ways all which must be united—a foreign loan, heavy pecuniary taxes, a tax in kind, and a bank founded on public and private credit.'[15]

Next on his agenda was marriage. In the autumn of 1779, Philip Schuyler, a former Major General in the Continental Army connected by marriage to the founders of the Dutch colony of New York, visited Philadelphia. His daughters, who accompanied him, went to see relatives in nearby Morristown, where they met Alexander. He flirted with the older daughter, but courted the younger,

---

[11] ibid, 72.
[12] ibid, 84.
[13] Cooke above n 1, 29.
[14] Syrett above n 2, Vol 2 1779–81, 400 et seq; From Alexander Hamilton to James Duane, [3 September 1780], *Founders Online*, National Archives.
[15] ibid.

Elizabeth. Despite Hamilton's lack of money and status Philip agreed to the marriage and became one of Hamilton's greatest supporters. The marriage took place on 14 December 1780. They had eight children. If Elizabeth was not an Abigail Adams, she was a steadfast supporter of her husband. Shortly before his death he described her as best of women, best of wives. From 1791 to 92 he had an affair with a young married woman, called Reynolds. Her husband discovered them and first blackmailed Hamilton for money and then, to escape his own criminal activities, revealed the affair to members of the government. The leader of the Senate, James Monroe, investigated; Hamilton admitted the truth of the allegation and handed over love letters in his possession. Monroe ensured that the letters were not made public, but he did show them to Jefferson, who some years later spread rumours about Hamilton's morality.

With the end of the war, Hamilton returned to New York. For admission to the New York bar, it was ordinarily necessary to serve a three year apprenticeship with a practising counsel. In January 1782, Congress suspended this requirement for those who had studied law, but given up their studies to enter the Revolutionary army. On the basis of his short period of legal studies at King's College, Hamilton applied for and was granted dispensation, allowing him three months to complete his studies. He applied for and was granted a further three months' extension. James Duane gave him the run of his considerable library. Though Hamilton read philosophical works on the nature of law, he soon discovered that British common law, adopted by American courts, depended on procedure, particularly the actions that could be brought on particular writs. To help his studies he wrote out a manual summarising procedure under headings such as Process, Joint Actions, Judgment, Execution, Pleas, Venue. It ran to 40,000 words and later in 1790 was published and became a standard manual for New York lawyers.[16] The New York profession being divided between attorneys and counsel on the English pattern, Alexander qualified as an attorney on 1 July 1782 and was admitted to the bar of the New York Supreme Court in Albany on 26 October of the same year.

Once admitted, he swiftly built up a substantial practice, being briefed in particular by a British business man called Church, who had helped finance the Revolutionary army.[17] During and after the Revolutionary War there was strong feeling in the United States against those within its borders who had remained loyal to Britain. The New York legislature passed a series of discriminatory acts against loyalists culminating in the Trespass Act of September 1793, which enabled patriots, who had fled leaving property behind British lines, to sue anyone who had occupied, damaged or destroyed it. In January 1784 Hamilton published a letter attacking the discriminatory legislation and arguing for generous treatment of loyalists.[18] Shortly after he was briefed to defend in an action for

[16] See McDonald above n 1, 52.
[17] ibid, 62.
[18] Syrett above n 2, Vol 3, 1782–86 483 et seq; 'A Letter from Phocion to the Considerate Citizens of New York' [1–27 January 1784] *Founders Online*, National Archives.

trespass brought in the New York City Court.[19] Mr Rutgers owned a brewery in New York City, but when the British invaded he fled. The British Commissary-General in New York took over the brewery for the use of the army and then let it to two British businessmen. They paid rent to him for two years and then on the orders of the British Commander-in-Chief to the local vestry for support of the poor. With the departure of the British, Rutgers sought £8000 damages as compensation for the period when the brewery was under occupation. He then died and his widow pursued his claim against the agent for the British businessmen, a New York merchant called James Waddington. The New York Trespass Act forbade a plea that military orders justified acts done during the British occupation. Hamilton nevertheless pleaded in defence the authorisation of the British army. Further, at the time the Trespass Act was passed the Confederation government had entered into a treaty of peace with the British government, providing that claims for damage or injury done by either party in consequence of the war between them were mutually relinquished. The Treaty had been ratified by the Confederation government.

Hamilton wrote a number of briefs for his own use (they were not served on the court) which are preserved and demonstrate his argument.[20] He argued that both the Articles of Confederation and the New York Constitution of 1777 adopted, as the basis of United States law, English law as it stood at 19 April 1775. Moreover, the *ius gentium* (law of the peoples) or natural law was part of English law and this included the laws of war, which allowed those who conquered territory to occupy and use the property of those they had defeated. The Trespass Act was passed contrary to the laws of war and so was void and also in breach of the Treaty of Paris. These propositions were supported by great erudition, citing amongst others the Dutch writer, Hugo Grotius, who had relied on natural law to define the laws of war in the early seventeenth century. Hamilton also relied on a number of philosophical works, particularly Emerich Vattel's *Law of Nations or the Principles of Natural Law,* which he had almost certainly come across in Duane's library. The case was heard in the New York City Court, before the Mayor and Recorder of the City and five aldermen. As luck would have it, the Mayor was John Duane.[21] Duane started his reasoned judgment by expressing 'the pleasure which we have received in seeing young gentlemen, just called to the bar, from active and honorable scenes of military life, achieving distinction as public speakers.' The court accepted that the laws of war were part of the English common law, which had translated to the United States. Whilst the New York legislature had an uncontrollable power to pass legislation, the law of nature or war could only be excluded by clear words and the Trespass Act did not contain such words. Hamilton's argument in relation to the peace treaty failed because Duane held it was aimed against public not private acts. On the facts, Mrs Rutgers was entitled to damages in respect of the period

---

[19] For an account of the case see J Goebel (ed), *The Law Practice of Alexander Hamilton: Documents and Commentary* (New York, Columbia University Press, 1964) Vol I 236.

[20] ibid, 340.

[21] For the judgment see Goebel above n 19, 402.

when permission was granted by the Commissary-General, because he did not have sufficient authority to take over enemy property; she was not entitled to any in respect of the period when rent was paid to the vestry on the orders of the Commander-in-Chief, because he did have authority. Though Hamilton would have seen his argument as one of principle, it did increase his practice, for he was retained in 44 similar cases.[22]

At the beginning of his judgment, Mayor Duane expressed some reticence about deciding important matters of principle at a relatively low judicial level. He was fortified by the thought that the case would be appealed to a higher court. This in fact did not happen; although Mrs Rutgers did institute an appeal, she settled her claim for £800 pounds and did not pursue the appeal. The notion that judges could overrule national and state statutes that were contrary to the Constitution became known as the doctrine of judicial review (a much wider concept than its meaning in English law). Hamilton was to define this doctrine in 1788, when he wrote that it is the duty of the courts 'to declare all acts contrary to the manifest tenor of the Constitution void.'[23] There was no question of the legislature being the judge of their own powers—the courts were designed to be an intermediate body between the people and the legislature, in order to keep the latter within the limits assigned to them. 'The constitution is the fundamental law and it falls to the judges to interpret it.' The decision in Rutgers case was not of great authority given that a local court decided it, but Hamilton's view of judicial review was eventually adopted by the Supreme Court.[24]

In 1787 Hamilton was chosen as a New York delegate to the Congress considering revision of the Constitution. Governor Clinton of New York was strongly opposed to increasing the power of the central government. New York was not simply the City, but the State of New York, where the population was largely comprised of small farmers; they saw big government as favouring commercial rather than farming interests and formed Governor Clinton's solid electoral base and now ensured that the other two delegates accorded with his views. Hamilton did not speak until the Convention had been sitting for a month and when he did so indicated that he had held back because of his relative youth (he was 32) and because he was conscious that the majority of the New York delegates disagreed with his views. Nevertheless he went on to address the Convention in terms most likely to alienate them.[25] His advocacy of a strong central government, including a strong executive, was buttressed by an admiration for the British Constitution, which was the best in the world—'the only one which unites public strength and individual security.' The King in England, inheriting

---

[22] Chernow above n 1, 199; they are set out in Goebel above n 19.

[23] Federalist Papers no 78 28 May 1788; Syrett above n 2, Vol IV, January 1787–May 1788, 655 et seq; The Federalist No 78 [28 May 1778], *Founders Online*, National Archives.

[24] Below Ch 15.

[25] Amongst the accounts of his speech are his original notes, Syrett above n 2, Vol IV January 1787–May 1788, 178–87; Alexander Hamilton's Notes [18 June 1787], *Founders Online*, National Archives; and also Madison's account in his journal, Syrett above n 2, Vol IV January 1787–May 1788, 187–95; James Madison's Version [18 June 1787] *Founders Online*, National Archives.

for life, was above corruption and so he recommended that, though there should be an elected lower house, both the President and Senators should be appointed for life. He made many detailed proposals, but whatever their sense, they were inevitably drowned out by what his audience took as monarchical views. This may explain why, shortly after, Hamilton left the Convention and, though he did return for short periods, played little part in its further deliberations and did not sign the Constitution.

Congress approved a draft of the new Constitution on 17 September 1787. On the 27th of that month the *New York Journal* published an article under the pseudonym Cato (actual author probably Clinton) strongly attacking its terms (Cato was a friend of Cicero and opponent of Julius Caesar and his supposed imperial ambitions). Similar articles appeared in the ensuing weeks. Over this period Hamilton was attending the Fall Session of the Supreme Court of New York in Albany.[26] Exactly a month after the Cato letter, a reply appeared in the *New York Independent Journal* under the pseudonym of Publius (Publius Valerius was a founder of the Roman Republic and had the nickname of Publicola, friend of the people). The author was Hamilton; if his conduct at the Congress indicated reservations about the effectiveness of the new draft, the Cato letters stung him into defending it. He stated that having given attentive consideration to it, 'I am clearly of opinion, it is your best interest to adopt it.' He tried to set the debate on an elevated level—the important question was 'whether societies of men are capable or not of establishing good government.' He opposed 'the interest of a certain class of man in every state to resist all changes which may hazard a diminution of the power, emolument and consequence of office held under the State establishment.'[27] This was the first of a series of letters that became known as the *Federalist Papers*. He found others to take part in the project—the first was John Jay, a prominent lawyer and leader of the Revolution in New York, soon to become first Chief Justice of the United States, who wrote numbers two to five, but then fell ill and effectively retired from the project. Then he persuaded James Madison, who was in New York following the end of the Congress, to contribute. All three wrote under the same pseudonym of Publius—in all between October and May 1798 some 77 letters appeared in a variety of New York journals, this increased to 85 when they were collected for later publication in 1808. Hamilton wrote over two-thirds of them and Madison about a third. The letters became a justly famous gloss on the Constitution. A particularly celebrated set, numbers eight to 11 appeared between 20 and 24 November. In number nine, which appeared on 21 November,[28] Hamilton wrote that a firm union would be of the utmost moment to the peace and liberty of the states as a barrier against domestic faction. Madison took up and

[26] See Introductory Note: The Federalist [27 October 1787–28 May 1788] Syrett above n 2, Vol IV January 1787–May 1788, 287–301,

[27] Syrett above n 2, Vol IV January 1787–May 1788, 301–06; Chernow above n 1 deals with the *Federalist Papers* in Ch 13.

[28] Syrett above n 2, Vol IV January 1787–May 1788, 333–39; The Federalist No 9 [21 November 1787], *Founders Online*, National Archives.

reinforced this theme in number 10, claiming that Montesquieu supported 'a kind of constitution that has all the internal advantages of a republican, together with the external force of a monarchical government ... a Confederate Republic.' Whereas the Cato letters inveighed against the possibility of a standing army, this series of letters saw such an army and a federal navy as protecting the union against external military threat and giving the United States authority in international politics and commerce. 'A vigorous national government ... would baffle all the combinations of European jealousy to restrain our growth.'[29] A national army should be of sufficient size to repel invasion, not so large as to lead to tyranny.[30]

The arguments in the Federalist Papers did not sway those who assembled on 17 June 1788 in Poughkeepsie, a newly established town halfway between New York City and the state capital at Albany, to debate ratification of the Constitution by the State of New York; initially there were 46 delegates who opposed ratification and 19 who favoured it, Hamilton being prominent among the minority. Attempts to reach a compromise centred on whether ratification could be subject to conditions. The delay in assembling, however, told against the majority. By the time the New York delegates met, there were already eight States which had ratified the Constitution and it came into effect on 21 June, when New Hampshire became the ninth. On 23 July, the Poughkeepsie Convention ratified without conditions, but in the stated confidence that the amendments which they proposed would receive an early consideration—amongst them a draft Bill of Rights. Hamilton argued in number 84 of the Federalist Papers against such a Bill—previous Bills in England were circumventing the monarchs who had destroyed specific rights; the American people had not been so deprived and retained all natural liberties intact.[31] Hamilton was to lose this battle.

When he wrote to John Duane in 1780 outlining his views on the form a new government should take, Hamilton suggested that Gouverneur Morris of New York,[32] who had experience in organising government finance, would make an ideal Secretary of State for the Treasury. George Washington was sworn as President on 30 April 1789 and established a Department of State (to deal with foreign affairs) and a War Department, and on 2 September 1789 the Treasury Department. This (though relatively small by European standards), was by far the largest of the three. The State Department had four clerks and the War Department three, whereas the Treasury had 30 clerks and a large network of tax collectors of various kinds.[33] Hamilton probably thought his national political days were for the moment over, but on 11 September Washington appointed him to the post of Secretary of State for the Treasury. On 21 September the

[29] The Federalist No 11 [24 November 1787]; Syrett above n 2, Vol IV January 1787–May 1788, 339–46.
[30] The Federalist No 8 [20 November 1787]; ibid, 326–33.
[31] The Federalist No 84 [28 May 1788]; ibid, 702–14.
[32] Gouverneur was a first name meaning 'baby boy' and does not indicate any office-holding.
[33] On this see Cooke above n 1, Ch Seven.

House of Representatives required him to prepare a report to make adequate provision for public finances. Apart from his own experience in commerce, he had already studied Chapter 10 of Book One of Vattel's *Law of Nations*, which dealt with managing money, exchange and commerce. He was also familiar with Adam Smith's *Wealth of Nations*.[34] The three reports he eventually produced for Congress were masterly.

By the time of his appointment, the lack of central government authority under the Articles of Confederation had led to financial drift.[35] Huge indebtedness had been incurred to pay for the Revolutionary War and the government had reneged on its obligations, both domestically and externally. There was a substantial government foreign debt of over 11 million dollars and, apart from government debt to individuals, some 25 million dollars of state debts. The value of land and the dollar had fallen steeply—the government had paid for supplies by printing more money. Hamilton's *First Report Relative to a Provision for the Support of Public Credit* was delivered on 14 January 1790.[36] At the outset it stated that 'every breach of public engagements, whether from choice or necessity, is in different degrees hurtful to public credit.' Amongst other measures, he proposed that the state debts should be assumed by the federal government. This caused dissension, in the first place because some states had small if any debt and others large debts—those with small debts felt they were discriminated against. Further many of those who had fought in the war had been given certificates of monies owed to them by the government, which they had sold on well below par. Hamilton now suggested that the present holders be compensated at face value, which many perceived as unfair to the former holders. Hamilton also proposed the creation of a sinking fund to deal with emergencies. Madison led the considerable opposition to his proposals. There was, however, at the same time a dispute about the siting of the national capital; the southern interest, which included Madison, was anxious that it should be placed on the Potomac River. Jefferson, who had recently returned from Paris, saw from his European experience the importance of public credit and arranged a dinner with himself, Madison and Hamilton, at which it was said a deal was struck—assumption of state debts in return for a capital on the Potomac. Whatever occurred (it may be that whatever did had little influence) in July 1790 Assumption and Residence Bills passed Congress ensuring just that result.

On 13 December 1790 Hamilton presented Congress with further proposals for establishing public credit, including that government debt be funded by taxes on distilled liquor and on the same date a further paper reporting on the necessity of a National Bank.[37] At this time there were three banks in

---

[34] Generally see *Introductory Note: Second Report on the Further Provision Necessary for Establishing Public Credit (Report on a National Bank)* 13 December 1790, Syrett above n 2, Vol VII September 1970–January 1791, 236–56.

[35] See Cooke above n 1.

[36] Syrett above n 2, Vol VI December 1789–August 1790, 65–110.

[37] *Final Version of the Second Report on the Further Provision Necessary for Establishing Public Credit (Report on a National Bank)* 13 December 1790, Syrett above n 2, Vol VII 305–42; generally on this see McDonald above n 1, 190 et seq and Cooke above n 1, Ch VIII.

America—that of New York, in whose establishment he had played a part, that of North America situated in Philadelphia and that of Massachusetts. Hamilton's studies on banking had led him to admire the role of the Bank of England in financing government and he pointed out in great detail the advantages of such a National Bank in the United States. He analysed how it would be underpinned by stock issues to investors, enabling it to lend beyond its reserves of coin or bullion. There should be a board of directors including the President. The bank was to have capitalization of 10 million dollars. Government would subscribe for two million dollars' worth of stock and eight million would be open to public subscription. The agrarian lobby saw this proposal as a means of furthering the interests of the merchant community and portrayed the proposed bill as an attempt by federal government to detract from the powers of states, which could charter their own banks. Nevertheless, in the course of 1790 there had been a financial boom, from which Hamilton drew personal credit. By mid February 1791, a Bill to create a National Bank had passed both Houses.

In the course of debate in Congress, however, the legality of the bill had been challenged and, before he was willing to sign it into law, Washington sought advice from Attorney General, Edmund Randolph, and Jefferson as to whether such a Bill was constitutional. They both advised that the Constitution contained no specific power to charter a bank and so it was unconstitutional. Washington sent both opinions to Hamilton, who presented a counter argument—if an object was defined in the Constitution, then any means to achieve it was implied; the Constitution provided that Congress had the power to make all laws necessary and proper to its specified powers.

> If the end be clearly comprehended within any of the specified powers, and if the measure have an obvious relation to that end, and is not forbidden by any particular provision of the constitution, it may safely be deemed to come within the compass of national authority.[38]

Washington was convinced by this argument—the executive power to regulate trade, collect taxes and provide for the defence of the nation justified the passage of the bill—and he signed it on 25 February 1791. Hamilton's purposive canon of constitutional interpretation was adopted by the Supreme Court in *McCullouch v Maryland*.[39]

Hamilton also saw the need for the United States to have a more broadly based economy. Before the Revolution, America had supplied Britain with raw materials and in return had received goods manufactured there. In January 1790, Congress asked Hamilton to supply a paper on how to encourage manufacture in the United States.[40] This was an area in which he had little experience and it took him until December 1791 to deliver his report.[41] He extolled

---

[38] Syrett above n 2, *Final Version of an Opinion on the Constitutionality of an Act to Establish a Bank* 23 February 1791, Vol VIII 97–134 at 107.

[39] 17 US 316 (1819); see below, ch 15.

[40] Cooke above n 1, 98 et seq.

[41] *Alexander Hamilton's Final Version of the Report on the Subject of Manufactures* 5 December 1791, Syrett above n 2, Vol X December 1791–January 1792 230 et seq.

the benefits which accrue from a mixed rather than a predominantly agrarian economy. His view was that an infant manufacturing economy required protection. He advocated moderate protective duties on imported manufactured goods and withdrawal of duties on raw materials necessary for home manufactures. He also proposed government spending on improved internal communication. He saw increase in manufacturing as leading to a partnership between farm and factory and between north and south, but his proposals were not received with enthusiasm by the agrarian lobby, who saw them as yet another invasion by central government and his proposals did not pass Congress. Nevertheless he set up a Society for Establishing Useful Manufactures, which issued a million dollars' worth of stock. In November of 1791, New Jersey granted it a Charter. Unfortunately, a financial panic in the spring of 1792 caused many who invested in it to lose their money. Hamilton pursued his aims on a piecemeal basis, but it was not until the latter nineteenth century that advocates of protectionism revived interest in his views.

As a result of all these arguments, hostility between Hamilton and Jefferson increased out of all proportion. Jefferson accused Hamilton of subverting American democracy—his financial plans would create a rich mercantile class, a new form of aristocracy with the President a virtual monarch. By the summer of 1792 both men were engaged, under pseudonyms, in warfare in the press. Jefferson went so far as to write to Washington that Hamilton was guilty of misdemeanours in public office. Washington tried to cool the antagonisms between his two principal ministers, but to no effect. On 23 January 1793 Jefferson engineered a resolution placed before Congress, accusing Hamilton of mishandling the public debt. Hamilton presented a detailed defence and Congress decisively rejected the resolution. Both men strayed beyond the remit of their office, interfering with the policies of the other, in particular, whilst Jefferson favoured the French Revolutionary government as an ally of the United States, Hamilton thought that Britain would still be the United States' principal trading partner and should be her ally. From 1792 onwards the French Revolutionary government became involved in war with various other European powers, which gained the support of Britain. Washington's declaration of neutrality caused Jefferson to resign on 31 December 1793. Hamilton felt that to place the Union on a safe economic base, it was necessary for there to be a period of peace with Britain and it was at his suggestion that John Jay, his old ally from the days of the *Federalist Papers,* was sent to London to iron out problems that had arisen under the treaty of 1783. The resulting treaty, known popularly or unpopularly as the Jay Treaty was ratified in 1795. The anti-federalists felt it was far too generous to Britain.

Like Jefferson before him, Hamilton tired of office and on 31 January 1795 he told Washington he intended to resign. When Adams became President in 1796, he continued Washington's policy of neutrality, but also considered it was prudent to re-establish an army in case of attack by either Britain or France. He planned to raise an army of 12,500 men and to that end reappointed Washington as Commander-in-Chief. This led in turn to Hamilton being appointed Inspector General of the Army, with the rank of Major General. Adams, however, delayed taking the new force to its full complement and, when eventually in 1800 France ceased to be hostile, it was disbanded. In the election of 1800 Jefferson and Aaron Burr each obtained the same number of votes in the Electoral College, both more than Adams. This meant that Congress had to decide which of Burr and Jefferson should be President; Hamilton was instrumental in achieving the choice of Jefferson, since he hated Burr even more.

Aaron Burr was a long standing political enemy of Hamilton in New York. Apart from supporting Jefferson against him for the Presidency, Hamilton had also helped to obtain his defeat in the election for the governorship of New York. Not long after, the *Albany Register* published an allegation that Hamilton had made derogatory remarks about Burr at a dinner and Burr demanded they be retracted. When Hamilton refused on the basis he did not recollect saying them, Burr challenged him to a duel, which Hamilton rashly accepted; it took place on 1 March 1804 and Hamilton, not yet 50, was killed.

No doubt he had a difficult personality; he was not politic in the good sense of the word. His antagonisms and lack of a personal political base undermined his potential achievements. Nevertheless, before he became Treasury Secretary, the United States remained in effect a confederation of nations; his contribution, both constitutionally and economically, led more than any other single influence to it becoming one nation.

15

Consolidation: John Marshall

JOHN MARSHALL WAS appointed Chief Justice of the Supreme Court of the United States in 1801 and served in that office for 35 years. He played an enormous role in defining the jurisdiction of the Court and the scope of the Constitution. He was born, the eldest of 15 children, in September 1755, in the relatively underdeveloped area in north east of Virginia known as the Northern Neck. Thomas Jefferson had been born in the same area about 12 years earlier and the fathers of both men were employed as surveyors by Lord Fairfax to map his vast undeveloped territory.[1] Both fathers in the male line had Welsh origins and on the female side the two boys were second cousins through connections to the prosperous plantation owners, the Randolphs. Both fathers were self-educated, but keen that their sons should better themselves. When Blackstone's *Commentaries* was published in America in 1772, Thomas Marshall was one of the first subscribers.[2] Whilst the Jeffersons moved from the Neck to the tidewater lands, Thomas built a log house in Germantown on the frontier of western development at that time; he subsequently moved out to the Piedmont at the edge of the Blue Ridge Mountains and later still on to the Shenandoah Valley in the Appalachians.[3] He became substantial enough, but nothing like as rich as the Jeffersons. As a boy John Marshall studied at home, reading from the library his father had built up, but even more crucially was given access to Lord Fairfax's library at Greenaway Court.[4] He read classical authors, such as Livy and Horace, and English authors, such as Shakespeare, Milton and Pope. One thing Jefferson and Marshall did share was a common interest in deism.[5]

In July 1775 the Virginian Assembly authorised the formation of two regular battalions of regular troops and 16 battalions of minutemen—reservists ostensibly ready to fight at one minute's notice. Marshall, just 20, joined the 350 strong Culpeper Minutemen and soon assumed command as a Second Lieutenant.[6] They looked a wild bunch—their yellow flag bore the image of a coiled serpent, with the message 'Don't Tread on Me'; they wore buckskin trousers and bucks' tails on their hats and carried tomahawks and scalping knives in their belts. No one could doubt their frontier experience. They saw armed service

---

[1] For a very detailed biography of Marshall see JE Smith, *John Marshall: Definer of a Nation* (New York, Henry Holt and Co, 1996); for early history of the Jeffersons, see above ch 11.
[2] Smith ibid, 75.
[3] For background on the north east of Virginia see Smith above n 1, 41.
[4] For Lord Fairfax see above ch 11.
[5] Smith above n 1, 36, 406.
[6] Smith above n 1, 45.

when the British were repelled at Norfolk, Virginia. Shortly after, the Marquis de Lafayette, who had come from France to support the Revolution, obtained permission from Washington to form an elite task force to harry the British; they were chosen for stamina and marksmanship (an early, perhaps the first, example of special forces). Marshall served with them for five years.

In early 1780 he went to join his father, who commanded an artillery unit at Yorktown, but there was little to do militarily at the time and John started to socialise in the town. There he met 14 year old Mary Ambler. When she was 16 he proposed to her, but was refused. He rode away, but she sent a cousin with a lock of her hair, who managed to catch him. John returned with his hair entwined with hers and they became engaged; she wore the hair in a locket and he wore it after her death. She came from an important family of Huguenot descent, but they had fallen on hard times. Unlike Jefferson, wealth did not come to him by marriage. The marriage took place on 3 January 1783.

Shortly after his first meeting with her, however, he had enrolled in a series of lectures organised by George Wythe at the College of William and Mary, which introduced him to Montesquieu's *Esprit des Lois (Spirit of the Law)*, advocating that the judiciary be a separate branch of government. At the end of July he applied to join the Virginia bar and was admitted on 28 August 1780. Much earlier Thomas Jefferson had built up a substantial legal practice particularly in the western parts of Virginia and, when he decided to concentrate on politics in 1774, passed it to his relative, Edmund Randolph. In 1780 Randolph allowed the young Marshall to use a room in his office and in due course, when Edmund became governor of Virginia in 1786, the practice passed to Marshall. He developed it on a wider basis, settling wills, arguing many of the cases regarding disputed title to land and defending criminals. In particular he represented the interests of the Fairfax family when the government of Virginia asserted that the proprietorial grant from Charles II, on which they based their title, was invalid, and started to grant title to others. He argued from Locke's standpoint that the people had a vested right to own property, which was superior to any right the government might claim.

In 1782 he entered politics as a representative in the Virginia House of Delegates. Like Hamilton, his political views were informed by his experience in the army. In a later *Autobiographical Sketch* he wrote:

> I partook largely of the sufferings and feelings of the army and my immediate entry into the state legislature opened my view to the causes which been chiefly instrumental in augmenting those suffering and the general tendency of state politics convinced me that no safe and permanent remedy could be found, but in a more efficient and better organized government.[7]

When an issue arose as to whether the legislature could examine the alleged misconduct of a magistrate under an Act of the Virginian legislature, Marshall

---

[7] John Marshall, *An Autobiographical Sketch* JS Adams (ed) (Ann Arbor, University of Michigan Press, 1937) 10.

was responsible for announcing the decision of the Council of Virginia that the Act was repugnant to the Articles of Confederation and so void.

When the new draft Constitution of the United States was referred to the States in the autumn of 1787 for ratification, there appeared to be a majority in the Virginian legislature against ratification. Marshall played a part in persuading the Assembly to refer ratification to a state convention.[8] Within that he argued strongly for ratification without amendment, arguing that the judiciary were the protectors of the Constitution, for who else would perform that role. If the legislature 'were to make a law not warranted by any of the powers enumerated, it would be considered by the Judges an infringement of the Constitution ... They would declare it void.'[9] It was clear the vote on ratification was to be close, but eventually it was in favour without amendment by 89 to 79 votes, though with a recommendation that it be amended in the form of the Virginia Charter of Liberties.

Thereafter he concentrated on his legal practice, moving to the state capital of Richmond and building a substantial house there for his growing family—he and Mary had 10 children, six of whom survived into adulthood. He described her as his 'solace', though she disliked travelling away from Richmond, which frequently kept them apart.[10] Marshall refused an invitation to stand for the national House of Representatives and the post of United States Attorney General in Virginia.[11] His single-minded pursuit of his profession led him swiftly to become a leader of the Virginian bar. He did accept an invitation from President Adams to go as one of three ministers on behalf of the United States to negotiate with the new Republican government in France in 1797; it ended in failure because of their refusal to give the French foreign minister, Talleyrand, a 'sweetener'.[12] Marshall's stance increased his public standing. He was finally persuaded by Washington to stand as a candidate for election to the House of Representatives in Congress and was elected, taking his seat in December 1799; he nevertheless resisted Adams' offer of a seat in the Supreme Court.[13] Within Congress he became a staunch supporter of the President and his moderate federalist approach and in June 1800 Adams appointed him Secretary of State. In the autumn of 1800 Adams lost the Presidential election, but, whilst he was still in office, Chief Justice Oliver Ellsworth resigned; Adams had the opportunity to appoint a successor.[14] It was now clear that the next government led by Jefferson would be anti-federalist and Adams wanted to ensure that the next Chief Justice was a federalist; Marshall had made his own views on a strong central government clear and Adams appointed him. That this was a political appointment was clear—Marshall had no judicial experience.

---

[8] Smith above n 1, 139.
[9] HA Johnson (ed), *Papers of John Marshall* (Chapel Hill NC, University of North Carolina Press, 2006) Vol I at 277.
[10] ibid, 75.
[11] Smith above n 1, 144.
[12] This was known as the 'XYZ affair'.
[13] On this period see Smith above n 1, ch 9.
[14] ibid, 282.

By now the government had moved to its new home in Washington.[15] The capital was still scarcely more than a village; there was no building for the Supreme Court and it was given a Committee Room in the newly built Capitol (note the echo of republican Rome). When Marshall took his oath of office in February 1801, his brethren attending him wore the red and ermine robes of the British judiciary, whilst he appeared in the plain black gown of the judges in the Virginian Court of Appeal. The Supreme Court had achieved little to date. It had reached no decisions in its first 18 months; from 1790–1800 the Chief Justices had been frequently seconded for diplomatic duties and only 63 opinions had been handed down. Now, when the Court was in session, the new Chief Justice persuaded all the Justices to stay in the same boarding house, so that they could discuss cases out of Court hours, and he also persuaded them wherever possible to produce a unanimous opinion.

From the beginning of his office, it is plain he was treating the English common law as received into its American equivalent. He frequently quoted Blackstone as a source and also referred to judgments of Lords Coke and Mansfield. He also adopted the English definition of obiter dicta which distinguishes between those judicial statements which are binding and those which, though valuable guides, are not. The first form the basis of the decision on the particular facts of the case; the second, while relating to the decision, are not relied on to reach its logical conclusion. Thus in *Cohens v Virginia*, in delivering the opinion of the Court, he stated:

> It is a maxim not to be disregarded, that general expressions in every opinion, are to be taken in connection with the case in which those expressions are used. If they go beyond the case, they may be respected, but ought not to control the judgment in a subsequent case when the very point is presented for decision.[16]

Nevertheless in some of the opinions he rendered, his broad statements on the meaning of the Constitution were at best peripherally pertinent to the decision on the facts. There may be a suspicion that the decision on the facts was a palliative for the wide-ranging statements, which were likely to attract opposition. A litigant who has won cannot dispute the decision!

There was, however, a vital difference between English and American jurisprudence. The English did not have a written constitution—theirs was an amalgam of some written documents, such as Magna Carta and the Bill of Rights, decisions of the courts and well established practice. 'According to the theory of the British constitution their parliament is omnipotent.'[17] The judiciary could not declare an Act of Parliament void. In the United States, on the other hand, the Constitution was supreme. Marshall took the view that no branch of government could breach it and that it was the role of the judiciary in the Supreme Court to ensure that the legislature and executive did not exceed

---

[15] ibid et seq.

[16] 1821 (6 Wheaton) 19 US 264 at 399; early reports of the opinions of the Supreme Court were recorded by private reporters, such as Wheaton—they were incorporated into US reports with the same pagination as the original report, so both references are given.

[17] *Trustees of Dartmouth College v Woodward* 1819 (4 Wheaton) 17 US 518 at 643.

their powers. 'All those who have framed written constitutions contemplate them as forming the fundamental and paramount law of the nations; the theory of every such government must be that an act of the legislature repugnant to the constitution is void.'[18] Moreover the judges in state courts are also bound by the Constitution, which

> states that it represents the supreme law of the land and the judges in every state shall be bound thereby; anything in the constitution of laws of any State to the contrary notwithstanding. The general government, though limited as to its objects, is supreme with respect to those objects.[19]

Gathered together, these statements reveal a clear federalist view of the Constitution, indeed Marshall regarded the Federalist Papers as in themselves authoritative.[20]

> The opinion of the Federalist has always been considered as of great authority. It is a complete commentary on our Constitution ... the part two of its authors performed in framing the Constitution put it very much in their power to explain the views with which it was framed.[21]

This is a somewhat selective view: Alexander Hamilton, who wrote the bulk of the Papers, played little direct part in drafting the Constitution. Marshall's views were expressed not in one grand piece, but piecemeal over several decades and it may be that this too resulted in less criticism than would otherwise be the case.

When someone has presided over a court for 35 years, it is impossible in short space to summarise all that he has achieved. What follows is a brief review of some of the leading cases in which Marshall delivered the opinion of the Supreme Court on matters touching the Constitution of the United States.

The relationship under the Constitution between the three branches of government was raised in one of the earliest cases that the Marshall Court decided. In February 1803, in the seminal case of *Marbury v Madison*,[22] it asserted its power in certain circumstances to police the actions of the other branches of government. When the site of a federal capital was decided, the states of Virginia and Maryland ceded land to the national government, in order that the City of Washington, when built on it, would not be part of any State—it was called the District of Columbia, Columbia being a poetic description of north America and was placed under the direct control of Congress. This was achieved by the Act Concerning the District of Columbia 1801, which additionally gave the President of the United States power to appoint the Mayor of Washington and Justices of the Peace to sit in two courts established within its boundaries. On the night before his term came to an end, President Adams nominated a number of Justices of the Peace for Washington, including Marbury. They became known as the 'midnight judges' and were mainly of federalist persuasion. Adams signed

---

[18] *Marbury v Madison* 1803 (1 Cranch) 5 US 137.
[19] *Cohens* above n 16 at 381.
[20] See above.
[21] *Cohens* above n 16 at 418.
[22] Above n 18.

their Commissions of the Peace and the Secretary of State (who holds the official seal of the United States) sealed them, but they were not delivered to the Justices, in fact they still lay on the Secretary's desk when Madison succeeded to that office. No doubt seeing them as political appointments, he left them where they were. Marbury applied to the Supreme Court for a writ of *mandamus* ordering Madison to deliver him his commission. *Mandamus* was a writ issuing out of the Court of King's Bench in England and used to control lower courts and officers of the executive, who failed to carry out their duties. Those receiving such a writ were called upon to make a return, ie reply to the writ. This was a process adopted by the American courts. Madison did not respond to the writ and no one argued his case before the court, which nevertheless tried to consider what arguments might have been advanced on his behalf.

The Court held that the appointment of the Justices was complete on their commission being signed and sealed—it was not necessary for the commissions to be delivered. Marbury had a right to his commission, which was his property. Relying on Blackstone, Marshall asserted that 'the very essence of civil liberty certainly consists in the right of every individual to claim the protection of the laws when he receives an injury.'[23] Where a head of department in the executive has a political discretion to act or not, the courts will not interfere, 'but where a specific duty is assigned by law and individual rights depend upon the performance of that duty, it seems equally clear that the individual who considers himself injured has a right to resort to the law of his country.'[24] The act of nomination and appointment were political acts; once they had occurred the executive discretion ended and the courts could order the executive to deliver the commission. As a matter of principle the Court upheld its right to control the executive in its non-political activities. This became known as part of the doctrine of judicial review—that is the power of the Supreme Court to decide whether, under the Constitution, a legislative or executive act is prohibited and, if not, whether it is likewise permissible.

Nevertheless Marbury did not get his commission; the Court held in favour of Madison, because on procedural grounds Marbury could not obtain a writ of *mandamus* from the Supreme Court. The Supreme Court had an appellate jurisdiction and only a limited original jurisdiction; *mandamus* could only be issued by a court of original jurisdiction and that which the Supreme Court held was not wide enough to grant the writ. The Court could have decided the case on this narrow point, without referring to any of the broader constitutional issues, but Marshall must have been keen to establish the authority of the Court over certain acts of the Executive. Although the right was asserted, Marshall was no doubt aware that there was no power under the Constitution for the Supreme Court to enforce its orders against the President. Finding for Madison on a jurisdictional point, left the Executive with no procedural challenge to the Court's constitutional decision.

[23] Above n 18, 162.
[24] ibid, 166.

In *Cohens v Virginia* the Court under Marshall's leadership asserted its power to judge disputes between individuals and states, though once again it found for the relevant state government on the facts.[25] A Federal Act of 1804 gave the City of Washington power to authorise the drawing of a lottery to finance improvements in the City, which ordinary taxation could not meet. Such a lottery was set up and the Cohen brothers sold tickets for it in Norfolk, Virginia, where state legislation prohibited the sale of lottery tickets. A criminal information was issued against them and in Norfolk County Quarter Sessions they claimed that the Congressional Act authorising the establishment of the lottery overrode the State legislation. The court ruled against them and they appealed ultimately to the Supreme Court. On the facts the Court held that the Congressional Act of 1804 only contemplated the issue of lottery tickets within the District of Columbia and affirmed the Norfolk court's ruling, though there was nothing in the 1804 Act limiting the area where tickets could be sold.[26] Before making this finding, however, the Court ruled that it had jurisdiction to hear cases between individuals and States:

> The American States, as well as the American people, have believed a close and firm Union to be essential to their liberty and to their happiness. They have been taught by experience that this Union cannot exist without a government for the whole; and they have been taught by the same experience that this government would be a mere shadow that must disappoint all their hopes, unless invested with large portions of that sovereignty which belongs to independent states[27] ... the Constitution states that it represents the supreme law of the land and the judges in every state shall be bound thereby; anything in the constitution or laws of any State to the contrary notwithstanding[28] ... a constitution is framed for ages to come and is designed to approach immortality as nearly as human institutions can approach it. Its course cannot always be tranquil ... there is certainly nothing in the circumstances under which our constitution was formed; nothing in the history of the times, which would justify the opinion that the confidence reposed in the States was so implicit as to leave in them and their tribunals, powers of resisting or defeating in the form of law, the legitimate measures of the Union[29] ... the constitution and laws of a State, so far as they are repugnant to the constitution and the laws of the United States, are absolutely void.[30]

Though in these two cases the Court adopted a narrow view on the facts, in general Marshall's Court adopted a purposive approach to the Constitution. In *McCullough v Maryland*[31] Acts of Congress had established a National Bank of the United States.[32] The Bank established a branch in Maryland and the State of Maryland passed legislation imposing taxes on it. McCullough, the manager of the branch, challenged the power of the State of Maryland to impose a tax on

---

[25] *Cohens* above n 16.
[26] ibid, 375.
[27] ibid, 380.
[28] ibid, 381.
[29] ibid, 387.
[30] ibid, 414.
[31] 1819 (4 Wheaton), 17 US 316.
[32] Above ch 14.

an organ of federal government. The Attorney General for Maryland adopted a frontal attack on national powers under the Constitution—the Constitution emanated not from the people but from the states, who retained sovereign power. The opinion delivered by Marshall firmly rejected this view. Although the Convention which framed the Constitution emanated from the states, its ratification was decided by conventions chosen in each state by the people. The Constitution itself stated it was ordained and established in the name of the people. The government of the United States was limited to exercising the powers conferred on it by the Constitution; there was no specific power to establish a bank, but there was nothing in the Constitution which excluded incidental or implied powers.[33] There were specific powers to tax, regulate commerce and to raise and support armies and navies. The Constitution gave the government power to pass all laws which were necessary and proper to carry into execution such specific powers as it had granted. Necessary meant no more than convenient or useful.

> Let the end be legitimate, let it be within the scope of the constitution, and all means which are appropriate, which are plainly adapted to that end, which are not prohibited, but consistent with the letter and spirit of the constitution are constitutional.[34]

States had no power, by taxation or otherwise, to retard, impede, burden, or in any manner control the operation of the Constitution as enacted by Congress. The Act passed by the Maryland legislature purporting to tax the National Bank was unconstitutional and void.[35]

The legislative powers of an individual State of the Union were also restrained in *Dartmouth College v Woodward*.[36] In 1754 the Reverend Eleazor Wheelock established Dartmouth College, partly at his private expense, as a charity school for the instruction of the native Indian population of America in the Christian religion. A board of trustees was established, which was self-perpetuating, and Dr Wheelock applied to King George III for a charter incorporating the college as a charity, which was granted. Local landowners contributed land in western New Hampshire, financial contributions were made and the college was established; thus it had acquired real and personal property. Its objects were enlarged to enable it to educate those of English descent in the Christian religion. In 1816 the trustees dismissed the then President of the college. The government of New Hampshire was unhappy with his dismissal and wished to reform the college to have a wider role in the state. The New Hampshire legislature passed an Act in June of that year increasing the number of trustees and giving the power to appoint them to the State Senate. It also created a board of overseers (including the principal officers of the state of New Hampshire) to control the more important acts of the trustees. The trustees then brought an action to recover the records, corporate seal and other corporate property of the college from the

---

[33] *McCullough* above n 31, 406.
[34] ibid, 413.
[35] ibid, 436.
[36] Above n 17.

state, but were denied by the Superior Court of New Hampshire. This decision was appealed to the Supreme Court.

The Court found that the Charter granted by George III had created a private corporation. A corporation was a convenient vehicle for managing in perpetuity the objects of individuals; an individual might pursue his private ends without becoming a public officer and so can a corporation. The Charter was not a grant of political power to the government of New Hampshire, but established a private institution endowed with the capacity to take property for objects unconnected with government.

> It is probable that no man ever was ... the founder of a college believing at the time, that an act of incorporation constitutes no security for the institution; believing that it is immediately to be deemed a public institution, whose funds are to be governed and applied not by the will of the donor, but by the will of the legislature.[37]

The act of incorporation under the Charter was effectively a contract between the donors and the college and Article I section 10 of the Constitution stated that no state legislature could, impair, weaken or cancel a contract. The Act of the New Hampshire legislature was contrary to the Constitution and so void.

Despite relying upon the necessity of a strong central government, Marshall was conscious of the degree of opposition there had been to the ratification of the Constitution and so he was ready on the right occasion to limit its effect. This was illustrated in *Barron v The Mayor and City Council of Baltimore*.[38] Barron owned a deep water wharf on the river at Baltimore, where he carried on a wharfing business. The City of Baltimore ordered the diversion of watercourses which fed into the river and this caused the river to silt up and made the wharf unusable. He sued for damages and relied on the wording of the Fifth Amendment, which stated (amongst other things) that private property should not be taken for public use without just compensation. The opinion of the court read by Marshall stated:

> It is universally understood, it is part of the history of the day, that the great revolution which established the constitution of the United States, was not effected without immense opposition. Serious fears were extensively entertained that those powers, which the patriot statesmen, who then watched over the interests of our country, deemed essential to union ... might be exercised in a manner dangerous to liberty. In every convention by which the constitution was adopted, amendments to guard against the abuse of power were recommended. These amendments demanded security against apprehended encroachments of the general government—not against those of local governments.[39]

The Court held that the Fifth Amendment restrained the power of central government and not that of the states. Each state, through its own Bill of Rights or Liberties, restricted the power of its own government and its citizens had to rely on them.

---

[37] ibid, 647.
[38] 1833 (7 Peters) 32 US 243.
[39] ibid, 250.

A strict reading of the Constitution with regard to relations with the native Americans appears less sympathetic to modern eyes. In *Johnson v M'Intosh* the plaintiff claimed the right to land granted to him by the Illinois and Pinnkershaw nations.[40] The Supreme Court held that that the grants did not give a title which would be recognised in the courts of the United States. Whilst the Indian nations had lawful occupancy of lands and could make their own arrangements allowing occupancy to others, they did not have complete sovereignty over their lands. All European powers recognised the principle that discovery gave title to the governments in whose name it was made and that created true sovereignty. In *Cherokee Nation v Georgia* the Cherokees sought to restrain the State of Georgia from seizing their lands and claiming sovereignty over them.[41] The Court held that, though the Constitution gave them power to try controversies between States of the Union and foreign states, the Cherokee Nation was not a foreign state. It was a dependent nation:

> They occupy territory to which we assert a title independent of their will, which takes effect in point of possession when their right to possession ceases. Meanwhile they are in a state of pupillage. Their relationship to the United States resembles that of a ward or guardian.[42]

Marshall's views on the Constitution inevitably collided with those of Jefferson. After an initial honeymoon period, the two men showed great hostility towards one another.[43] There was enough in their backgrounds, particularly the distinction between Marshall's military service and Jefferson's continued civilian life during the revolutionary war, to cause enmity. Additionally Washington was a hero of Marshall and between 1805 and 1808 he wrote a five volume life of the ex-President. Jefferson openly criticized Washington. Marshall came to regard Jefferson as fundamentally dishonest. Jefferson showed his attitude to Marshall in a letter to the editor of the *Richmond Enquirer* in 1820, when he wrote that the Justices of the Supreme Court 'consider themselves secure for life' and

> skulk from responsibility ... An opinion is huddled up in conclave, perhaps by a majority of one, delivered as if unanimous and with silent acquiescence of lazy or timid associates led by a crafty chief judge, who sophisticates the law to his mind, by the turn of his own reasoning.[44]

This antagonism was exacerbated by the trial of Aaron Burr.[45] Burr had been Vice President during Jefferson's first term, but, after he killed Alexander Hamilton in a duel,[46] his political career seemed to have ended. In 1805 he travelled to the western territories in Ohio and Louisiana. What precisely he intended was never

---

[40] 1823 (8 Wheaton) 21 US 543.
[41] 1831 (5 Peters) 30 US 1.
[42] ibid, 17.
[43] Smith above n 1, 11.
[44] 'Letter to Thomas Ritchie Dec 25, 1820' *Works of Thomas Jefferson* (ed) PL Ford (New York and London, GP Putnam's Sons, 1905) 175–78.
[45] RK Newmyer, *The Treason Trial of Aaron Burr: Law, Politics, and the Character Wars of the New Nation* (Cambridge, Cambridge University Press, 2012).
[46] Above ch 14.

clearly established, but he did form a band of 80 armed men, according to him for defence in case of war with Spain. Jefferson became convinced his intentions were treasonous and issued a warrant for his arrest. Eventually in 1807 he was tried in Richmond for treason before Marshall sitting as a judge at first instance. Jefferson tried to mastermind the trial from behind the scenes, but the evidence was thin. A letter was produced by Jefferson's ally, General Wilkinson, purporting to show treasonous intent, but it turned out to be in the General's hand, he claiming it as a copy of the original which was lost. In any event the Constitution, following earlier English law, required in Article III section 3 that there could be no conviction in such a case without proof of some overt act of treason witnessed by two persons. Marshall ruled there was none and the jury acquitted. Jefferson was furious and talked of impeaching Marshall.

Like Jefferson, Marshall was somewhat ambivalent on the subject of slavery. He owned slaves, though not on the scale of the Jeffersons, but gave his personal slave the opportunity of freedom on his death. In his judicial capacity, he considered the slave trade, as opposed to the condition of slavery, in the case of *The Antelope*.[47] The background facts were somewhat complicated. The vessel was found by a revenue cutter off the coast of Florida and brought into port in Savannah, Georgia. It was captained and crewed by American citizens, but was owned by Spaniards resident in Havana; it contained somewhere around 160 Africans. It appeared the vessel had been subject to capture and release and that the slaves on board had been taken at different times and in varying circumstances. They were originally intended for Brazil, which was under Portuguese rule. The captain of the vessel claimed ownership of the slaves as being taken in war. The Spanish and Portuguese vice consuls each claimed a portion of the slaves as belonging to their subjects, though the Portuguese consul could not say which Portuguese owned them. The government of the United States argued on behalf of the slaves that they had been transported from foreign parts in contravention of United States law and were entitled to their freedom under the law of nature. In delivering the opinion of the Court on the legality of slavery, Marshall distinguished the law of nature and the law of nations:

> That it is contrary to the law of nature will scarcely be denied. That every man has a natural right to the fruits of his own labour is generally admitted, and that no other person can rightfully deprive him of those fruits and appropriate them against his will seems to be the necessary result of this admission. But from the earliest times, war has existed and war confers rights in which all have acquiesced. Among the most enlightened nations of antiquity, one of these was that the victor might enslave the vanquished. This, which was the usage of all, could not be pronounced repugnant to the law of nations … Both Europe and America embarked in it and for nearly two centuries it was carried on without opposition and without censure. A jurist could not say that a practice thus supported was illegal.[48]

---

[47] 1825 (10 Wheaton) 23 US 66.
[48] ibid, at 120.

On the facts, the Spanish had proved they owned part of the slaves on board the vessel and they should be returned to them; the remainder, whose ownership could not be proved, were to be delivered to the government of the United States to be dealt with according to the law of the United States. On the other hand, in *Boyce v Anderson* slaves had been killed in a steamboat accident and the liability of the steamboat owners depended on whether they were cargo or persons.[49] Marshall, delivering the opinion of the court, said 'a slave has volition, and has feelings, which cannot be entirely disregarded ... in the nature of things and in his character he resembles a passenger, not a package of goods.' His general attitude was to abhor the practice of slavery, but to oppose its outright abolition, because it was not practicable or attainable; he preferred to let it gradually die out.[50]

Marshall remained in office until his death at the age of 79 in 1835. At his wish he was buried at the side of his wife with a plain tombstone simply recording his birth, marriage and death. The opinions to which he was party demonstrate, whatever popular sentiment might have wished, a determination to apply what he judged to be the law; if his opinion were criticized as too legalistic, he would have regarded that as sufficient praise. In the end his main claim to fame was the establishment, even the creation, of a Court which under the Constitution was an equal part of the state.

[49] 1829 (2 Peters) 27 US 150.
[50] Smith above n 1, 458–59.

16

Slavery Abolished: Abraham Lincoln

ABRAHAM LINCOLN WAS yet another future politician born in a log cabin—on 12 February 1809 at Sinking Spring Farm, Kentucky, in an area known as the Barrens.[1] His family had moved from Norfolk in England in the 1630s to settle in Virginia.[2] In modern speak, they were losers and gradually moved further and further west. By the time of Abraham's birth they were on the western frontier of white settlement, where life was tough. It was an area plagued by mosquitoes in summer and snow storms in winter and the white settlers clashed with the native Americans. Abraham's paternal grandfather was killed by one on his farm on the Kentucky border. Later the Lincoln family moved north to Illinois and in 1822 Abraham enlisted in the militia to resist an invasion by Chief Black Hawk, who was trying to retake lands he had transferred earlier to settlers.

Abraham's father, Thomas, having been orphaned at an early age and having few means, mortgaged land from the government, a liability eventually paid off by Abraham. Thomas did not believe in educating his son and punished him if he caught him reading; Abraham was used by his father for heavy land clearing and farming. The young man was tall and strong and spent a good deal of time splitting branches into rails and hunting with his father. In these western lands, it was the custom for sons up to the age of 21 to hand their fathers any earnings they received. Abraham did this, but greatly resented having to do so; after he left home, he had nothing to do with his father, refusing even to visit him on his deathbed. Later he claimed that the servitude he experienced as a young man impacted on his views on slavery—'I want every man to have the chance, and I believe a black man is entitled to it, in which he can better his condition.'[3]

His family were Baptists, who as a religious group were known for their generous treatment of black people, recognising them as equal human beings and welcoming them into their church. Whether his family's religion influenced Abraham is difficult to say, because he himself took no part in organised religion and was opposed to the Calvinism of the frontier churches. John Stuart,

---

[1] Biographies of Lincoln include M Burlingame, *Abraham Lincoln: A Life* (Baltimore MD, John Hopkins University Press, 2008)—very exhaustive; DH Donald, *Lincoln* (New York, Touchstone, 1996); an excellent concise account is found in JM McPherson, *Abraham Lincoln* (New York, Oxford University Press, 2009).

[2] For early life see Burlingame ibid, 1–70 and McPherson ibid, 1–6.

[3] RP Basler (ed), *Collected Works of Abraham Lincoln* (New Brunswick NJ, Rutgers University Press, 1953) IV 24–25. The Abraham Lincoln Association has made these available online at http://quod.lib.umich.edu/l/lincoln/

a lawyer who later took Abraham under his wing, described him as an open infidel bordering on the atheistic, who did not acknowledge Jesus as the son of God.[4] When Abraham was attacked as a religious sceptic during an election campaign in 1846, he was more circumspect, saying that though he was never a member of an organised church, he had never denied the truth of the scripture. He plainly was opposed to slavery from an early age. In 1828, when he was 19, he left home with a friend to travel on a flat boat transporting farm produce down the Ohio and Mississippi rivers to New Orleans. In the course of that journey some men were brought aboard—'ten or a dozen slaves shackled with irons. The sight was a continual torment to me.'[5]

Map showing states eventually established on North West Territories

When Abraham was seven the family moved north from Kentucky to Indiana, where they lived on a number of small farms, and then when he was 21 to Illinois. These moves were not without significance, for Kentucky was a slave state and Indiana and Illinois were not. The early colonists recognised the Appalachian mountain chain as the natural boundary of their lands. Beyond that was an area known as the North West Territories, ceded under the peace treaty of 1783 from Great Britain to the United States. It ran from the Great Lakes in the north and tapered down to the 50th parallel, contained the great Ohio River valley and was inhabited largely by native American tribes. In 1787 Congress passed the North West Ordinance, which provided that the area should

[4] Burlingame above n 1, 250.
[5] McPherson above n 1; Basler above n 3, II 97.

be governed as territories, until there were sufficient settlers to justify recognition as a state. The Ordinance forbade the practice of slavery in the territories. Kentucky, which ran west from Virginia, was not part of these territories and obtained statehood in 1792 as a slave state. Indiana and Illinois were part of the territories. Indiana obtained statehood in 1816 and Illinois in 1818 and their Constitutions forbade the practice of slavery.

In 1830 Abraham moved from the family home to New Salem, Illinois, and made his own way in a variety of jobs including postmaster and surveyor and opened a general store with a partner; it failed because of the partner's behaviour, but Abraham paid off all of the debts. This may have been the beginning of his reputation as 'honest Abe'; he never lost his Kentucky accent or some rough forms of speech—as President he often said 'ain't' instead of 'isn't'. He was a teller of homespun tales. This all-American image no doubt helped him later electorally. In New Salem he met a justice of the peace, called Greene, who became almost a surrogate father to him; Abraham accompanied Greene to court and was encouraged to study law. He also met an attorney called John Stuart, who lent him law books and eventually took him as a partner in his law firm in Springfield. Abraham was admitted to the Illinois bar on 9 September 1836.[6] Thereafter, between periods of political office, he practised law until he became President. At first this was a small time prairie practice, dealing with local disputes as he rode the eighth circuit in Illinois. Later in the 1850s the rate of expansion west increased and with it the came the railroads. Between 1850 and 1860 the price of land in Illinois doubled and that in Chicago trebled. Railroad suits and a general increase in commercial cases led to him becoming a substantial lawyer. He also appeared in criminal libel cases, which were prevalent, particularly where accusations of adultery or fornication had been made, and also handled divorce cases and occasionally crime; he gained a considerable reputation as a trial and appellate advocate.[7]

On 4 November 1842, Abraham married Mary Todd; they had four sons. He did seek her views on political matters, but they were temperamentally ill-suited. She was more ambitious for him than he was for himself and, once the wife of a Congressman and then President, was always anxious to maintain her dignity at the expense of others.

John Stuart was the leader of the Whig Party in the Illinois House of Representatives and Lincoln fell under his political influence. By this time their opponents, the Democratic Party, favoured as little government control as possible. Lincoln stated the Whig view in a *Fragment on Government*: 'the legitimate object of government is to do for the people whatever needs to be done, but which they cannot do at all, or do so well themselves.'[8] Between 1834 and 1842 he sat for various periods in the Whig interest in the Illinois House of Representatives, but, finding he could not get the political preferment he wished, retired again to his practice in Springfield.

---

[6] Burlingame above n 1, 87.
[7] ibid, 315 et seq.
[8] Basler above n 3, Vol II 220.

What triggered his return to politics was the passage through the national Congress of the Kansas/Nebraska Act in 1854, effectively enabling slave owning to spread westwards. The political conflict that arose after the passage of this Act led eventually to civil war; the argument was not about the abolition of slavery where it already existed, but about its further extension. The immediate background to the civil war is complicated. To the west of the North West Territories was the enormous area of Louisiana, which was originally under French rule. It was purchased by the United States government from the Napoleonic government in 1803.[9] In 1819 the territory of Missouri on the eastern edge of the Louisiana territory applied to become a state of the union allowed to practice slavery. This caused immense controversy, settled only by the so-called Missouri Compromise of 1820—a Federal statute was passed forbidding the practice of slavery in the Louisiana territory north of 36 degrees 30 minutes latitude, but an exception was made to allow it be practised in Missouri. Thereafter pressure built from the southern states to be allowed to expand westwards and take slavery with them. In 1848 the United States defeated Mexico in an expansionist war and in the resulting peace large tracts of land were ceded to the victors. In February 1850, Jefferson Davis, who was to become the President of the Confederate States during the Civil War, addressed Congress saying that the population of both whites and slaves in the southern states was expanding, while the soil they farmed was becoming less and less fertile. He argued that slaves were well suited to working in the hot conditions found in New Mexico and Texas and also in the newly discovered gold and silver mines further west.[10] The spread of slavery to these new territories should be permitted.

The southerners found an unlikely ally. Stephen Douglas was a Chicago lawyer and Democratic Senator for Illinois. He was not a slave owner; his passions were popular democratic government, where the people decided within their states what best suited them, and the spread of commerce. Proposals were in the air for the construction of the first transcontinental railway; the south wanted a southern route; Douglas wanted it to run west from Chicago and this would take it across the Louisiana territory. The southern senators agreed to support the northern route in return for Douglas supporting the extension of slavery westwards. Douglas secured the passage of the federal Kansas/Nebraska Act in 1854, creating two huge new territories in central Louisiana, which would be free when they became states to decide whether to allow the practice of slavery. It was against the spirit of the North West Ordinance and drove a coach and horses through the Missouri Compromise.

The passage of the Act split both the Whigs and the Democrats. Lincoln, amongst others, saw the need for a new political alignment to prevent the spread of slavery and on 6 July 1854 he attended a convention of a new Republican Party, which proposed a slate of anti-slavery candidates for national elections. In

---

[9] Above ch 11.
[10] C Eaton, *Jefferson Davis* (New York, Free Press, 1977) 72.

the period that followed, Lincoln made some 175 speeches opposing the spread of slavery.[11]

On 16 October 1854, he delivered a famous address at Peoria south east of Chicago.[12] He described his personal hatred of the

> monstrous injustice of slavery itself. I hate it because it deprives our republican exam-ple of its just influence in the world—enables the enemies of free institutions, with plausibility, to taunt us as hypocrites—causes the real friends of freedom to doubt our sincerity, and especially because it forces so many really good men amongst ourselves into an open war with the very fundamental principles of civil liberty—criticizing the Declaration of Independence, and insisting that there is no right principle of actions but *self-interest*.[13]

He was prepared to acknowledge that the southern states had not originated slavery, that it was difficult to conceive a satisfactory method to free those who were in existing slavery—it was not possible to make them political or social equals.

> But all this, to my judgment furnishes no more excuse for permitting slavery to go into our own free territory, than it would for reviving the African slave trade by law. The law which forbids the bringing of slaves *from* Africa, and that which has so long forbid the taking them *to* Nebraska, can hardly be distinguished on moral principle.[14]

The extension of slavery within the United States was inconsistent with aboli-tion of the slave trade, in which the southern states had acquiesced.

His central argument was inconsistency between the Declaration of Independ-ence and slavery.

> The just powers of governments are derived from the consent of the governed. Now the relation of masters and slave is ... a total violation of this principle. The master not only governs the slave without his consent, but he governs him by a set of rules altogether different from those which he prescribes for himself ... Let it not be said I am contending for the establishment of political and social equality between the whites and blacks ... I am combating what is set up as a moral argument for allowing them to be taken where they have never yet been.[15]

Later in the same speech, he added:

> Near eighty years ago we began by declaring that all men are created equal, but now from that beginning we have run down to the other declaration, that for SOME men to enslave OTHERS is a 'sacred right of self-government.' These principles cannot stand together.[16]

He was, however, prepared to prioritise: 'Much as I hate slavery, I would con-sent to the extension rather than see the Union dissolved.'

---

[11] McPherson above n 1, 15.
[12] Basler above n 3, Vol II 248 et seq.
[13] ibid, 255.
[14] ibid, 256.
[15] ibid, 266.
[16] ibid, 275.

On 16 June 1858, Lincoln was nominated as the Illinois Republican candidate for the national Senate in the elections to be held in the fall of that year. In his acceptance speech he said:

> A house divided against itself cannot stand. I believe this government cannot endure permanently half slave and half free. I do not expect the Union to be dissolved—I do not expect the house to fall—but I do expect it will cease to be divided. It will become all one thing or all the other.[17]

The reference to the divided house echoed the words of Christ in the gospel according to St Mark;[18] it would have been recognised by his audience and underlined the seriousness of his purpose. It presaged a fight to what he regarded as a just conclusion, though in reality he did not think the south would secede. As much as any other quotation it sealed the southerner's view that he was not a man to compromise. The Democratic candidate standing against him was the same Senator Stephen Douglas. In the period leading up to the election the two candidates publicly debated in seven locations in Illinois. The battle lines were drawn. Douglas asked 'why cannot the nation, part slave and part free, continue as our fathers made it forever?' Lincoln responded:

> [O]ur fathers *did not* make this nation half slave and half free, or part slave and part free. I insist that they found the institution of slavery existing here. They did not make it so, but they left it so because they knew of no way to get rid of it at that time.[19]

Although the debates took place in Illinois, they received national coverage. When the election came, although Lincoln narrowly won the popular vote, Douglas won decisively in the state legislature and became Senator for Illinois.

Attention now turned to the Presidential election due to take place in 1860. The favourite for the Republican nomination was the New York lawyer William Seward, though Lincoln's name began to appear in the press as a possible Vice-Presidential candidate. Rumours spread that the slave states would secede from the Union if a Republican President were elected. Lincoln received an invitation to speak in New York and on 27 February 1860 addressed a large audience organised by the Young Men's Republican Union in the Cooper's building. He started with a detailed consideration of the views of those who had signed the Constitution, to demonstrate that a majority of them favoured Congressional control of the spread of slavery beyond the states where it had currently been practised. He went on to address the southern states directly:

> [Y]ou will break up the Union rather than submit to a denial of your Constitutional Rights. This has a somewhat reckless sound; but it would be palliated if not fully justified, were we proposing, by the mere force of numbers to deprive you of some right, plainly written down in the Constitution. But we are proposing no such thing. When you make these declarations, you have a specific ... allusion to an assumed

---

17 Basler above n 3, Vol II 461–69.
18 Mark 3:25.
19 Sixth Debate with Stephen A Douglas at Quincy, Illinois, Basler above n 3, Vol III 245–83, at 276.

Constitutional right of yours, to take slaves into federal territories, and to hold them there as property. But no such right is specifically written in the Constitution.[20]

The speech had a big public impact and further invitations led to him speaking in Hartford Connecticut and New Haven in March.

In May 1760 the Republican Party assembled in Convention in Chicago. Other candidates, in particular Seward, were still much better known than Lincoln, but the latter's supporters campaigned for him to be everyone's second choice when votes came to be transferred. On the first ballot Seward secured nearly four times the votes that Lincoln received, but eventually Lincoln secured the nomination on the third ballot. In the election that followed the Democrats split their vote between Douglas, a northern, and Breckenridge, a southern candidate. As a result on 6 November Lincoln won a decisive victory. On 20 December South Carolina seceded from the Union. By February 1861, Florida, Mississippi, Alabama, Georgia and Texas had followed suit and on 11 March a Constitution of the Confederate States of America was adopted and Jefferson Davis chosen as its President. Ironically he was in favour of the gradual emancipation of slaves, but segregating them once free.[21] Lincoln was inaugurated as President on 4 May 1861 and in his address to the nation sought to be conciliatory. He undertook that he would not interfere with slavery in the states where it already existed and would enforce the Fugitive Slave Act, by which slaves were returned to their masters. He would not appoint office holders in the southern states who were obnoxious to their inhabitants. He was, however, insistent that there was no legal right to secede from the Constitution. His words fell on deaf ears—Lincoln's earlier unequivocal opposition to slavery meant the south would not trust him.

Lincoln was determined that the Union should not commence armed hostilities. Outside Charleston harbour in South Carolina was Fort Sumter. The building of the fort had started in 1829, but it was not yet completed and had few cannons in working order. It was occupied by troops loyal to the Union. The governor of South Carolina ordered its surrender. To try the temper of the Confederates, Lincoln informed the governor that an attempt would be made to provision the fort, but if this were not resisted no attempt would be made to arm the garrison. On 12 April 1861 the Confederate forces fired on the fort. The next day it surrendered. The Civil War had begun.[22]

Lincoln called up 75,000 militia. In the earlier Revolutionary War a smaller, but more mobile patriot force, had defeated a larger, better equipped British force; that position now appeared to be reversed. It was the Unionist army which was stronger and better equipped, the Confederates who were more mobile. In the course of the war some 2.2 million men fought on the Union side and 620,000 on the Confederate. At first, the Confederates were probably better led by General Robert E Lee, who turned down an offer of command in the Union

[20] Burlingame above n 1, 582.
[21] Eaton above n 10, 69.
[22] McPherson above n 1, 32–33.

army to support his home state; he took command of the Confederate army in 1862. Lincoln suffered, as the British did in the Revolutionary War, from generals who were overcautious and would not press home an advantage. He wrote to two of his generals:

> I state my general idea of this war to be that we have *greater* numbers and the enemy has the *greater* facility of concentrating forces upon points of collision: that we must fail, unless we can find some way of making *our* advantage an overmatch for *his*, and that this can only be done by menacing him with superior forces at *different* points at the *same* time.[23]

It was not until he put General Ulysses S Grant in charge of the Union army early in 1864 that he found a leader who agreed with his tactics.

When Virginia seceded, the only route from Washington DC to the south ran through Maryland, which contained many Confederate sympathisers. On 27 April 1861, Lincoln issued an order to General Winfield Scott authorising him to suspend the writ of *habeas corpus* at or near a line between Philadelphia and Washington, if public safety required it.[24] *Habeas corpus* was an ancient English writ issued by the Crown requiring anyone who held another prisoner to produce him to the Court of King's Bench and justify his detention. On 25 May Union troops arrested John Merryman for recruiting, training and leading a company in Maryland for Confederate service. Merryman sought a writ of *habeas corpus* from the Chief Justice of the Supreme Court, John Taney, who ruled that the President had no power under the Constitution to suspend *habeas corpus*.[25] There was provision in Article I section 9 of the Constitution for the writ to be suspended, when in cases of rebellion public safety might require it, but the article did not state who might suspend it. Taney ruled that as the article was in a section dealing with legislative powers, only Congress could suspend it. There followed an uneasy stand-off, in which various attempts were made by Congress to authorise a suspension of the writ, but Lincoln was uneasy about availing himself of them for fear of surrendering the principle. The argument on his behalf was that the particular provision was originally in a section of the Constitution dealing with powers of the judiciary and removed to Article I by the Committee of Detail, presumably as a matter of style. Moreover, the Constitution makers must have known that decisions to suspend the writ might have to be made urgently and that could be done under the President's powers as Commander-in-Chief, but not under the much slower process of obtaining sanction from Congress. The matter was not resolved by the end of the war, though there has been academic support for Lincoln's view.[26]

The fortunes of war swung to and fro. From early on the Unionist press were urging the President to outlaw slavery, but he held back. In 1862 he published

---

[23] Basler above n 3, Vol V 98.
[24] JA Dueholm, *Lincoln's Suspension of the Writ of Habeas Corpus: An Historical and Constitutional Analysis* (Jo Abraham Lincoln Association XXIX Issue 2 2008) 47–66.
[25] *Ex parte Merryman* 17 Fed Cas 144.
[26] ibid.

a letter in several newspapers stating 'my paramount object in this struggle *is* to save the Union, and is *not* either to save or destroy slavery.'[27] Modern armaments caused terrible casualties; by the end of the conflict over 600,000 had perished. In September of 1862 Union and Confederate armies met at Antietam Creek on the Potomac River in Maryland. In bitter fighting the Confederates lost 14,000 and the Union 12,000 men. Lincoln's views hardened. On 22 September, he issued a preliminary proclamation indicating that, if the rebellion had not ceased by 1 January 1863, he would emancipate all slaves in the Confederate states. Rebellion continued and on that date he signed an executive order that all slaves in any state or part of a state in rebellion with the United States shall be forever free.[28] This was not done simply as a matter of principle, but to weaken the southern economy; the Union army began recruiting black soldiers, some 200,000 by the end of the war.

In the early part of the war, Lee had fought mainly on Confederate territory, but in the summer of 1863 he advanced for the first time into northern territory, closing in on Harrisburg in Pennsylvania; he met up with a large Union army near Gettysburg to the west of Philadelphia. The Union army was led by General Mead, who stationed his men on higher ground. A fierce battle was fought between 1 and 3 July, both sides again suffering heavy losses, but the end result was that Lee retreated. Lincoln was furious that Meade did not pursue him.[29] A local attorney raised funds to provide a cemetery for Union soldiers who had died in the battle and on 18 November Lincoln came to a ceremony consecrating the ground. A famous orator from Massachusetts, called Edward Everett, made the principal address; the Philadelphia Daily Age recorded that 'seldom has a man talked so long and said so little.'[30] Lincoln followed with what has become known as the Gettysburg address; it consisted of just 272 words:

Four score and seven years ago[31] our fathers brought forth on this continent, a new nation, conceived in Liberty, and dedicated to the proposition that all men are created equal. Now we are engaged in a great civil war, testing whether that nation or any nation so conceived and so dedicated, can long endure. We are met on a great battlefield of that war. We have come to dedicate a portion of that field as a final resting place for those who here gave their lives that that nation might live. It is altogether fitting and proper that we should do this. But, in a larger sense, we cannot dedicate—we cannot consecrate—we cannot hallow—this ground. The brave men, living and dead, who struggled here, have consecrated it, far above our poor power to add or detract. The world will little note, nor long remember what we say here, but it can never forget what they did here. It is for the living, rather, to be dedicated here to the unfinished work, which they who fought here have thus far so nobly advanced. It is rather for us to be here dedicated to the great task remaining before us—that from these honored dead we take increased devotion to that cause for which they gave the last full measure

---

[27] Basler above n 3, Vol V 388.
[28] McPherson above n 1, 46.
[29] ibid, 39; Burlingame above n 1, 511.
[30] Cited Burlingame above n 1, 568; *Philadelphia Daily Age* (21 November 1863).
[31] A reference to the Declaration of Independence.

of devotion—that we here highly resolve that these dead shall not have died in vain—that this nation, under God, shall have a new birth of freedom—and that government of the people, by the people, for the people, shall not perish from the earth.[32]

After Gettysburg the war became bogged down and the possibilities of a swift conclusion receded. Voices urging a negotiated peace were raised particularly among Democrats. Lincoln now made it clear that he would not compromise on the integrity of the union or the abandonment of slavery.[33] At the Republican Party Convention in June 1864, he was again nominated as Presidential candidate and persuaded the Convention to pass resolutions demanding no compromise with the rebels and that the Constitution be amended to terminate and forever prohibit the existence of slavery.[34] The Democratic Convention showed a considerable split between war and peace parties, but there was a real possibility that their candidate, George McClellan, might win the election.[35] He was nominated on 29 August. On 3 September a telegram reached the President Washington with the news that a Union army under the command of General Sherman had taken Atlanta in Georgia. Shortly before a Union fleet had sunk the Confederate ironclad warship Tennessee. The war was on the turn. Whilst there had been heavy losses on both sides, the Union had greater human resources to replace those lost. The Presidential campaign was bitterly fought with many racist allegations against the President, but on 8 November he won the popular vote and by a landslide in the Electoral College. On 4 March 1865 he was sworn in and in his inaugural address promised that, to achieve a true and lasting peace, there would be malice towards none and charity towards all. By 1 April, General Grant had encircled Petersburg in Virginia and the Confederates evacuated their capital of Richmond. On 9 April Lee surrendered his Army of Virginia. Five days later Lincoln went to watch a comedy at the Ford theatre in Washington; a young actor, John Wilkes Booth, who was a Confederate sympathiser, gained access to the presidential box and shot him in the back of the head; he died the next morning. Other Confederate armies surrendered over the ensuing months and the rebellion was officially declared ended on 20 August 1866 by Lincoln's successor, Andrew Johnson.

Lincoln's growing determination to end slavery had borne fruit before his death. To that end the Senate had approved a Thirteenth Amendment to the Constitution on 8 April 1864. It only passed in the House of Representatives after a political struggle on 31 January 1865. It was not until after Lincoln's assassination that it was ratified on 6 December 1865. It reads:

Neither slavery nor involuntary servitude, except as a punishment for crime whereof the party shall have been duly convicted, shall exist within the United States or any place subject to its jurisdiction.

---

[32] There are a number of versions which can be found online under the Speeches and Writings of Abraham Lincoln.
[33] Burlingame above n 1, 669–70.
[34] ibid, 642.
[35] ibid, 681–88.

There followed a constitutional conflict over the power of Congress to give practical effect to the Amendment. In 1865 the complicated history of what was to become the Civil Rights Act 1866 began. When elected for a second term, President Lincoln had chosen a southerner, Andrew Johnson, as his vice President, in an attempt to heal the wounds of war. When, after Lincoln's assassination, Johnson took over the reins of the Presidency, it soon became apparent that he was a staunch defender of the rights of states against those of central government. The Civil Rights Bill originally came before Congress in 1865, providing that all persons born in the United States (save for Indians who were not taxed) of every race or colour were citizens of the state and had the same right to make and enforce contracts, to sue, be parties and give evidence in court, to inherit, lease, sell, hold and convey real and personal property as white citizens. Congressman James Wilson, introducing the Bill to the House of Representatives, stated that it was intended that regulation of suffrage should be controlled by states; the Bill did not intend that all citizens should sit on juries and or that their children should attend the same schools.[36] With these assurances, Congress passed the Bill. President Johnson, however, took the view the Bill represented too great an incursion into the powers of the states and twice vetoed it. When Congress again passed the Bill by a two-thirds majority, it became law on 9 July 1866. Nevertheless serious doubts remained as to its constitutionality, opponents arguing that Congress had no power under the Constitution to pass such an Act.

Meanwhile in June 1866 Congress passed a Fourteenth Amendment to the Constitution, providing that all citizens of the United States had equal protection under the law.[37] Additionally, it gave Congress the power to enforce its provisions by appropriate legislation. The Amendment was not ratified by the States until 9 July 1868 and so was not effective when the Civil Rights Act 1866 became law.

The power to enact appropriate legislation was purportedly exercised in 1875, when Congress passed the Civil Rights Act 1875 specifically providing for equal treatment for all citizens in public accommodation and transportation and prohibiting the exclusion of any citizen from jury service. In 1883, a series of cases were amalgamated for a single hearing before the Supreme Court in the *Civil Rights Cases*.[38] The Court held that the 1875 Act was unconstitutional on the grounds that the Constitution gave no power to Congress to regulate states' relations with private citizens. In 1896 in *Plessy v Ferguson*,[39] the Supreme Court ruled that, provided the facilities provided on transport were equal, black and white citizens could be separated. Segregation was lawful.

In fact, the Reconstruction period showed a determination on the part of many southern states to maintain white supremacy. Supplying the war effort had

---

[36] Congressional Globe, House of Reprs, 39 Congress, 1st Session 1117.
[37] Compare above, ch 13.
[38] 109 US 3.
[39] 163 US 537.

made northern industrialists and merchants rich;[40] in the course of the conflict bank deposits had risen from 150 million to 240 million dollars. Advances in mechanical engineering had produced a range of products from sewing machines to reapers; railways were laid. The victors could afford to be magnanimous. Confederate soldiers from generals down were pardoned. The southern states repealed their secession instruments and were left largely free to reconstitute themselves and to regulate their relations with freed blacks. Local codes were introduced, in general giving black citizens the right to hold property, to sue or be sued, to have legal marriages and offspring. At the same time, some provided that black testimony in court could only be received where one party was black. The right of blacks to break contracts of labour before the end of their term was restricted. In some states they were forbidden to handle firearms and other weapons and in some to possess alcoholic beverages. The resolution of these problems would have to wait 150 years.[41]

After his death, Lincoln's coffin was taken on a special funeral train by a circuitous route to Springfield Illinois, where he was buried. He has been commemorated with his image on United States bank notes, on Mount Rushmore, his Memorial in Washington and in the Hall of Presidents in Disneyland.

[40] See JH Franklin, *Reconstruction after the Civil War* 3rd edn (Chicago IL, University of Chicago Press, 2013).
[41] Below, ch 19.

17

The World Stage: Woodrow Wilson

WOODROW WILSON WAS a reluctant lawyer. In 1874 his father obtained a teaching post at a theological college in Princeton and Woodrow took the opportunity to join the College of New Jersey to study political philosophy and history. He graduated in 1879 and went on to study law at the University of Virginia. He found the law a harsh task master: 'when one has nothing but law served in all its dryness, it gets monotonous'.[1] He dropped out before the end of his first year, although he still intended to follow a career in the law; he read for admission to the Georgia bar, was admitted in October 1882 and set up a practice with a fellow graduate in Atlanta. Ironically, a man who was to bestride the world stage failed to attract many clients. He was, however, interested in the academic approach to law. In 1883, his father agreed to fund his study of political science at John Hopkins University. In 1885, he published *Congressional Government* and was awarded a PhD on the strength of it. He is the only President of the United States to be thus qualified. In 1890, he was offered and accepted a professorship in Jurisprudence and Political Economy at Princeton.[2] He taught law. In 1902, he published a *History of the American People*. Princeton at this time was not the prestigious Ivy League college that we know today. In 1902 the Trustees of Princeton offered him the post of President of the College and he set about reforming its organisation, trying to turn it into a graduate college. His writing showed him a liberal, proposing state intervention to protect the weak. His position and writing drew him to the notice of the Democratic Party machine and, although he had little political experience, in 1910 he was elected Governor of New Jersey.

It was by now obvious that, whilst the everyday business of the law bored him, he was attracted by a broader philosophical approach to the subject. This may be partly because of his upbringing. His grandparents had both emigrated from Northern Ireland on the same boat in 1807. They married and settled in Ohio, producing 10 children, the youngest of whom was Woodrow's father, Joseph. Grandfather James supported the Confederate cause in the Civil War.[3] The family were of Scottish/Northern Irish descent, devout Presbyterians and played an important role in spreading their version of Christianity. Wilson was born in 1856 when his father was minister in Staunton, Virginia. He was not christened

---

[1] A Heckscher, *Woodrow Wilson* (New York, Prentice Hall & IBD, 1991) 48.
[2] KA Clements and EA Cheezum, *Woodrow Wilson* (Washington DC, CQ Press, 2003) 16.
[3] See Heckscher above n 1, 12.

Woodrow, but adopted that name later, since it was his mother's family name. In 1857 Woodrow's father was appointed to a ministry in Augusta, Georgia and eventually to a seminary in Princeton. He became clerk to the General Assembly of the Presbyterian Church. In 1883 Woodrow married Ellen, the daughter of a Presbyterian minister. His religious upbringing undoubtedly contributed to the high moral tone of his later political life.

As Governor of New Jersey he established a reputation as a progressive reformer who was ready to stand up to the party bosses.[4] Legislation was passed establishing primary elections before appointment to office, preventing corruption, setting up a Public Utilities Commission with regulatory powers and creating a fund subsidised by employers to compensate employees injured at work. On the back of this record he threw his hat into the ring for the Presidential elections of 1912. At the Baltimore Democratic Convention that year, he was not the obvious choice as nominee.[5] The big battalions preferred James 'Champ' Clarke, the Speaker of the House of Representatives; when the Convention opened Wilson commanded only half the votes that the 'Champ' did. There was a third candidate, called Underwood. In the early voting the 'Champ' took the lead, but could not reach a majority of the votes. Vote followed vote, with Wilson representing himself as the lone rider, facing down the party machine. It took 25 ballots for him to be chosen as Democratic nominee.

It was his good fortune that the Republicans split. The party chose the incumbent President, William Taft, who was known to be unpopular with the public. His opponent for the nomination was former President Theodore Roosevelt. When Taft was chosen as candidate, Roosevelt stormed out of the Republican Convention and formed a new Progressive Party. Wilson too stood on a progressive ticket, but with the advantage that he now used the well established Democratic Party machine. When in November 1912 the result of the Presidential election was announced, Wilson had 435 votes in the Electoral College to Roosevelt's 11 and Taft's 8.[6]

The Democratic Party also secured a majority in both Houses of Congress and Wilson was able to deliver his election promises.[7] He demonstrated his attachment to a free market by abolishing or reducing tariffs set on imports. He introduced a federal income tax, set up a Federal Reserve Bank with powers to regulate the financial sector under the supervision of the Treasury and established a Trade Commission to regulate the power of monopolies. All of this on its own would have established him as a President of note. Britain's Declaration of War against Germany on 4 August 1914, however, meant that Wilson's reputation thereafter would depend on how he managed relations between the United States and the European combatants.

The First World War broke out because of a network of treaties, alliances and assurances, which drew the European powers into a conflict, which with

---

[4] See Clements and Cheezum above n 2, 24–25.
[5] See Heckscher above n 1, 245.
[6] Clements and Cheezum above n 1, 251.
[7] JA Thompson, *Woodrow Wilson* (London, Routledge, 2002) 73 et seq.

hindsight was unnecessary; Wilson regarded these agreements as the prod-
uct of old-style diplomacy which had to go. On 28 June 1914, the heir to the
Austro-Hungarian Empire, Archduke Franz Ferdinand, was assassinated by a
Serbian. On 5 July, Germany assured Austria of her support, if she went to
war with Serbia. On 28 July Austria did so. The Serbians were slavs and so
Russia mobilised in support of pan-slavism. On the 31 July, Italy declared war
on Russia and Germany and then the Ottoman Empire signed a secret treaty
with Germany, undertaking mutual support. On 3 August, Germany declared
war on France and requested Belgium that German troops could pass through
her territory, so as to avoid French defences. Belgium refused, but Germany
nevertheless invaded Belgium. The neutrality of Belgium was guaranteed by the
Treaty of London in 1839. Britain, which was a signatory, declared war on
Germany on 4 August and on the same date America declared its neutrality. Serbia declared war on Germany. France was bound by treaty obligations to Russia
and declared war on Germany. The German Army marched through Belgium
and into France to a point within 35 miles of Paris, but in so doing exposed a
flank which the French attacked, causing the Germans to retreat and dig in—the
beginning of trench warfare. The rest of the war was an uneasy stalemate, very
costly both in terms of lives and economically.

By racial background and democratic inclination, Wilson favoured Britain.
His book on *Congressional Government* contrasted the American Constitution
with the unwritten British one, favouring the British model. Nevertheless the
United States had a well established policy of neutrality in relation to European
affairs. Many of those who emigrated to America did so to escape the restrictions of European life. George Washington in his farewell address warned
the American people not to get embroiled in European political and military
affairs.[8] Moreover there was a sizable and vocal German minority among the
citizens of the United States. American businessmen were keen to ensure that
their trade with the European belligerents remained unaffected. Wilson's policy,
therefore, was to maintain neutrality and protect American business. He nevertheless saw a neutral stance could give him a powerful role as mediator between
the combatants.

The British government immediately declared a blockade of Germany on
15 August 1914.[9] Britain had the most powerful navy in the world and it
was therefore feasible to intercept vessels trying to reach ports on Germany's
Baltic coast. Blockading an enemy country had been regarded as legal since the
seventeenth century and admiralty law had rules about the capture of vessels
belonging to the enemy (prize ships) or belonging to neutrals, but carrying goods
to aid a combatant's war effort.[10] Britain, when announcing the blockade, set
out a list of goods it would treat as contraband, if destined for the central powers of Germany and Austro-Hungary. The list included food. The Germans complained that Britain was trying to starve them into submission. Matters got more

---

[8] T Wilson, *The Myriad Faces of War* (London, Polity Press, 1986).
[9] MR Floyd, *Abandoning American Neutrality* (NY, Palgrave Macmillan US, 2013) 11.
[10] Generally on this topic see Floyd ibid, ch 3.

complicated when American merchants took to sending goods, particularly rubber and copper essential to the production of heavy artillery, to neutral countries such as Holland and those in Scandinavia for onward despatch to the central powers. To meet this problem, Britain divided cargoes found on neutral vessels into two classes: absolute contraband was defined as material clearly destined for Germany to aid its war effort; conditional contraband was where the final destination and the purpose of the goods was not clear; in such a case the shipper had to demonstrate that the goods were not intended to aid the German war effort.

There was a further problem that before the war 70 per cent of American exports to Europe were carried in British and German vessels. Britain insisted that if American merchants bought German ships to fly under the American flag, they had to demonstrate that they were not intending to trade with Germany. Another ruse used by some American shippers was to send goods in parts that once assembled would be used in the German war effort; in particular submarine parts were despatched in this way. There was a legal precedent condemning such conduct. During the American Civil War the British had supplied a vessel called the SS Alabama to the Confederates as a carcass not fitted out for war. Once the Confederates had fitted it out, it inflicted considerable damage on Unionist forces. Subsequently an international tribunal declared that Britain had breached international law and ordered the British government to pay over 15 million dollars in reparation. There was also the additional problem that Britain did not have sufficient industrial output to support the war effort or funds to purchase weapons from America. Was it permissible to make loans to one belligerent?

In these circumstances maintaining neutrality was not simple. Wilson was faced with exporters, such as Goodyear Tyres, complaining that their trade was being ruined and by leaders of the German community in America complaining that he was not acting neutrally. In the 1914 mid-term elections to Congress, German voters in the United States voted strongly Republican—the Democrats lost 58 seats in the House of Representatives. It did not prove possible to control the situation with rules of general application and in the end Britain and the United States agreed to deal with this plethora of problems on a case-by-case basis.

Wilson wrote immediately after the declarations of war to the Kaiser of Germany, the Austrian Emperor, the President of France and the King of England offering to help the cause of peace. He received no encouragement. Once the Germans had been forced into partial retreat and dug in, neither side was interested in mediation, because neither felt they had achieved sufficient.[11] The Germans had done their cause no good when in late August 1914 they declared a policy of *schrecklichkeit*, strictly 'frightfulness', towards the citizens of Belgium, burning down houses and in a few cases executing civilians; Antwerp was reduced to ashes. Britain was not prepared to come to the negotiating table unless compensation to Belgium was on the agenda; Germany would have none

[11] See Floyd above n 9, 11.

of that. The American government continued to try to arrange mediation, but to no avail.[12]

America's progress towards war was incremental. Wilson appears genuinely to have wished to remain neutral and mediate an end to the fighting. He was also acutely aware of the need, if the United States was to become a combatant, that American public opinion should support such a move. There was a triangle of competing interests. Americans wanted to remain out of the conflict, but still to be able to trade freely with the world, including the combatants. With stalemate on the western front, Britain wanted to use the power of its navy to isolate Germany. Germany wanted to break the stranglehold of the British navy and to be able to trade freely with the world. A point came when Germany started to sink merchant vessels. It took time for the effect of this to turn American public opinion, but in the end it did.

The British blockade proved successful. Over a one year period the value of trade between the United States and Germany fell to a tenth of its value before the outbreak of war.[13] Over the same period the value of trade between the United States and Britain rose by 55 million pounds. Treating food as contraband was causing acute shortages in Germany. In January 1915 the Kaiser accepted a plan to blockade Britain with U-boats.[14] On 18 February, Germany declared all waters around the British Isles a war zone; enemy merchant ships within those waters would be destroyed and neutral shipping was warned not to enter the zone. Wilson instructed the United States' Ambassador in Berlin to inform the German government that the United States did not regard a submarine cordon as a legitimate form of warfare—German vessels could stop and search merchant shipping for contraband, but no more. The German government was told it would be held strictly accountable for any injury to American lives or property. This prompted Germany to offer to withdraw the U-boat cordon, if Britain allowed free passage of foodstuffs. Britain refused. Foreign Secretary Sir Edward Grey stated that if Germany meant that their commerce could go free upon the sea in time of war, whilst she made war on other nations, that was not fair.[15] On 28 March 1915 a German U-boat sank a merchant vessel called the Falaba sailing from Liverpool to Sierra Leone. One American citizen was amongst those lost. The New York Times condemned this as a crime against civilisation.[16] This was followed by attacks on two United States' merchant vessels. Then, on 1 May 1915, an English registered passenger liner, the Lusitania, which was part of the Cunard line, sailed from New York for Liverpool. On 7 May it was sunk by a torpedo some 11 miles off the Irish coast; well over 1000 passengers, including 128 US citizens, perished. Although this is popularly seen as a key moment leading to American entry into the war, Wilson remained reluctant to pledge American troops. Three days after the sinking he addressed a large public meeting in the Convention Hall in Philadelphia, telling them that

[12] ibid, 23.
[13] See Floyd above n 9, 129.
[14] ibid, ch 3.
[15] ibid, 137.
[16] ibid, ch 5.

'there is such a thing as a man being so right that he does not need to convince others by force that he is right.'[17] The German response was that Britain was arming merchant vessels to attack submarines.[18] In fact the Lusitania was built with a large contribution from the British government with a view to arming it at a later stage. At one point it was registered as an armed vessel, but it never was equipped for war and the registration was withdrawn. In the summer of 1915 the United States' Ambassador to Berlin reported to his government that German public opinion approved the sinking of the Lusitania and expected Germany to win the war.[19] At the same time, the German government wanted some reward for the sacrifices of war, including retaining control of Belgium.

In June 1915, American Secretary of State Bryan resigned to be replaced by Lansing, who was much more pro-British. In July Wilson gave instructions to increase military preparedness. He went on to approve a substantial loan to Britain, but did not make this public.[20] In November 1916 Wilson won a second term as President. Matters took a significant turn in early 1917, when the German government announced a policy of unrestricted submarine warfare. The German High Command were taking a calculated risk. They foresaw that attacks on United States' registered vessels would draw the United States into the conflict, but considered that Germany could force an end to the war before the Americans made a significant contribution. The United States' entry into the war became even more likely when the British intercepted a telegram from the German foreign minister to the German ambassador to Mexico, Arthur Zimmerman, offering a German/Mexican alliance against the United States, with a promise that Texas, New Mexico and Arizona would be ceded to Mexico when the Americans were defeated.[21] Still Wilson held back from entering the war. On 3 February 1917, he addressed both Houses of Congress. He expressed disbelief that Germany would act indiscriminately against American vessels. 'We shall not believe that they are hostile to us, unless and until we are obliged to believe it.'[22] Americans were forced to believe it when in March 1917 four United States merchant vessels were sunk in the Atlantic with a loss of 15 American lives.[23] On 17 March 1917 news arrived of the fall of the Tsarist government in Russia, which left Germany free to move troops to the western front. On 20 March, Wilson again addressed both Houses of Congress, announcing that the United States was at war with Germany.

The German gamble nearly came off. In early 1917 the US army comprised only 130,000 men, ranking as the seventeenth in size of all nations. Wilson called for an army of half a million, chosen upon the basis of universal liability

---

[17] ibid, 128.
[18] ibid, 129.
[19] ibid, 153.
[20] ibid, 171.
[21] See Heckscher above n 1, 426 and *Papers of Woodrow Wilson* (ed) AS Link (Princeton NJ, Princeton University Press, 1966) A 41: 108–12 (hereinafter referred to as *PWW*).
[22] Heckscher above n 1, 128–29.
[23] ibid, 435.

to serve.[24] It was still going to take time to train such an army and transport meaningful numbers to Europe. The German army had been reinforced too and launched what they thought would be a final offensive in March 1918; it showed every sign of succeeding. It was not until the end of May that General Pershing arrived in France with a division of regular American soldiers.[25] By the end of June, however, there were a million American soldiers in France. It was becoming clear that Germany had miscalculated. On 27 September 1918, Wilson announced that in making peace the United States would not discriminate between those to whom it wished to be just and to those to whom it did not wish to be just.[26] The German High Command responded with a request for an Armistice, which came into effect on 11 November 1918.

Whilst the United States had joined the Allies and forced an end to hostilities, Wilson remained suspicious of their aims. He had learnt of a secret treaty, which had drawn Italy and Romania into the war on the side of the Allies and that there were murmurings amongst the Allies of a punitive peace. Wilson saw his mission as securing the genuine peace of the world. As far back as September 1917, he had set up a committee to formulate the United States' aims for peace.[27] He received a memorandum from them on 18 December 1917.[28] It was on the basis of this document that he began secretly to prepare his famous Fourteen Points for a lasting peace. On 8 January 1918, he revealed them to Congress. He had made no attempt to consult his European Allies.

The preamble declared that the day of conquest and aggrandisement was gone; so were secret covenants. The United States demanded that the world be made safe for every peace loving nation that wishes to live its own life and determine its own institutions. Point I called for open covenants of peace, openly arrived at. Point II called for absolute freedom of navigation upon the seas outside territorial waters alike in peace and war, except the seas might be closed in whole or in part by international action for the enforcement of international covenants. Point III called for removal of all economic barriers to equality of trade. Point IV called for adequate guarantees that national armaments would be reduced to the lowest point consistent with domestic safety. Point V required a free, open-minded and absolutely impartial adjustment of colonial claims, based upon a strict observance of the principle that in determining all such questions of sovereignty, the interests of the populations concerned must have equal right with the equitable claims of the government whose right is to be determined. Points VI to XIII dealt with specific problems of sovereignty in Europe. German troops were to be evacuated from Russia and Belgium, which should have its sovereignty restored. Likewise German soldiers should quit France and Alsace and Lorraine (taken from France by Germany in 1870) should be restored to France. The peoples of the Austro-Hungarian Empire should be accorded the freest opportunity

---

[24] See Thompson above n 7, 153.
[25] ibid, 153.
[26] ibid, 174.
[27] ibid, 161; *PWW* above n 21, 44: 220–21.
[28] ibid 45: 550–59.

for autonomous development. In particular Romania, Serbia and Montenegro were to be freed. Non-Turkish peoples under the control of the Ottoman Empire were to have the opportunity of autonomy. An independent Polish state would be formed with access to the sea. Point XIV provided that 'a general association of nations must be formed under specific covenants for the purpose of affording mutual guarantees of political independence and territorial integrity to great and small states alike.'

Within this idealistic document three principal strands appear: that diplomacy should be open; that the peoples of the world should be enabled to determine their own sovereignty; and that there should be an international League of Nations. These ideas ran counter to such existing ideas as secret diplomacy, empire and national freedom of action. Nevertheless, the ecstatic send off he received when he sailed from New York on 4 December 1918 and the welcoming crowds in Brest and Paris,[29] must have encouraged Wilson to think that he was engaged on a mission that would save the world. Although the Republican opposition had supported the war and Wilson's vision of a League of Nations, he did not invite a single member of that party to join his delegation, which was to prove a mistake.[30] He was obviously aware of possible antagonisms between the Allies. During the war, the United States called itself an associate of the Allies rather than an ally.[31] The American party were instructed not give any impression of a special relationship with Britain, though they did work closely with them in Paris.

Neither autonomy established by the will of the people, nor an international league to preserve peace were original ideas. The American Revolution was the prime example of a people establishing a government independent of their former masters. That American independence was not the unanimous idea of the American people is evidenced by the fact that a good number fought on the British side in the Revolutionary War. When South American states began to achieve independence from the European empires of Spain and Portugal, President Monroe produced a formula in 1823, which warned that any attempt to colonise or re-colonise these countries would be regarded by the United States as an act of aggression against itself. The idea that subject states in empires should determine their own fate was entirely foreign to the European powers, whose self-interest lay in maintaining and even increasing their empires.

As for a League of Nations, in 1795 Immanuel Kant had written a pamphlet entitled *Perpetual Peace—a Philosophical Sketch*, which envisaged nation states rationally accepting a peaceful world order, though this did not involve any international body policing its aims. The Concert of Europe sought after the Napoleonic Wars to establish a balance of power between the European states, but this led to secret treaties and mutual guarantees, which were seen in the end to have led to the disastrous 1914-18 war. This was the first war where the

---

[29] Margaret MacMillan, *Peacemakers: Six Months that Changed the World: The Paris Peace Conference of 1919 and Its Attempt to End War* (London, John Murray, 2003).
[30] ibid, 14.
[31] ibid.

antagonists used the fruits of industrialisation to annihilate vast numbers of young men. Unsurprisingly it led to peace movements. In the autumn of 1914 an English political scientist called Dickinson and a former British Ambassador to the United States, Lord Bryce, formed a peace league and coined the phrase League of Nations. An organisation called a League to Enforce Peace with similar aims was formed in the United States. In early 1915 when the Germans objected to the British blockade of her ports, the English Foreign Secretary, Sir Edward Grey, wrote that if

> Germany would enter some League of Nations where she would give and accept the same security that other nations gave and accepted rules against war breaking out between them, their expenditures on armaments might be reduced and new rules to secure freedom of the seas made.[32]

Wilson was cherry picking ideas of others, but their adoption by a President of the United States gave them a currency and weight they had hitherto lacked.

In 1916 Wilson had tried to inspire an audience of salesmen with 'the thought that you are Americans and are meant to carry liberty and justice and the principles of humanity where ever you go.'[33] He approached peace negotiations in 1918 from a moral high ground. He told a journalist that the peace was not to be one of loot or spoliation.[34] On the boat to France, he stated he sought peace, not victory.[35] He was soon to find that the Alliance of European nations, which had finally won the war, were in no mood to be lectured to by the idealistic leader of a nation, which had only fought for a few months. Their financial position was in stark contrast to that of America, where business had boomed on the back of armaments sold to the Allies. At the beginning of the war, the United States had a net debt of 3.7 billion dollars; after the war they had a credit of about the same amount.[36] A good deal of the armaments purchased by Britain and its allies had been on the back of loans from the United States government. The Secretary to the United States Treasury wrote to Wilson expressing grave concern about the possibility of debts by the Allies being reduced.[37] The moral high ground was likely to be windswept.

Proceedings at the Peace Conference in Paris started with a meeting of the leaders of Britain, France, the United States, Italy and Japan and their Foreign Secretaries. These were to be the five nations which formed a Supreme Council to decide on the content of the treaty; others with interests had to make application to it. Delegates quickly agreed that the creation of a League of Nations would be dealt with as part of the eventual treaty. Wilson was appointed chairman of a committee to establish a constitution. He did not want one which gave specific powers in specific situations, but simply mutual guarantees of political

---

[32] Floyd above n 9, 137.

[33] NG Levin, *Woodrow Wilson and World Politics: America's Response to War and Revolution* (New York, Oxford University Press USA, 1968) vii 18.

[34] See Thompson above n 7, 190; *PWW* above n 21, 51: 372.

[35] Thompson above n 7, 193.

[36] ibid, 190.

[37] Cited ibid, 192; *PWW* above n 21, 53: 441–42.

independence and territorial integrity. He wanted the methods by which these guarantees were enforced to grow organically in the manner that the common law in England had evolved.[38] He was reluctant in any event to commit United States' forces to actions commanded by the League, because this was likely to provoke opposition at home.[39] Eventually clause 10 of the Peace Treaty provided that

> the Members of the League undertake to respect and observe against external aggression the territorial integrity and existing political independence of all Members of the League. In case of any such aggression the Council [of the League] shall advise upon the means by which this obligation shall be fulfilled.

Despite this initial agreement, it soon became clear that the European Allies had different agendas between themselves and also with the United States. Georges Clemenceau, the French Prime Minister, still saw the old European balance of power as the best way of securing peace, provided German power was destroyed.[40] He made it clear that France required Germany to pay for the damage done to his country and people; for him a peace had to be punitive.[41] There were precedents for this; in 1815, at the end of the Napoleonic Wars, France had been required to pay reparations to the various Allies who had defeated them and in 1871 Germany had required France to pay them for the cost of their war against France.[42] The French demanded not only that their former provinces of Alsace/Lorraine be returned, but also that they would be allowed to annex the Saar region to the east of the Rhine, with its coal mines and heavy industry, to compensate for the German destruction of their French counterparts. This was in flat contradiction to the generous peace which Wilson sought. It was, however, understandable—France had not only suffered huge human losses and injury, but had endured a lengthy occupation of a large swathe of its territory. Britain had suffered great human loss and economic loss, but it not been occupied; it did not seek European territory, but insisted on Germany funding pensions for the families of those killed and for the injured. In any event, Britain had achieved one of its principal aims—the capture of the German fleet, which had sailed from Kiel to Scapa Flow off the north of Scotland, where it remained with its German crews still on board.[43] Italy wanted to annex the German-speaking south Tyrol to give it a secure border in the Alps—there was a pre-existing obligation under the Treaty of London in 1915, which preceded Italy's entry into the war, that South Tyrol would be ceded to Italy after the war. Italy also wanted a large swathe of territory down the eastern Adriatic, including

---

[38] Thompson above n 7, 198–99; *PWW* above n 21, 47: 198–99.
[39] Thompson above n 7, 200.
[40] MacMillan above n 29, 30.
[41] Generally for an account of the peace negotiations see MacMillan above n 29, and Heckscher above n 1, 513–62.
[42] See MacMillan above n 29, 201.
[43] MacMillan above n 29, 50 and 167–68.

part of Istria and Dalmatia.[44] These were also coveted by Serbia, now part of a larger Yugoslavia.[45] A re-created Poland wanted a much enlarged state.[46]

If this did not make matters difficult enough, there were three Empires to be dismantled—the German, Austro Hungarian and Ottoman; together these covered large areas of Europe, the Middle East and Africa and were viewed with covetous eyes. France wanted to extend its influence in North Africa and both England and France to do so in the Middle East.[47] They made a secret deal to divide the old Ottoman Empire in the Middle East effectively between their two interests.[48] Britain had its eye on German East Africa and South Africa on German South West Africa, Italy on Somalia.[49] Much further east the Japanese (who had joined the allied cause) wanted to annex German concessions in China[50] and Australia and New Zealand (who had supplied many soldiers, who died or were injured) wanted to annex various islands in the Pacific.[51] This is a brief and incomplete summary of the territorial ambitions of the European nations, sufficient to show they were the antithesis of Wilson's doctrine of self-determination. The French saw annexation as a way of spreading civilisation, notably their own.[52] Wilson was opposed to any form of annexation or colonisation.[53] Many of those attending the Peace Conference must have thought the process would be simple, but in reality it was unworkable. It was an ambitious attempt to settle peace worldwide. Competing interests inevitably meant that compromises had to be made. The eventual treaty contained 440 clauses.

If self-determination seemed a beautiful idea, practical problems about securing it became apparent. Some plebiscites were held in Europe. In 1920, one was held in Schleswig Holstein, an area between Germany and Denmark; the southern area voted to be part of Germany and the northern area to be part of Denmark, and the area accordingly divided. Poland had already declared its independence and there was a general desire on the part of the principal Allies to support her and give her access to the Baltic sea.[54] This was to be done by creating a Polish corridor along the river Vistula to the port of Danzig. The original plan was amended by reducing the size of the corridor and making Danzig a free rather than a Polish port. The recreated Polish state was largely Catholic and a mainly protestant area originally in the corridor, called Allenstein, voted to remain in East Prussia. Upper Silesia was a large source of coal to Germany, but a plebiscite resulted in its division into two halves, one going to Poland and

[44] ibid, 120.
[45] ibid, ch 9.
[46] ibid, 227 et seq.
[47] ibid, 397 et seq.
[48] ibid, 107.
[49] ibid.
[50] ibid, 320 and 456.
[51] ibid, 112.
[52] ibid, 39.
[53] ibid, 107.
[54] ibid, 227–32.

the other to Germany. The new Yugoslavia and Romania both laid claim to a prosperous farming area on the Banat plain between their two countries and as the result of a plebiscite it was divided between the two. One was also held in Carinthia, resulting in its division between Yugoslavia and Austria.[55]

Other decisions were made unilaterally. Wilson supported the return of Alsace-Lorraine to France, but opposed any transfer of sovereignty of territory east of the Rhine; in the end a compromise was reached allowing the French to control the output of the coal mines in the Saar valley for 15 years. When a plebiscite was taken in the Saar in 1935, its inhabitants voted by an overwhelming majority to be part of Germany.[56] Wilson, in the end, compromised on Italy's claims and agreed to the South Tyrol becoming part of her territory. Her claims to the Istrian coast were largely granted and her claim to the port of Fiume apparently solved by making it a Free City.[57] Czechoslovakia was given large areas of the former Austro-Hungarian Empire, including the largely German-speaking Sudetenland.

The real problem with the division of European territory, was that the two countries not to be given a voice in their future were Germany and Austria. Large German populations were left under foreign control. There were three million German speakers in the Sudetenland;[58] the provision of a Polish corridor through East Prussia left nearly two million under Polish control;[59] a quarter of a million Austrians in South Tyrol found themselves now Italians.[60] In all Germany lost about 13 per cent of its territory and 10 per cent of its population.[61] On top of all this, Germany and Austria were forbidden to unite[62] and the Commission created to fix the amount of reparation did so at a value equal to six and a half million pounds.[63] In fact in the end Germany paid only just over a million pounds.[64] The Germans, who had sought an armistice on the back of Wilson's promise of a just peace felt betrayed. German naval officers, still in charge of their vessels at Scapa Flow, scuppered their fleet. The Nazi Party were subsequently able to rise to power on the portrayal of an unjust peace and march into the Sudetenland, Poland and eventually Austria.

Wilson sought to head off the European Allies' desire to annex portions of the old Empires by adopting the idea of a mandate suggested by the South African Prime Minster, General Smuts. This placed former colonies not yet ready for self-government under the mandate (or command) of protecting powers.[65] The protecting powers, however, were placed under an obligation to advance

[55] ibid, 262.
[56] ibid, 212.
[57] ibid, 300.
[58] ibid, 147.
[59] ibid, 227.
[60] ibid, 300.
[61] ibid, 495.
[62] ibid, 490.
[63] ibid, 203.
[64] ibid, 490.
[65] ibid, 94 et seq.

the mandate to the point where the mandated nation achieved independence. This plan was adopted by the Peace Conference and incorporated in the Peace Treaty.[66] Thus the former German South West Africa was placed under a mandate in favour of South Africa and Palestine under a British mandate. France initially opposed the idea of mandates, particularly because it was concerned that it would not be able to recruit troops from mandated territories. Wilson and Lloyd George assured the French they would be able to do so and the French accepted mandates of Togoland and Cameroon.

Britain and France had been planning during the war, without consultation, to divide the Middle East into separate spheres of influence. A Declaration was made in 1915 in the name of the British Foreign Secretary, Arthur Balfour, that a homeland would be provided for Jews in Palestine—he expressed the view that the Arabs would not resist the appropriation of this little notch of territory, though there were 700,000 of them in Palestine.[67] There was some competition between France and Britain for the Palestinian mandate, but British forces had taken Palestine from the Turks and were awarded it. The French obtained influence in another slice of trouble, Syria and Lebanon. Another example of a cavalier approach to indigenous minorities can be seen in the creation of modern Iraq. Areas around Mosul, Baghdad and Basra were lumped together, regardless of the fact that the area had populations which were half Shia and a quarter Sunni, who were bitterly antagonistic.[68] Prince Faisal was installed as a King who would need British protection. These are all names that have become chillingly familiar.

The economist, John Maynard Keynes, was part of the English delegation to the peace conference. In 1919 he published *The Economic Consequences of the Peace*, in which he savagely attacked the Allies for their lack of foresight that a punitive peace would lead to further conflict. He was equally unimpressed by Woodrow Wilson:

> When it came to practice his ideas were nebulous and incomplete. He had no plan, no scheme, no constructive ideas whatever for clothing with the flesh of life the commandments which he had thundered from the White House. He could have preached a sermon on any of them or addressed a stately prayer to the Almighty for their fulfilment; but he could not frame their concrete application to the state of Europe.

Keynes obviously detected Wilson's Presbyterian background. He did, however, confirm that Wilson's opinion that a magnanimous peace was most likely to result in an ordered future was right.

Negotiations leading up to a draft treaty took nearly six months and the Treaty of Versailles was not presented to the Germans until 7 May 1919. They had taken no part in the negotiations and, although they delayed to the eleventh hour had no alternative but to sign, which they did humiliatingly in Louis XIV's Hall of Mirrors in Versailles. The whole process had been wearing and Wilson

[66] See Thompson above n 7, 202.
[67] MacMillan above n 29, 432.
[68] ibid, 395 et seq.

now took the stance there could be no amendment to the Treaty.[69] Under the Constitution of the United States, no treaty was binding unless approved by a two-thirds majority of both Houses. The 1918 mid-term elections in the United States had given the Republicans a majority in both Houses of Congress. Their leader, Theodore Roosevelt, denounced Clause 10 of the Treaty, establishing the League of Nations, as an unconditional surrender by the President. Roosevelt died on 19 January 1919 and was succeeded as Republican leader by Henry Cabot Lodge, but he too sought to amend many of the clauses of the Treaty. In the summer of 1919 Wilson toured the country trying to drum up support for ratification, but this did nothing to assuage the Republicans. They put forward an amendment to Clause 10 whereby the involvement of United States troops under the banner of the League could only take place with an act or resolution of Congress approving it.[70] In the end, however, Congress rejected the treaty altogether in November 1919. In the 1920 Presidential election the Republican ticket of Harding and Coolidge defeated the Democrats Cox and Franklin Roosevelt. The United States did not become a member of the League of Nations.

On 20 January 1920, shortly after Wilson's presidency ended, a League of Nations dedicated to the prevention of war through collective security came into being without American participation. Wilson was by then a sick man and he died on 3 February 1924. His highly principled views had failed to convince a majority of his countrymen or the European powers. A League of Nations without the backing of the United States was probably bound to fail and proved unable to prevent the aggression of the Axis powers in 1939.

At this point it might reasonably be asked 'what did Woodrow Wilson do to make America; had his efforts not ended largely in failure?' If his ideas of a magnanimous peace and self-determination did not gain acceptance at Versailles, their wisdom was nevertheless recognised at the end of the Second World War; by 1945 Germany was wrecked and the Marshall (no relation of John, but a Second War General) Plan contributed hugely to the re-development of a strong German State. After defeat in war, Germany achieved much of what she had sought in the economic miracle that placed her in a powerful position in the post-war world. She now had a truly democratic government. The League of Nations was replaced in 1946 by the United Nations, of which the United States was a member and provided a headquarters in New York.

It is ironic that the phrase self-determination derives from the German *Selbstbestimmungsrecht*, a principle which was deployed in support of the unification of Germany from its many principalities. Wilson's vision of a new peaceful order is reflected in the United Nations Charter. One of its purposes and principles stated in Article 1 is the development of 'friendly relations among nations based on respect for the principle of equal rights and self-determination of peoples.' On 14 December 1960 the General Assembly of the United Nations adopted Resolution 1514 (XV) which granted the right to colonial peoples

---

[69] ibid, 211.
[70] ibid, 234.

to determine their own sovereignty. This has led to the dismantling of the old European Empires and the creation of many independent nations. If the United Nations is seen only to have had partial success, if self-determination has often been distorted and exploited, if the conduct of newly created nations has led to corruption, it is nevertheless reasonable to suggest that Wilson's Fourteen Points have had a considerable impact upon relations between states in the twenty-first century and for the better.

What is clear is that President Wilson played a pivotal role in the United States becoming leading player on the world stage. He started his presidency adopting the principle of American neutrality. Events forced a change of view. Although he was able to take American public opinion with him part of the way, it was wary of going the whole way. It took the Japanese bombing of Pearl Harbor to bring the United States into the Second World War and permanently onto the world stage. Its progession from isolation remains the legacy of a man who saw further than his contemporaries, but also a man who built on the traditions of his revolutionary forbears.

18

Legal Dynamism: Oliver Wendell Holmes Junior and Louis Brandeis

OLIVER WENDELL HOLMES Junior took his seat as a Justice of the Supreme Court of the United States in 1902; **Louis Brandeis** joined him there in 1916. Holmes retired in 1932 and Brandeis in 1939. They became known as the great dissenters, frequently finding their 'progressive' views opposed to those of their colleagues. Nevertheless, these views strongly influenced later Supreme Court decisions.

Given the role of the Supreme Court defined under Chief Justice Marshall, it is not surprising that it came to play a decisive role in the legal and social development of the United States. To highlight particular justices from the many who have contributed to this process is inevitably invidious; all that is attempted here is an illustration of how personal factors may influence the opinions of the Court. Though Holmes and Brandeis frequently joined judicial forces, they were different personalities; Holmes was the more academic, philosophical, Brandeis the fact cruncher. The Holmes family were of Scottish and English Presbyterian background, though Oliver developed an interest in Unitarianism.[1] He was born in 1841, by which time his family were part of upper class Boston society—his father (also Oliver) was a physician, but also a noted writer, who coined the phrase the 'Boston Brahmins' to describe the social and literary set of which he was a part. Oliver junior entered Harvard at the age of 16; his mother, Amelia Jackson, was a fervent abolitionist and in 1861 he withdrew from college to fight in the civil war, taking a commission in the Massachusetts' Volunteers and seeing a great deal of fighting and slaughter. The extent of this disillusioned him and, at the end of his three-year commission, he returned to Harvard and entered the law school. He graduated in 1866 and was admitted to the Boston bar in 1867, developing a very successful practice. He nevertheless retained a strong academic interest, becoming a lecturer in jurisprudence in the Harvard Law School in 1871. He edited Kent's Commentaries on the Law of America. In 1882 he left Harvard to sit as a Justice of the Supreme Court of Massachusetts and in 1902 President Theodore Roosevelt nominated him for a seat on the Supreme Court of the United States.

---

[1] See RKL Collins, *The Fundamental Holmes* (Cambridge, Cambridge University Press, 2010); GE White, *Oliver Wendell Holmes* (Oxford, Oxford University Press, 2006).

The family of Louis Brandeis was of German-Jewish origin; they settled for some years in Prague, before his immediate family emigrated to Louisville, Kentucky in 1848, when there was a considerable German community there.[2] Louis never joined a synagogue or advertised his Jewish origins; he assimilated and saw Jewish values in American democracy.[3] When, however, during the First World War, the idea of a Jewish state in Palestine was mooted, he became a Zionist, organising a Jewish Congress to support democracy in the United States and Jews abroad. He was to become the first Jewish Justice of the Supreme Court. In Louisville his father developed a business as a grain merchant. Louis was born there in 1856. In 1875 he gained entrance to the Harvard Law School—unlike most students he did not have an undergraduate degree, but passed examinations demonstrating knowledge of Blackstone and Latin. Dean Langdell was currently reorganising the syllabus to provide study on a systematic basis.[4] Louis was introduced to Boston society by a well connected fellow student, called Samuel Warren, and was said to have become more Brahmin than the Boston Brahmins.[5] When Warren married, he became annoyed at the way the press intruded and Brandeis and he combined to write an article suggesting there should be a law of privacy, offering protection from prurient curiosity.[6] Brandeis was admitted to the bar in Missouri in 1878 and almost immediately Warren, who had gone to work in Holmes' office, suggested that Louis and he set up in practice together in Boston. They did and Holmes came to the opening of the new firm. They prospered (though Warren left the firm after a few years to attend to family business) and for the next 27 years Brandeis practised law at the Boston bar. He bought a house on Otis Street.

Both Holmes and Brandeis were anglophiles. In 1873 Brandeis's father had closed his business and taken his family on a tour of Europe and later Louis himself went to England and expressed his admiration of English men and women.[7] At the end of his time at Harvard, Holmes travelled to England and met John Stuart Mill.[8] He showed his admiration of English (or at least Irish) women more practically than Brandeis; in 1889, on one of his many visits to England, he met Claire Fitzpatrick, Lady Castletown. They formed a close friendship and met whenever he came to England—he stayed as her guest at the Castletown estate in Ireland. His letters to her were sufficiently affectionate that he asked her to destroy them, but she did not. Holmes also developed a friendship with the English legal historian Frederick Pollock, with whom he likewise corresponded.[9]

In 1880 Holmes was invited by the Lowell Institute to deliver 12 lectures on the common law, in which he explored its English origins and development in

---

[2] See L Baker *Brandeis and Frankfurter* (New York, Harper & Row, 1984); MI Urofsky, *Louis D Brandeis and the Progressive Tradition* (Boston MA, Scott Foresman & Co, 1981).

[3] See Baker ibid, 941 and Urofsky ibid, 90.

[4] Baker above n 2, 23.

[5] Urofsky above n 2, 4.

[6] Baker above n 2, 30.

[7] ibid, 31.

[8] Collins above n 1, 47.

[9] MD Howe (ed), *Holmes—Pollock Letters* (Cambridge MA, Harvard University Press, 1941).

the United States.[10] They were sufficiently successful to be published under the title *Common Law*, which went through many editions. In its opening pages he expressed a philosophical view of the law, which informed his opinions for the rest of his career:

> The life of the law has not been logic: it has been experience. The felt necessities of the time, the prevalent moral and political theories, institutions of public policy, avowed and unconscious, even the prejudices which judges share with their fellow men, have had a good deal more to do than the syllogism in determining the rules by which men should be governed. The law embodies the history of a nation's development through many centuries and it cannot be dealt with as if it contained only the axioms and corollaries of a book of mathematics. In order to know what it is, we must know what it has been and what it tends to become. We must alternately consult history and existing theories of legislation. But the most difficult labor will be to understand the combination of the two into new products at every stage. The substance of the law at any given time pretty nearly corresponds, so far as it goes, with what is then understood to be convenient, but its form and machinery, and the degree to which it is able to work out desired results, depend very much upon its past.[11]

There had been an enormous change in the nature of American society since the Declaration of Independence. Following the Civil War, there was great economic expansion. Jefferson's idea of a nation of small farmers had been overtaken by the growth of large commercial monopolies and a powerful press. Holmes saw a growing imbalance of power, which needed to be addressed. Darwin's *Origin of the Species* had been published in 1859 and Holmes saw the law as evolving to meet new conditions.[12]

Brandeis went even further down this route. His wife had sisters who were members of the American Consumers' Association. In 1907 the Association invited him to argue a case before the Supreme Court about the legality of a statute passed by the Oregon legislature limiting the hours that women could be contracted to work to 10 hours; anyone employing them for longer was liable to a criminal sanction. Carl Muller was a laundry owner, who was convicted of breaking the terms of the statute and his appeal eventually reached the Supreme Court. In England the appellate hearings are conducted orally, with only short written skeleton arguments submitted beforehand. In the United States the advocates submit lengthy written submissions and currently have the right to address the court only for a limited time; the nature of the written brief developed very much from what became known as the *Brandeis brief* in the *Muller* case. In fact two briefs were submitted to the court on behalf of the defendant state of Oregon, one signed by the advocate appointed by the state and Brandeis and the other, much larger brief, signed only by Brandeis. In the earlier case of *Lochner v New York*,[13] the Supreme Court had declared a

---

[10] ibid, 51.
[11] OW Holmes Jr, *Common Law* with introduction by GE White (Cambridge MA, Belknap Press, 2009).
[12] cf White above n 1, 51.
[13] 198 US 45 (1905).

New York law limiting the hours that bakers could work unconstitutional, because it breached a guarantee of freedom of contract under the Fourteenth Amendment. The court relied on the fact that the statute did not involve the safety, morals or welfare of the bakers. The decision was by a five to four majority, Holmes being among the dissentients. Brandeis as an advocate saw a loophole. Male bakers could work whatever hours were required, but arguably female workers were more vulnerable. His personal brief (compiled with the help of the Consumers' Association) was over 100 pages long and packed with information about the experience in the laundry trade in Europe, medical reports on the effect the trade had on workers and a report from the Massachusetts Bureau of Statistics, which stated that laundry work was so fatiguing that few could endure the labour from month to month. The Court unanimously (including Holmes) accepted Brandeis' argument, differentiated the effect work had on women, and confirmed Muller's conviction.

The *Brandeis brief* went beyond evidence put before the lower courts. The English tradition is that evidence upon which judgment is based must be properly part of the court record, either at first instance or on appeal, and only exceptionally may the court take judicial notice of notorious facts without further evidence. Once he was appointed a member of the Supreme Court, Brandeis went much further than this. In *Jay Burns Bakery v Bryan* in 1924 counsel for the appellant argued that a Nebraska State law, prescribing minimum and maximum weights for loaves of bread, was unconstitutional.[14] The majority of the Justices held that the prescription for a maximum weight was not reasonably related to any need to prevent short weights of loaves and so was unconstitutional. Brandeis delivered a dissenting judgment, in which Holmes concurred, upholding the state's right to regulate commerce. In the course of his judgment, Brandeis relied upon data from other states showing the beneficial effect of similar laws.

> Much evidence referred to by me is not in the record, nor could it have been included. It is the history of the experience gained under similar legislation … the Court should acquire knowledge, and must, in my opinion, take judicial notice, whenever required to perform the delicate judicial task here involved.[15]

It becomes obvious why Holmes and Brandeis were called progressives. Brandeis had met Woodrow Wilson in 1912 and was frequently consulted by him in the period leading up to the Wilson Presidency. In 1908 Wilson had written 'living political constitutions must be Darwinian in structure and in practice.'[16] The power Marshall abrogated to the Supreme Court to declare legislative acts unconstitutional gave the opportunity to regulate social behaviour. Judges in all jurisdictions have been labelled as conservative or liberal in varying degrees. In the United States the appointment of judges is often politically motivated,

[14] 264 US 504.
[15] ibid, 514.
[16] W Wilson, *Constitutional Government in America* (New York, Columbia University Press, 1917)

each administration at state or national level appointing judges who seem to be sympathetic to the particular administration's political colours. From 1921 to 1930 the US Supreme Court was presided over by the former President and now Chief Justice, William Taft, and was regarded as a conservative court, which is no doubt why Holmes and Brandeis so frequently dissented. Of course, all argument in the courts of the United States has to be presented within the confines of the Constitution. If Holmes preferred a developing constitution, on a Darwinian model, others favoured the idea of originalism—that interpretation of the Constitution should be confined to establishing the original meaning or intent of the Constitution. The tension between the two approaches resulted sometimes in an uneasy compromise.

Schenck v US in 1919 may be such a case.[17] In delivering the unanimous opinion of the Court, Holmes coined a phrase which has found a place in American culture and even been used as the title to a 1994 spy film—*a clear and present danger*. In question was the provision in the First Amendment forbidding the making of any law abridging freedom of speech. Shortly after the United States entered the First World War, Congress passed the Espionage Act 1917, section 3 of which subjected anyone who obstructed the enlistment of members of the armed services to criminal penalties. When the draft was introduced Schenck, who was secretary to the Socialist Society, circulated some 15,000 copies of a pamphlet alleging that conscription was involuntary servitude and so banned under the Thirteenth Amendment and urging men to resist the draft; amongst other charges he was indicted for conspiracy to breach section 3, convicted and sentenced to 10 years' imprisonment. The Supreme Court affirmed his conviction. Dealing with the suggested breach of the First Amendment Holmes, concurring with the majority, stated:

> [T]he character of every act depends upon the circumstances in which it is done. The most stringent protection of free speech would not protect a man in falsely shouting fire in a theatre and causing panic ... The question in every case is whether the words used are used in such circumstances and are of such a nature as to create a clear and present danger that they will bring about the substantive evils that Congress had a right to prevent. It is a question of proximity and degree. When a nation is at war many things that might be said in time of peace are such a hindrance to its effort that their utterance will not be endured so long as men fight and that no Court could regard them as protected by any constitutional right.[18]

The opinion was delivered on 3 March 1919 and was subjected to academic criticism for its invasion of free speech. Brandeis was also a concurring member of the Court. In October of the same year a similar point came before the Court in *Abrams v US*[19] and the two, concurring in a single dissenting judgment, tried to restrict the clear and present danger test. In August 1918, the American government dispatched two expeditionary forces to Russia, partly to

---

[17] 249 US 47.
[18] ibid, 51.
[19] 250 US 616.

protect arms previously sent to the deposed Tsarist government and partly to intervene against the Bolsheviks. Abrams was one of five men of Russian origin and anarchist persuasion, who distributed pamphlets abusing President Wilson for ordering the expeditions and alleging they were part of a capitalist conspiracy against the Bolsheviks; Americans were urged to give no support to the war effort and strike rather than manufacture munitions. The five men alleged that their convictions for conspiring to breach the Espionage Act itself breached the free speech requirement of the First Amendment. A majority opinion of seven justices applied the clear and present danger test and affirmed the convictions. The dissenting opinion stressed that, under the Espionage Act, the actions of the defendants had to be carried out with intent to cripple or hinder the prosecution of the war; there might be many criticisms of the war effort which had the likely consequence of hindering it, but they would not breach the Act unless that was the proximate motive of a specific act, which was not the case here. This is somewhat unconvincing reasoning, but more important was the view the opinion expressed on freedom of speech:

> The principle of the right to free speech is always the same. It is only the present danger of immediate evil or an intent to bring it about that warrants Congress in setting a limit to the expression of opinion, where private rights are not concerned. Congress certainly cannot forbid all effort to change the mind of the country ... the best test of truth is the power of the thought to get itself accepted in the competition of the market ... That at any rate is the theory of our Constitution. It is an experiment, as all life is an experiment ... we should be eternally vigilant against attempt to check the expression of opinions that we loathe and believe to be fraught with death, unless they so imminently threaten immediate interference with the lawful and pressing purposes of the law that immediate check is required to save the country.[20]

The Schenck test has never been overruled, but it has been 'reworked, redefined, renounced, reconceptualized and revitalized.'[21] Much later in 1978 in *Landmark Communications v Virginia*,[22] the Virginia legislature had passed a law making it a crime to report proceedings before a judicial review commission. The commission was considering the conduct of a judge and the *Virginian Pilot* newspaper revealed his identity. The parent company of the paper was convicted under the state statute and the Supreme Court of Virginia confirmed the conviction. The Supreme Court ruled that the Virginian statute was unconstitutional. Chief Justice Warren Burger delivered the unanimous opinion:

> The Supreme Court of Virginia relied on the 'clear and present danger' test in rejecting Landmark's claim. We question the relevance of that standard here; moreover we cannot accept the mechanical application of the test, which led that court to its conclusion ... properly applied, the test requires a court to make its own inquiry into the imminence and magnitude of the danger said to flow from the particular utterance, and then to balance the character of the evil, as well as its likelihood, against the necessity for free and unfettered expression.[23]

[20] ibid, 628.
[21] Collins above n 1, 'Epilogue: The Long Shadow' at 368.
[22] 435 US 829.
[23] ibid, 843.

The great dissenters also tried to influence the effect of labour law. By the early twentieth century the use of child labour was widespread through the United States. Although national Congress had no right in this context to intervene within an individual state, it did have the power under the 'Commerce Clause' of the Constitution to regulate commerce. In 1916 it passed a statute prohibiting the transportation across state boundaries of goods manufactured with child labour.[24] In *Hammer v Dagenhart* in 1918 the majority in the Supreme Court ruled the statute unconstitutional:[25] Congress's power to regulate interstate traffic only extended to products that were in themselves harmful. Holmes wrote a powerful dissenting judgment arguing that that evil of premature and excessive child labour was preeminently a case for Congress exercising its regulatory powers to the full. In 1941 the Supreme Court in *US v Darby* reversed the decision and adopted Holmes' reasoning.[26]

Through the early twentieth century there was a big increase in union activity in the United States. The Taft court regularly restricted its legality and Holmes and Brandeis dissented. In 1917 in *The Hitchman Coal and Coke Company v Mitchell* a union had organised a number of strikes at the Hitchman mines.[27] The company then insisted on clauses in contracts of employment that employees should not be members of a union. A union official went to the mines and recruited employees as members of the union. The company sought an injunction to restrain such activity. The majority in the Supreme Court held they were entitled to one. 'The same liberty which enables men to form unions ... entitles other men to remain independent of the union and other employers to agree with them to employ no man who owes any allegiance or obligation to the union.'[28] Brandeis delivered a dissenting opinion that it was not permissible to coerce a potential employee into non-union employment. Holmes and Brandeis also failed to stop the Court outlawing secondary picketing.[29]

They also intervened in law and order issues. In *Ziang Sung Wan v US* in 1924 a man suspected of murder was taken into custody when he was already sick.[30] He was held without arrest for eight days and continually questioned. On the ninth day he was arrested. Eventually he signed a confession, though a doctor who saw him shortly after stated that he was in pain and vomiting and would not have known what he was signing. The Supreme Court, in a unanimous opinion delivered by Brandeis, ruled that the confession should not have been admitted in evidence and quashed the conviction. Brandeis was not so successful in *Olmstead v US* in 1924.[31] In the prohibition era, Olmstead was a bootlegger or dealer in prohibited liquor, who used a telephone booth to arrange his illegal

---

[24] Baker above n 2, 198.
[25] 247 US 251.
[26] 312 US 100.
[27] 245 US 229.
[28] ibid, 230.
[29] *Truax v Corrigan* 257 US 312; *Duplex Printing Co v Deering* 254 US 443.
[30] 266 US 1.
[31] 277 US 438.

deliveries; the Federal Bureau of Investigation tapped the phone. The Fourth Amendment protected citizens from unreasonable searches and seizures and the Fifth from self-incrimination. The majority opinion upheld his conviction following English authorities which stated that evidence illegally obtained could nevertheless be admitted in evidence. Brandeis in a dissenting judgment, harking back to his earlier interest in privacy, ruled that the phone tapping was in breach of the Constitution:

> Decency, security and liberty alike demand that government officials shall be subject to the same rules of conduct that are commands to the citizen. In a government of laws, existence of the government will be imperiled ... if the Government becomes a lawbreaker; it breeds contempt for the law.[32]

Holmes in a separate judgment said 'I think it is a less evil that some criminals should escape than that the government should play an ignoble part.'[33] In 1967 a later court effectively overruled the majority decision in *Olmstead* in *Katz v US*.[34] Katz was an illegal gambler whose phone was tapped and the Supreme Court now held that this was a breach of the Fourth and Fifth Amendments. Later, the Foreign Intelligence Surveillance Act 1978 set up a court to oversee surveillance by federal agencies of those suspected of spying on the United States.

Being at the cutting edge of current thought can be a trap. In 1927 both Holmes and Brandeis were on the court which authorised the sterilisation of a young woman said to be an imbecile. The background was that Francis Galton, a cousin to Charles Darwin and in his own right an eminent scientist and statistician, published a book in 1869 entitled *Hereditary Genius*, in which he examined the extent to which eminence was derived from heredity, coining the term 'eugenics' to cover this new area of enquiry. Though concerned with how to improve human intelligence, his book did contain the suggestion that the 'weak' could be housed in celibate monasteries. His ideas spawned great interest, particularly in the United States, where courses in eugenics were established in many academic institutions, some attracting funding from philanthropic foundations supported by the Rothschilds, Carnegie and Kellogg. Improving the human race appeared a good idea, until German scientists and Nazi politicians adopted it with chilling results. In 1906 the Virginia Legislature passed an Act establishing colonies for Epileptics and the Feebleminded and in 1924 a Sterilization Act gave the superintendent of such an institution power to order the sterilisation of an inmate if the superintendent was of the opinion that this was in the best interests of the patient and society. The board of directors of the colony had to approve the decision, with a right of appeal to the Circuit Court of the local county. The Circuit Court of Amherst County ruled that Carrie Buck was 'the probable potential parent of socially inadequate offspring and that she may be sexually sterilized without detriment to her general health.' Carrie

---

[32] ibid, 485.
[33] ibid, 470.
[34] 389 US 347.

appealed to the Supreme Court of Virginia and eventually to the Supreme Court. The short opinion of the Court was delivered by Holmes.[35]

Brendan Wolfe gives an account of the background facts and first instance hearing in the *Encyclopedia of Virginia*.[36] Carrie was the illegitimate daughter of a woman described as a low grade moron, earlier committed to the Amherst colony. Carrie was brought up by foster parents and, at the age of 18, herself produced an illegitimate child, which she said was the result of a rape. It was this birth which caused her foster parents to seek her committal to the same institution. It may be noted that in Britain the Mental Deficiency Act 1913 (replacing the Idiocy Act 1896) provided for similar committals in the case of those who were feebleminded or morally defective and young women were committed to mental institutions on account of their supposed promiscuity. The evidence that Carrie was actually mentally impaired seems to have been rather thin.

The opinion of the Court (delivered by Holmes) simply acted on the finding of the Amherst court that Carrie was feebleminded. The argument on behalf of Carrie was that she was denied due process and protection of the law under the Fourteenth amendment. The argument was rejected:

> We have seen more than once that the public welfare may call upon the best citizens for their lives. It would seem strange if it could not call upon those who already sap the strength of the State for these lesser sacrifices, often not felt to be such by those concerned, in order to prevent our being swamped with incompetence. It is better for all the world if, instead of waiting to execute degenerate offspring for crime or to let them starve for their imbecility, society can prevent those who are manifestly unfit from continuing their kind. The principle that sustains compulsory vaccination is broad enough to cover cutting the Fallopian tubes. Three generations of imbeciles is enough.[37]

---

[35] 274 US 200 (1927).
[36] www.encyclopediavirginia.org, *Buck v Bell*; he does not state his source.
[37] Above n 35, 207.

19

Social Intervention: Earl Warren

IN AUGUST 1908 there were serious race riots in Springfield, Illinois, in which a white mob killed a number of black Americans. Horrified by such violence, a largely white group formed the National Association for the Advancement of Colored People (NAACP) and announced its formation on the centenary of Lincoln's birth. Its programme to eliminate racial discrimination initially had a slow effect, but the Second World War, in which blacks and whites both served in the Armed forces, proved a catalyst; reformers turned to the Supreme Court, which in a series of landmark cases changed the legal framework governing relations between blacks and whites. *Oliver Brown v Board of Education of Topeka* was initially argued in 1952 before a court presided over by Chief Justice Vinson; the Justices were at this stage divided and Vinson persuaded them to order it be reargued.[1] Before that could happen, two important events occurred: Dwight Eisenhower was elected Republican President and Vinson died. Eisenhower had earmarked **Earl Warren** for the Supreme Court, but only after a period as Solicitor General. In October 1953, however, the President made a recess appointment of Earl Warren to the Court and he heard the reargument in *Brown* in December of that year; his appointment as Chief Justice was approved by the Senate in March 1954. On 17 May 1954 he delivered the unanimous opinion of the Court declaring the segregation of black and white pupils in public schools unconstitutional. This was the first opinion of his tenure and the beginning of the 'Warren court'. The term was originally coined by critics, who felt the Supreme Court under his leadership too liberal. In his *Memoirs*[2] Warren wrote:

> Directly after *Brown* Southern congressmen signed and introduced into the Congressional Record the so called Southern Manifesto, pledging they would use every means at their command to overcome *Brown* and several of them personally told me that I had stabbed them in the back.[3]

MJ Horowitz in *The Warren Court and the Pursuit of Justice* described the court over which Warren presided as 'having initiated a unique and revolutionary chapter in American constitutional history, a constitutional revolution.'[4]

---

[1] 347 US 483.
[2] E Warren, *Memoirs of Earl Warren* (Garden City NY, Doubleday, 1977).
[3] ibid, 4.
[4] MJ Horowitz, *The Warren Court and the Pursuit of Justice* (New York, Hill and Wang, 1998) 3.

On the face of it, Warren was an unlikely candidate for Chief Justice and an even more unlikely candidate to head a liberal court. At the time of his appointment, he had never held any judicial office and had not been in a courtroom for over 20 years. When he was sworn in he had to borrow judicial robes, which were too big for him.[5] His eight brethren were all Democratic appointees. Warren was not only the first Republican appointee for many years, but appeared to have a conservative record. As a law officer in California he had gained a reputation for taking a tough line on crime and labour organisation. He had criticised some of Roosevelt's New Deal legislation. He had been a member of the Natural Sons of the West, which had an anti-Asian reputation, and he supported internment of American nationals of Japanese descent after Pearl Harbor.[6] He also supported eugenic sterilisation. There was, however, another side to him. His record as longtime Governor of California showed a concern for the disadvantaged. He had created a modern hospital service, improved prisons, increased old age pensions and unemployment benefit. He had improved police procedures; alongside being tough on crime, he was convinced that the police should behave fairly. He rejected the view that he had changed his ideas over time, though he did express regret at his support of the internment of citizens of Japanese origin.[7] So far as the opinion of the Court in *Brown* was concerned, he wrote that he never gave a second thought to his decision to support desegregation:

> I had been reared in California, had attended public schools and the University of California and had sat in classroom with blacks and members of almost every minority group ... The real credit for achieving unanimity, in my opinion, should go to those Justices who were born and reared in that part of the nation where segregation was a way of life and where everyone knew the greatest emotional opposition to the decision would be forthcoming.[8]

The Court over which he was to preside was divided in judicial approach, in particular between Justices Frankfurter and Jackson on the one hand and Douglas and Black on the other. Frankfurter was in favour of judicial restraint, that is leaving matters concerning policy to the legislature. The Supreme Court in the 1920s and 1930s had declared some of President Roosevelt's New Deal legislation unconstitutional. Frankfurter, who was a supporter of Roosevelt, felt that the Court had exceeded its proper role—a statute should only be struck down when its terms were so outside the limits of supportable judgment as to constitute disregard of reason.[9] Jackson, though siding with Frankfurter, had a more limited agenda; he agreed that the Supreme Court should not intervene in legislation aimed at economic regulation, but in other areas, such as due process and equal protection under the Constitution, he felt it could intervene.[10]

---

[5] M Belknap, *The Supreme Court Under Earl Warren* (Columbia SC, The University of South Carolina, 2005) 1.

[6] ibid, 4 and 30.

[7] Warren above n 2, 4 and 149.

[8] ibid, 4; the southern Justices were Black (Alabama), Reed (Kentucky) and Clark (Texas).

[9] ibid, 14.

[10] ibid, 15.

In general terms, Black and Douglas believed the court had an obligation to declare unconstitutional Acts which penalised the disadvantaged. In addition to these philosophical differences, there was personal antagonism between Frankfurter and some of his brethren, who regarded him as arrogant; he had a sharp tongue and was reported as saying that the death of Vinson was the first evidence he had seen that there was a God.[11] To this fractious court, Warren brought great political skill.

He was born in California in 1891, the son of Norwegian and Swedish immigrants. He read political science and then graduated in law from Berkeley University and was admitted to the California bar in 1917. After a period of private practice he was chosen as District Attorney for Alameda County in California in 1925 and made State Attorney General in 1938. In private life he was a prominent Freemason, becoming Grand Master for California in 1935. In 1942 he was elected Governor of California, serving in all for three terms.

Warren was not a man for the academic approach. He made up his mind what the right decision was and then often left the writing of the opinion to his law clerks (these were usually young men who had distinguished themselves in the top law schools).[12] Now, however, he wrote and delivered the opinion of the Court in *Brown*. The hearings consolidated cases from four states—Kansas, South Carolina, Virginia and Delaware—where black children were not allowed to enrol in schools attended by white children, but were educated in separate schools provided by the state. Oliver Brown was the father of a black boy, who with other parents appealed decisions of District Courts, which had refused to rule that segregated education was a breach of the Fourteenth Amendment. On his behalf it was alleged that segregated schools were not equal. In fact, the Board of Education of Topeka had already adopted a policy of gradual deseg-regation and did not appear before the Court; briefs were, however, put in by the states involved in opposing the appeal. Lower courts had relied on *Plessy v Ferguson*,[13] where the Supreme Court had ruled in 1896 that equal but sepa-rate facilities on public transport were lawful.[14] The NAACP had put in an *amicus* brief in *Brown* inviting the Court to overrule *Plessy*. When the case was first considered by Vinson's court, there was a reluctance to do so.[15] The case was set down for re-argument and the Justice Department was asked to submit a brief and, despite some reluctance from President Eisenhower, the Attorney General accepted that segregation was unconstitutional. There remained doubts among the Justices as to the effect any opinion against segregation might have in the southern states. Some doubted presciently whether it would be enforceable. Warren, however, was clear that segregation was unconstitutional and, after a good deal of cajoling, even arm twisting, he achieved a unanimous court.[16]

---

[11] ibid, 26.
[12] ibid, 21.
[13] 163 US 537.
[14] See above ch 16.
[15] Belknap above n 29.
[16] ibid 32–34.

In departing from the decision in *Plessy*, the Court's opinion relied on the marked changes in American society since the 1890s when

in the South, the movement toward free common schools, supported by general taxation, had not yet taken hold. Education of white children was largely in the hands of private groups. Education of Negroes was almost nonexistent, and practically all of the race were illiterate. In fact, any education of Negroes was forbidden by law in some states. Today, in contrast, many Negroes have achieved outstanding success in the arts and sciences, as well as in the business and professional world ... Even in the North, the conditions of public education did not approximate those existing today ...[17]

Today, education is perhaps the most important function of state and local governments. Compulsory school attendance laws and the great expenditures for education both demonstrate our recognition of the importance of education to our democratic society ... We come then to the question presented: does segregation of children in public schools solely on the basis of race, even though the physical facilities and other 'tangible' factors may be equal, deprive the children of the minority group of equal educational opportunities? We believe that it does ... to separate them from others of similar age and qualifications, solely because of their race generates a feeling of inferiority as to their status in the community that may affect their hearts and minds in a way unlikely to be undone ...[18]

We conclude that, in the field of education, the doctrine of 'separate but equal' has no place. Separate educational facilities are inherently unequal.[19]

The segregation of children in schools on the basis of racial origin was a breach of the Fourteenth Amendment.

The decision was not universally accepted. It became clear that education authorities in some southern states were ignoring the decision or only implementing it slowly. The earlier opinion of the Court gave no guidance on how desegregation should be implemented and on 31 May 1955 the Court issued an Implementation Decree.[20] This gave local courts some latitude in requiring the orderly elimination of segregation; school boards could be given time to effect it, provided they made a prompt and reasonable start.

Popular opposition continued; when nine black students were enrolled in 1957 at the High School in Little Rock, Arkansas, a mob prevented their entering the building and it was only after President Eisenhower sent members of the 101st Airborne Division to protect them that they were admitted. The Governor of Arkansas thereupon closed all public schools. In December 1957 the Supreme Court condemned him for acting as if Arkansas was not bound by decisions of the Court and ordered their reopening.[21]

In the wake of *Brown*, the test in *Plessy* was abandoned in relation to public transport. Sarah Keys was an African American serving in the Women's

---

[17] Above n 1, 489.
[18] ibid, 493–94.
[19] ibid, 495.
[20] 349 US 294.
[21] *Faubus v Aaron* 361 US 197.

Army Corps; she travelled in uniform from her base in New Jersey to her home in North Carolina on a bus that was travelling interstate. When she reached Roanoke Rapids in North Carolina, a new driver required her to move from a seat reserved for white people. She refused, was arrested, kept in custody for several hours and fined $25. Her father contacted the NAACP who filed a complaint on her behalf with the Interstate Commerce Commission. In November 1955 they upheld her complaint and six days later Rosa Parks refused to move from her seat on a segregated bus in Montgomery, Alabama. The following year the Supreme Court presided over by Warren affirmed that the state legislation in Alabama requiring segregated transportation was unconstitutional.[22]

In 1957 Congress passed a statute establishing equal voting rights regardless of racial origin and in 1964 the Kennedy administration, concerned at the slow progress towards desegregation, prepared a fresh Civil Rights Act, which forbade discrimination on the ground of race, colour, religion or national origin in most public places. It gave the Attorney General power to enforce desegregation in schools. President Kennedy was assassinated before it was passed by Congress, but a strong plea from his successor President Lyndon Johnson secured its later passage. Although an Act of Congress was felt necessary, the Supreme Court had shown the way.

In 1968 problems concerning the constitutionality of statutes passed by Congress in relation to civil rights arose for consideration again by another Court, on which Earl Warren presided, in *Jones v Mayer Co*.[23] By 1871 great concern had been aroused by racial attacks made by the Klu Klux Klan. President Ulysses Grant brought bills before Congress providing for the suspension of *habeas corpus* where necessary to curb racially inspired violence and that anyone depriving a citizen of the United States of any of his rights, immunities or privileges under the Constitution or law was liable to an action for damages or other redress. In the instant case, this provision was considered alongside the provision of the Civil Rights Act, 1866, which provided that all citizens of whatever colour or race had the same right to purchase and lease property as white citizens. In 1965 the petitioner filed a complaint in the District Court for the Eastern District of Missouri that the respondents had refused to sell him a house for the sole reason that he was a Negro. Lower courts held that the 1866 and 1871 Statutes did not apply to private sales. The Supreme Court, reversing them, held that the 1866 Statute barred all racial discrimination, private as well as public, in the sale or rental of property and was a valid exercise of the power of Congress to enforce the Thirteenth Amendment. Justice Stewart, reading the opinion of the Court stated:

> Congress has the power under the Thirteenth Amendment rationally to determine what are the badges and the incidents of slavery, and the authority to translate that determination into effective legislation ...[24]

---

[22] *Browder v Gayle* 352 US 903.
[23] 392 US 409.
[24] ibid, 440.

Negro citizens, North and South, who saw in the Thirteenth Amendment a promise of freedom—freedom to 'go and come and go at pleasure' and to 'buy and sell when they please'—would be left with 'a mere paper guarantee' if Congress were powerless to assure that a dollar in the hands of a Negro will purchase the same thing as a dollar in the hands of a white man.[25]

Whilst Warren had been a tough law enforcer as Attorney General in California, he believed that the criminal law process should be conducted fairly. The Court that has been given his name delivered a number of important opinions in this area, of which the following are simply examples. In *Gideon v Wainwright* Gideon was charged with entering a poolroom in Panama City, Florida and stealing money from vending machines.[26] In Florida this ranked as a felony. He had no funds to pay for a defence attorney and, on being arraigned, he asked for counsel to be assigned to him; this was refused, as under Florida law counsel were only assigned in capital cases, which this was not. He defended himself, was convicted and sentenced to five years' imprisonment; having failed in his application for *habeas corpus* in lower courts, he appealed to the Supreme Court, claiming that his conviction without counsel assigned violated the Sixth Amendment, which provided that 'in all criminal prosecutions the accused shall enjoy the right ... to have the Assistance of Counsel for his defence.' This raised an important constitutional question: the first eight amendments to the Constitution established rights that were binding on federal courts; did they also bind state courts as a result of the Fourteenth Amendment's due process provisions? There had been an earlier decision of the Supreme Court in 1942 in *Betts v Brady* in which it was held that a defendant charged in a state court with robbery did not have a right to representation,[27] but more recently in *Mapp v Ohio*,[28] where police in Cleveland, Ohio, had carried out a forcible search without a warrant and found some pornographic material, the Court had ruled that the protection provided by the Fourth Amendment against unreasonable searches applied in state law by virtue of the Fourteenth Amendment and articles seized illegally were not admissible in evidence.

In *Gideon*, Chief Justice Warren, though a member of the Court, did not deliver the opinion; he was conscious that unlike his fellow justices, he had no judicial experience before his appointment and initially he asked another Justice to chair the conference of the judges before an opinion was formulated; not infrequently he left it to his brethren to write and deliver an opinion. In this case it was delivered by Justice Black, with Warren's concurrence. He expressed the test of whether the Sixth Amendment was applicable in a state court thus: 'is it a denial of fundamental fairness, shocking to the universal sense of justice?' If so it was applicable in a state court by reason of the Fourteenth Amendment. In the case of a trial for felony in a state court, the guarantee in the Sixth Amendment

---

[25] ibid, 443.
[26] 372 US 335.
[27] 316 US 455.
[28] 367 US 643.

of representation by counsel was fundamental and the failure to grant Gideon counsel was unconstitutional. The Court overruled the decision in *Betts*.

Warren did deliver the opinion of the Court in the pivotal case of *Miranda v Arizona* in 1966.[29] It is a decision which demonstrates how English common law came to be deployed in the United States. The hearing involved appeals in four criminal cases where an accused had been interrogated by police, in some instances for lengthy periods, without being told of his right to remain silent or to have legal representation. The Supreme Court held by a majority that none of the convictions in the four cases could be upheld.

The majority opinion Warren delivered traced the origin of the right to silence from seventeenth century English practice. The English criminal courts did not admit evidence from a defendant until 1898 and even then it was voluntary. From the late fifteenth century to 1641, however, the Crown used courts separate from the common law courts to enforce some parts of criminal law, such as criminal conspiracies, and also to secure religious uniformity. These were the prerogative courts of Star Chamber and High Commission. On occasion, they used torture to extract confessions and, if a suspect refused to answer questions, he was subjected to severe physical punishments, such as prolonged whipping or even removal of an ear. For instance, in 1638 John Lilburne published pamphlets proclaiming the rights of freeborn Englishmen and criticising the King. The royal government forbade publishing without a licence from the Stationers' Company and Lilburne had none. The Company reported him to the Star Chamber, which required him to answer whether he had published these pamphlets. He refused to do so and claimed the fundamental right that 'no man's conscience ought to be racked by oaths imposed to answer to questions concerning himself in matters criminal or pretended to be so.' The Star Chamber ordered he be whipped from Fleet Street to Westminster, set in the pillory, fined and imprisoned. These courts understandably became unpopular and in 1641 the so-called Rump of the Long Parliament, controlled by opponents of King Charles I, abolished them. Under the Commonwealth government of Oliver Cromwell, Lilburne appealed to the House of Lords who recognised his right to remain silent and compensated him. As a matter of practice in the English courts, it became established that if a person remained silent when questioned by an investigating authority or in court, that could not be used as evidence against him.

The Fifth Amendment to the United States Constitution provides that 'no person ... shall be compelled in any criminal case to be a witness against himself, nor to be deprived of life, liberty or property, without due process of law.' In *Malloy v Hogan*[30] the court had earlier held the protection of the Fifth Amendment applied in state as well as federal courts, which the Court in the case of *Miranda* affirmed. They now also gave their opinion that the Fifth Amendment applied to police interrogations and that due process included the right on such occasions to be advised by counsel. The opinion reviewed earlier reports

[29] 384 US 436.
[30] 378 US 1.

on police interrogation techniques, which had included beating, hanging and whipping, and pointed out that as recently as 1965 police in King's County, New York State, had beaten and whipped and pressed lighted cigarette butts on the buttocks of a potential witness to compel him to make a statement incriminating a suspect. It also considered manuals currently issued to police interrogators setting out how to place psychological pressure on a suspect to obtain a confession. The Court went on to say:

> Today, then, there can be no doubt that the Fifth Amendment privilege is available outside of criminal court proceedings, and serves to protect persons in all settings in which their freedom of action is curtailed in any significant way from being compelled to incriminate themselves. We have concluded that without proper safeguards, the process of in-custody interrogation of persons suspected or accused of crime contains inherently compelling pressures which work to undermine the individual's will to resist and compel him to speak where he would not otherwise do so freely. In order to combat these pressures and to permit a full opportunity to exercise the privilege against self-incrimination, the accused must be adequately and effectively apprised of his rights, and the exercise of those rights must be fully honored ...[31]

> [W]e hold that an individual held for interrogation must be clearly informed that he has the right to consult with a lawyer and to have the lawyer with him during interrogation under the system for protecting the privilege we delineate today. As with the warning of the right to remain silent and that anything stated can be used in evidence against him, this warning is an absolute prerequisite to interrogation. No amount of circumstantial evidence that the person may have been aware of this right will suffice to stand in its stead. Only through such a warning is there ascertainable assurance that the accused was aware of the right.[32]

The guarantees contained in the Fifth Amendment are effectively embedded in American law. In Great Britain, however, parliament may and has curtailed the right to silence. Under sections 34–37 of the Criminal Justice and Public Order Act 1994 a jury may draw inferences that they consider reasonable from the accused's failure to mention, when questioned by the police, facts upon which he later relies in his defence and from his failure to testify at trial. The jury have to be directed that he still has a right to remain silent, that the burden of proof remains on the prosecution and that silence alone cannot found a conviction. These provisions seem to have stemmed from a conviction that an innocent man has nothing to hide by speaking out. They lead to what is sometimes an uneasy compromise, since the right to remain silent and the drawing of adverse inferences are mutually incompatible.

In the course of the nineteenth and twentieth centuries the demography of the United States changed. Population in some counties increased hugely, whilst the number of candidates they could elect in state elections was based upon much lower census figures.[33] Any attempt to put this right would involve a measure of social engineering. The Alabama Constitution of 1901 provided that the method

---

[31] Above n 29, 467.
[32] ibid, 471–72.
[33] Belknap above n 5, 120.

of apportioning seats in the two houses of the legislature should be by population. Every 10 years there was to be a census, after which such an apportion-
ment should be made. No census had been held in Alabama since 1900 and
there had been considerable shifts in population since then. In August 1961 the
inhabitants of Jefferson County made complaint to their District Court that they
now suffered such serious discrimination in the allocation of seats to votes that
their constitutional rights to equal suffrage in free and equal elections and equal
protection under the law had been breached—in effect they were complaining of
gerrymandering by the State authorities. By the time the complaint was heard,
a quarter of the population of Alabama could elect a majority in the legislature.
The District Court accepted that their constitutional rights had been violated.
In 1964 that decision was argued on appeal to the Supreme Court under the
title *Reynolds v Sims*.[34] Warren delivered the majority opinion. All who voted
in national or state elections had the right to an equal vote apportioned on a
population basis:

> Once the geographical unit for which a representative is to be chosen is designated, all
> who participate in the election are to have an equal vote—whatever their race, what-
> ever their sex and whatever their occupation, whatever their income and wherever
> their home may be in that geographical unit ... the conception of political quality from
> the Declaration of Independence to Lincoln's Gettysburg Address ... can only mean
> one thing—one person one vote.[35]

He went on to assert that 'legislators represent people, not trees or acres.
Legislators are elected by voters, not farms or cities or economic interests.' The
Court would not sanction minority control of state legislatures. A practical
approach was required:

> [T]he Equal Protection clause requires that a State make an honest and good faith
> effort to construct districts in both houses of its legislature, as nearly of equal popu-
> lation as is practicable ... Mathematical exactness or precision is hardly a workable
> constitutional requirement.

The decision of the Warren court which has caused most controversy was *Roe
v Wade* in 1973,[36] because it required the Court to consider two contradictory
emotive propositions—a woman's right to control her body and the right of
her foetus to life. In June 1969 Norma McCorvey, a single woman living in
Dallas County, Texas, found she was pregnant for the third time and tried to
find a doctor to abort her foetus. The Texas Penal Code (dating originally from
1857) made it a criminal offence to procure or attempt to procure an abortion,
except on medical advice to save the life of the mother. Norma's life was not
endangered by her pregnancy. She was referred to two young women attorneys,
recently graduated from the University of Texas Law School, who agreed to help
her. Her child was born, but the attorneys sought a declaration in the federal
courts on her behalf that the provision restricting abortion in the Texas law code

---

[34] 377 US 533; see also *Baker v Carr* 319 US 583.
[35] In fact quoting from an earlier decision of the court in *Gray v Sanders* 372 US 368.
[36] 410 US 113.

was unconstitutional. The case was titled *Roe v Wade* to give her anonymity;[37] Henry Wade was the Attorney General for Dallas County, Texas. The two young attorneys argued the case to and in the Supreme Court, which heard them in December 1970, though the opinion of the Court was not delivered until January 1973, presumably indicating the difficulty and importance of the decision. The Court then declared that the relevant provision of the Texan Criminal Code was unconstitutional.

The majority decision of eight (including Earl Warren) was delivered by Justice Blackmun. The Court noted that state legislation limiting abortions was of relatively recent origin during the nineteenth century. True to the tradition of the *Brandeis brief*, it reviewed the practice of abortion in the Persian Empire and ancient Greece and Rome, and the effect of the Hippocratic oath and English and American common and statute law. It considered reports from the American Medical Association, which seemed polarised on the issue. Crucially, it went on to consider whether there was a right to privacy in the Constitution sufficient to protect a woman's decision to abort, concluding that there was:

> This right of privacy, whether it be founded in the Fourteenth Amendment's concept of personal liberty and restrictions on state action, as we feel it is, or, as the District Court determined, in the Ninth Amendment's reservation of rights to the people, is broad enough to encompass a woman's decision whether or not to terminate her pregnancy. The detriment that the State would impose upon the pregnant woman by denying this choice altogether is apparent. Specific and direct harm medically diagnosable even in early pregnancy may be involved. Maternity, or additional offspring, may force upon the woman a distressful life and future. Psychological harm may be imminent. Mental and physical health may be taxed by childcare. There is also the distress for all concerned, associated with the unwanted child, and there is the problem of bringing a child into a family already unable, psychologically and otherwise, to care for it. In other cases, as in this one, the additional difficulties and continuing stigma of unwed motherhood may be involved. All these are factors the woman and her responsible physician necessarily will consider in consultation.[38]

This did not mean, however, that a woman had an unfettered right to terminate. The state had an interest in ensuring proper medical procedures and in protecting potential life. It was not the intention of those who drafted the Constitution, including its Amendments, to include a foetus in its definition of a person. The Court were unable to find an overriding argument when life should be regarded as commencing, but medical opinion did regard a foetus as viable, in the sense of being able to live outside the womb without independent support, as occurring about the 28th week of pregnancy (though it might occur slightly earlier). Accordingly, for legal purposes they divided the pregnancy notionally into three equal periods, in which the right of the mother was to be treated differently. Because Texas criminal code did not take into account all the interests affecting

---

[37] In medieval English law, parties in certain property actions were given the fictitious names of John/Jane Roe to allow points to be decided effectively on a theoretical basis. The American courts have adopted this device in some instances to afford parties anonymity.

[38] Above n 36, 153.

the different stages in the course of a pregnancy, it did violate the Fourteenth Amendment. The criteria for deciding on a termination or not were:

(a) prior to approximately the end of the first trimester, the abortion decision and its effectuation must be left to the medical judgment of the pregnant woman's attending physician

(b) for the stage subsequent to approximately the end of the first trimester, the State, in promoting its interest in the health of the mother, may, if it chooses, regulate abortion procedure in ways that are reasonably related to maternal health.

(c) for the stage subsequent to viability, the State in promoting its interest in the potentiality of life, may if it chooses, regulate, and even proscribe, abortion except where necessary, in appropriate judgment, for the preservation of the life and health of the mother.[39]

This was a situation where the Court felt, in accordance with its role under the Constitution, able to make a policy decision, rather than leaving it to Congress. The decision was sufficiently controversial to lead to demonstrations by the right to life lobby. Various challenges to it, stimulated by Republican administrations, were made but failed. By 1992 the composition of the Supreme Court had become more conservative and a fresh challenge was mounted. It was widely anticipated that the challenge would succeed; whether it did is considered later.[40]

The Warren Court made many other decisions of note, but those selected perhaps illustrate Wendell Holmes's view that the life of the law is experience.[41]

---

[39] ibid, 164–65.
[40] Below ch 21.
[41] Above ch 18.

20

The President Under the Law: Archibald Cox and Richard Nixon

D URING THE LEAD up to the presidential election of November 1972, the Democratic Party established a campaign office in the Watergate Building in Washington DC. In June of that year, five intruders were arrested inside the building and eventually charged with illegal wiretapping, eavesdropping and theft of documents. Two young reporters on the Washington Post, Carl Bernstein and Bob Woodward, were approached by an anonymous source (subsequently revealed to be William Felt junior, a deputy director in the Federal Bureau of Investigation), who revealed that one of the burglars was associated with the Committee for the Re-Election of President Nixon. The source continued to leak information to the reporters, as an FBI investigation uncovered a paper trail to a slush fund run by the Committee, which had been used to pay the burglars. In the end the trail was to lead to the prosecution of many of those who were part of or associated with the Nixon administration, to impeachment proceedings in Congress against the President and his ultimate resignation.[1]

Richard Nixon was the only President of the United States ever to resign his office; **Archibald Cox** was a Special Prosecutor appointed by the United States' Attorney General to investigate the part played by members of the Nixon administration in the Watergate affair. The two men were contemporaries— Cox born in May 1912 and Nixon in January 1913. Both trained and practised for a time as lawyers. Nixon qualified at Duke University, North Carolina and practiced in California for five years, before military service in the Navy. Cox qualified at Harvard as one of those at the top of his year, worked as a clerk to Learned Hand, Chief Judge of the United States Court of Appeals Second Circuit and then in private practice in Boston. He became expert in labour law and, during the Second World War, worked in a mediation service designed to reduce disputes in industries supplying the war effort. After the war, Nixon devoted himself to Republican politics. He became a Congressman and Senator and then served as Vice-President under Eisenhower. In 1968 he was elected President of the United States and re-elected in 1972. In the early sixties, however, he

---

[1] See K Gormley, *Archibald Cox: Conscience of a Nation* (Cambridge MA, De Capo Press, 1997); J Doyle, *Not Above the Law: The Battles of Watergate Prosecutors Cox and Jaworski: A Behind-the-Scenes Account* (New York, Morrow, 1977).

had lost a presidential election to John F Kennedy and one for governorship of California and this may have caused him to become involved in a campaign of dirty tricks against his political opponents during the 1972 election. It was to cause his downfall.

After the war, Cox became an academic lawyer at Harvard; he specialised in constitutional law and was delivering a lecture on the Warren court when the invitation arrived to act as Special Prosecutor in the Watergate affair. On the face of it he was an odd choice for a Republican Attorney General to make, since he had advised Kennedy's Democratic administration on labour issues. As Solicitor General for four and half years under that administration, he had argued cases on behalf of the government in the Supreme Court, including those concerning civil rights and re-apportionment of votes, but he had no experience as a criminal trial lawyer. It was the insistence of the Senate Judiciary Committee, in confirmation hearings on the nomination of a new Attorney General, that a truly independent investigation of the Watergate affair was essential, that led to his appointment as a special prosecutor. As it turned out, the brief crucially required a constitutional lawyer. Conversations the President had had in the Oval Office with his advisers had been tape recorded; when this was discovered, Cox sought to obtain the tapes by a *subpoena duces tecum* (an order to produce evidence). The President denied involvement in the dirty tricks campaign and claimed executive privilege against disclosing the tapes. The argument on disclosure went all the way to the Supreme Court, which eventually held that the President could not be the sole judge of whether it was appropriate to disclose. He had an executive privilege, but that was subject to bounds, particularly where the evidence he held related to a criminal trial. The President was subject to the law.

Nixon was re-elected President in November 1972, ironically by a landslide majority. The trial of the Watergate intruders commenced in January 1973 in the Federal District Courthouse in Washington DC. Judge John Sirica presided. He usually tried the run of the mill criminal charges heard in any federal district court, far from the constitutional issues this case was to raise. He was the son of an Italian immigrant hairdresser and literally a tough customer, having paid his way through law school by boxing professionally. Some of the defendants pleaded guilty; Gordon Liddy and James McCord fought, but were convicted. The prosecution conducted the trial on a short rein, confined to the facts of the illegal entry and its immediate purpose, but after conviction McCord wrote a letter to the judge alleging that political pressure had been brought on the defendants to plead guilty and that some of the witnesses in the trial had given perjured evidence (something some of them later admitted). Judge Sirica read the letter out in open court. On 30 January 1973 the intruders and some of the organisers of the break-in were sentenced to long prison terms, though in due course they only served a small part of them.

On the 20 January 1973, Nixon was sworn in as President and on 28 April he nominated Elliot Richardson as United States Attorney General. Like other nominations, this had to be approved by the Senate Judiciary Committee. Richardson had been Secretary of State for Defence and was very much a Nixon loyalist. The Judiciary Committee explored how Richardson would investigate the Watergate affair. His intention was to appoint an Assistant Attorney General within the Justice Department to do so, but with responsibility to him. The Committee regarded this as unacceptable and insisted on the appointment of a Special Prosecutor.

At this stage it is necessary to understand something of how the administration of justice in the United States works and in particular the role of Attorney General.[2] The title derives from its English counterpart. Originally it referred to anyone who held a general power of attorney on behalf of another. It then became used to describe the principal legal adviser to the English government. His junior minister is called the Solicitor General. Both are Members of Parliament, but neither are members of the cabinet. The Attorney is head of the English bar. The head of the justice system is the Minister of Justice (he also holds the historic office of Lord Chancellor). He is a member of the cabinet and on occasion speaks for the judiciary. In the United States, on the other hand, the Attorney General *is* a member of the cabinet and head of the Department of Justice. The Solicitor General advises the government and argues before the Supreme Court pleas that concern organs of government. He decides which of these pleas are put before the Court. Cox as Solicitor General under the Kennedy administration argued such cases as *Reynolds v Sims*. Law officers in both countries occupy a curious position; they are ministers and so political, but there are professional and political restraints on their advice—it must be impartial. In the United States, where an investigation involving a member of the government is called for, it is the practice for the Attorney General to appoint a Special Prosecutor (now called an Independent Prosecutor).

In this case, the Judiciary Committee insisted on an undertaking from Richardson that the special prosecutor must be appointed on terms that he could investigate all criminal offences which might have been committed by members of the White House Staff and the President's political appointees and that he could only be dismissed for extraordinary impropriety.[3] Richardson tried to find an experienced trial lawyer, who would be acceptable on a cross-party basis, but the four people he first approached turned the post down. Cox, when approached, was willing, subject to negotiation of further conditions. He foresaw the possibility of a claim of executive privilege—there was no specific provision in the Constitution for Presidential privilege from disclosure, but, before his elevation to the Supreme Court, Justice Rehnquist had been employed in the Justice Department and developed the concept. Understanding this, Cox insisted that he had authority to contest all claims to executive privilege raised by those being investigated and Richardson accepted this. It was the custom that Special Prosecutors did not generally hold press conferences; Cox saw the difficulty of investigating those close to the President and the necessity to be able to take public opinion with him. He was granted authority to report periodically to

[2] L Caplan, *The Tenth Justice: The Solicitor General and the Rule of Law* (New York, Alfred A Knopf, 1987).
[3] Doyle above n 1, 41 et seq.

the public. On these terms he accepted the appointment and was sworn in on 25 May 1973.

He proceeded swiftly. Previously the investigation was headed by Henry Peterson, chief of the criminal division in the Justice Department, who, when interviewed by Cox, claimed confidentiality in respect of his conversations with the President. He did reveal, however, that Nixon had told him that his in-house counsel, John Dean, had told him that the prosecution were offering him immunity if he disclosed what he knew. Petersen had told the President that Dean had not been offered immunity, to which the President had replied that Dean's words were on tape. Following this, Cox met with representatives of the administration and asked for any tapes of conversations between the President and Dean and also a log of all their meetings. A response was delayed. On the 13 July 1973, a White House assistant, called Butterfield, was interviewed prior to appearing before the Senate Committee investigating the Watergate affair and disclosed that all conversations in the Oval office were recorded. Logs of meetings between the President and Dean were disclosed and Cox was able to issue nine *subpoenas duces tecum* for production of specific tapes. Special Counsel to the President accepted service of the subpoenas.[4] On 25 July 1973 the President's reply was received: 'it would be inconsistent with the public interest and with the Constitutional position of the Presidency to make available recordings of meetings and telephone conversations in which I was a participant and I must respectfully decline to do so.'[5]

By this time a Grand Jury were considering whether to hand down indictments in relation to the Watergate affair. This procedure has been abolished in England, but in the United States continues as a means of preferring indictments, where the jury determines there is a case to answer. The grand jury was sitting in private and Cox visited them, explained the necessity for the subpoenas and they authorised him to seek them on their behalf. They went into open court and affirmed their position to Judge Sirica. Because of the President's refusal to produce the tapes, Cox applied for an order to show cause why they should not be produced. The hearing took place before Judge Sirica. Cox argued it as Special Prosecutor and Charles Wright, Professor of Law and a constitutional expert at the University of Texas, argued it on behalf of the President. Wright argued that, in all the years since the Constitution was ratified, never had any court in the United States ordered what Cox now sought. There were 400 federal judges and if this order were granted it would be a free pass for any one of them to grant access to the President's personal papers. Cox replied: 'This is not just an accusation, but there is strong evidence to believe that the integrity of the Executive officers has been corrupted, although the extent of it is not yet clear.' He went on to quote an exchange between James I of England and Chief Justice Coke, in which the King had said 'that I am to be under the law, that is treason to aver';

[4] Gormley above n 1, 290.
[5] Richard Milhous (ed) *Public Papers of the Presidents of the United States: Richard M Nixon, 1973* (Ann Arbor MI, University of Michigan Library, 2005).

Coke had replied 'non sub homine sed Deo ex lege' (not under man, but under God and the law). In August 1973, Judge Sirica ordered the President to hand over the nine tapes to him personally, so that he could review them privately and decide whether they should be disclosed.

In October 1973, the President ordered Richardson to dismiss Cox; Richardson refused and resigned. The Solicitor General was persuaded to do so and Cox was replaced as special prosecutor by Leon Jaworski. The President still refused to comply with the subpoena. On 1 March 1974 the Grand Jury handed down an indictment charging seven named individuals, who were part of the President's staff, with conspiracy to defraud the United States and to obstruct justice. Although he was not charged with these offences (he was immune from prosecution during office) the President was named as a co-conspirator. An appeal against production under the subpoenas had been lodged and not yet determined. After failed attempts between the parties to arrive at some middle course, this aspect of the case eventually reached the Supreme Court, which gave its opinion on 8 July 1974.

The majority opinion of the court was delivered by Chief Justice Warren Burger.[6] Nixon had appointed him as Chief Justice in 1969 in succession to Earl Warren. Burger was seen as having a more conservative bent than Warren and no doubt the President's advisers saw him as likely to be sympathetic to a claim of executive privilege. In delivering the opinion of the Court, Burger pointed out that there had been no previous opinion of the Court defining the scope of judicial power over enforcement of a *subpoena* seeking confidential Presidential communications; other exercises of power, however, by the Executive and Legislative branches had been found invalid as in conflict with the Constitution. The importance of protecting confidential communications between high government officials and those who advise them was too plain to require discussion. At the same time

> neither the doctrine of separation of powers nor the need for confidentiality of high-level communications, without more, can sustain an absolute, unqualified Presidential privilege of immunity from judicial process under all circumstances. The President's need for complete candor and objectivity from advisers calls for great deference from the courts. However, when the privilege depends solely on the broad, undifferentiated claim of public interest in the confidentiality of such conversations, a confrontation with other values arises. Absent a claim of need to protect military, diplomatic, or sensitive national security secrets, we find it difficult to accept the argument that even the very important interest in confidentiality of Presidential communications is significantly diminished by production of such material for *in camera* inspection with all the protection that a district court will be obliged to provide ...[7]

> [W]e have elected to employ an adversary system of criminal justice ... the need to develop all relevant facts in the adversary system is both fundamental and comprehensive. The ends of criminal justice would be defeated if judgments were to be founded on a partial or speculative presentation of the facts ...[8]

[6] *United States v Nixon*, 418 US 683.
[7] ibid, 706.
[8] ibid, 709.

The Sixth Amendment explicitly confers upon every defendant in a criminal trial the right 'to be confronted with the witnesses against him (and) to have compulsory process for obtaining witnesses in his favor.' Moreover, the Fifth Amendment also guarantees that no person shall be deprived of liberty without due process of law.[9]

The Court held that there was a presumption in favour of presidential confidentiality, but Judge Sirica had properly balanced that with the need to make available evidence that was admissible and relevant in the criminal proceedings. His order was affirmed. Although Cox had not argued the case before the Supreme Court, it had upheld his reasoning. Some tapes were released, which revealed that the President had clearly been involved at least in covering up the dirty tricks that had been played.

On the 27 July the House of Representatives Judiciary Committee voted to commence impeachment proceedings against the President for obstructing the course of justice. On 8 August Nixon resigned. In September his successor, President Ford, pardoned him.

Nearly 50 people were convicted of a variety of criminal offences in connection with the Watergate affair, many of them qualified lawyers. They included two former Attorneys General. The President himself had been a partner in a commercial firm in California for some years, before joining the government service. This inevitably led to criticism of the American Bar Association's regulation of its members. In 1977 the Association set up a Commission to evaluate professional conduct and this led in 1983 to the publication of *Model Rules of Professional Conduct*, which stressed the importance of honesty in all legal dealings. Courses on professional conduct were made obligatory in all university law courses.

If the Watergate affair is, at first sight, an unsavoury incident in an account of those who made America, Archibald in fact achieved what Lord Coke had attempted in seventeenth century England, namely a legal ruling from the highest court that the Head of State was subject to the law.

---

[9] ibid, 417.

21

The Glass Ceiling: Sandra O'Connor and Ruth Bader Ginsburg

I F ABIGAIL ADAMS had been alive on 19 July 1981, she would have jumped for joy, for that was the day when **Sandra O'Connor** was the first woman to be appointed a Justice of the Supreme Court.[1] 12 years later **Ruth Bader Ginsburg** followed her onto the Supreme Court bench.[2] They were born three years apart, Sandra in 1930 and Ruth in 1933; one of Irish extraction, the other of Jewish, they mirror two of the great migrations to the United States. Sandra was brought up on a ranch in Arizona,[3] Ruth in New York City. Sandra was educated at Stanford University and then Stanford Law School; she worked on the *Stanford Law Review* with William Rehnquist, under whom she later served when he was Chief Justice. Ruth was educated at Cornell University and Harvard Law School. Both women suffered gender discrimination at the outset of their careers. Sandra applied for employment after graduation to 40 law firms, but did not receive a single interview.[4] Ruth was turned down for a clerkship with Supreme Court Justice Frankfurter, because she was a woman.[5] She did obtain a clerkship to a judge in a District Court.

In the end Sandra did gain employment as a deputy district attorney, but only after she offered to work for no salary. In 1965 she was promoted to Assistant Attorney General for Arizona. She entered politics for the Republican Party, eventually becoming majority leader in the Arizona Senate and thereafter served as an appellate judge in Arizona. In 1981 President Reagan rang her and said he was nominating her as an Associate Justice of the Supreme Court, asking her if that was alright. It was.

Ruth worked for a time in Sweden and was impressed by the number of women in law schools and the legal profession. She was from the beginning of her career a champion of equality for women under the Constitution, writing a standard work on the subject of women's rights and arguing cases on the subject before the Supreme Court. Initially she followed an academic legal career at

---

[1] See D Abrams, *Sandra Day O'Connor* (New York, Infobase Publishing, 2009).

[2] See LN Bayer, *Ruth Bader Ginsburg* (New York, Chelsea House Publications, 2000); S Dodson, *The Legacy of Ruth Bader Ginsburg* (Cambridge, Cambridge University Press, 2015).

[3] SD O'Connor and HA Day, *Lazy B; Growing up on a Cattle Ranch in the American Southwest* (New York, Random House, 2002).

[4] Interview on *Fresh Air* (5 March 2013).

[5] N Lewis *New York Times* (15 June 1993).

Rutgers and Columbia Universities and then was appointed by President Carter to the United States Court of Appeals for the District of Columbia; in 1993 President Clinton appointed her to the Supreme Court. Both women married and had a family.

As a generality, O'Connor has been seen as allying herself with the conservative wing of the Court and Ginsburg with the liberal wing. Both women, however, have shown pragmatism based on the particular facts of a case and a distrust of wide propositions of law, which might come back to bite. At the time of O'Connor's appointment, Chief Justice William Rehnquist was generally recognised as the leader of the conservative faction. She concurred with him a majority of the time.[6] On occasion, however, she has disappointed conservative critics of the Supreme Court. As the composition of the Bench changed over time, she found herself giving the deciding opinion in a number of critical cases, particularly those governing sexual relations and minorities. She was given the title of 'swing voter', with the surface meaning that she swung the decision, but with an undercurrent of suggestion that she was unreliable, swinging this way and that. She rightly felt this was unfair.

The difference between the two women's approach was sometimes a fine one. This is illustrated by two cases decided in 2003, in suits brought against Michigan University and Michigan School of Law respectively. The admission procedures of both institutions included criteria which sought to affirm a diverse student intake. The admission procedure for the University had a number of criteria, which were used to mark applicants out of a total score of 100. Those from ethnic or racial minorities, however, were automatically awarded 20 starting points, which in practice meant that all applicants from those groups gained admittance. The admission procedures of the Law School also included the achievement of racial and ethnic diversity as one of its criteria, but each candidate had to be considered against a wide ranging set of values. In the case of the University, O'Connor supported (as did Rehnquist) the majority opinion that, while the attainment of diversity in student bodies was a legitimate aim of state educational institutions, the award of 20 starting points breached the equal opportunity provision in the Fourteenth Amendment, because it was too arbitrary.[7] Ginsburg dissented from this opinion on the ground that the affirmative action taken by the University was freely disclosed and better than a system which depended on nods and winks. On the other hand, both women concurred in the majority opinion in *Grutter v Bollinger* that the Law School's criteria were not in breach of the Amendment, because they did not include an arbitrary award of points, but required individual assessment of applicants over a wide range of criteria, of which racial diversity was only one.[8]

---

[6] RJ Jackson and T Vjgnarajah, 'Nine Justices, Ten Years:, a Statistical Retrospective' (2004) 118(1) *Harvard Law Review* 510–23 at 521.
[7] *Gratz v Bollinger* 539 US 244.
[8] 539 US 306.

The two women were on opposite sides of the fence in 1995 in *Missouri v Jenkins*.[9] The desegregation of schools after the decision in *Brown* was supervised by District Courts.[10] The process took a long time. Problems arose in Kansas City (mirrored elsewhere), where students in inner city schools were up to 90 per cent black and those in the suburban schools largely white. It was said there had been a white exodus from the inner city. One solution to this (which had aroused great opposition) was bussing children from one school to another to even out the racial imbalance. The scheme which the District Court in Missouri sought to enforce was different. It proposed that the overall standard of schools throughout the city should be raised by investment in infrastructure and salaries of teachers and the creation of high standard 'magnet' schools to attract all races. The programme, aimed at 'desegregated attractiveness' in schools, was hugely expensive. The State of Missouri challenged the District Court's power to order such a costly process. The majority opinion, delivered by Chief Justice Rehnquist with O'Connor concurring, held that the aim of any desegregation scheme must be to restore the victims of desegregation to the position they would have been in but for segregation. Missouri had already taken great steps to that end. Any scheme should take into account the interest of the state and local authorities in managing their affairs. The proposed scheme was financially open-ended and beyond the remedial power of the District Court. It was unconstitutional. The minority opinion was delivered by Justice Souter with Ginsburg concurring. In their view the case had been submitted under limited points and the basis of the majority decision had not been fully argued before the Court. This returns to the argument, first raised by Brandeis, as to whether the Supreme Court can go beyond the briefs submitted to it and promote its own policy.

O'Connor and Ginsburg also took opposing views in *Bush v Gore* in 2000.[11] The presidential election had been so close that its result depended on the count in Florida, which had been flawed. The Florida Court of Appeals had ordered a recount, but the majority in the Supreme Court, including O'Connor, stayed it. A deadline for the recount had been set, which would not allow the process to be properly and fairly executed. A minority, including Ginsburg, favoured the recount.

Perhaps O'Connor's most important and decisive intervention came before Ginsburg's appointment, when the case of *Roe v Wade* was reconsidered. By 1992 the composition of the Supreme Court had changed markedly—of the justices who had decided *Roe v Wade* only one, Blackmun, remained and of the nine justices, who were now members of the court, eight were Republican nominees and regarded as conservatives. There was an expectation that the Court would overturn *Roe v Wade*.

---

[9] 515 US 70.
[10] Above ch 19.
[11] 531 US 98.

The Pennsylvania Legislature had passed a statute requiring various conditions to be satisfied before a pregnancy could be terminated; these included the woman's informed consent, notification to her husband, or parent if a minor, and a definition of a medical emergency if that were the ground for the termination. In *Planned Parenthood of Southeastern Pennsylvania v Casey, Governor of Pennsylvania* the constitutionality of the state Act was challenged;[12] a District court had held the restrictions unconstitutional, but a Circuit Appeal Court upheld all except husband notification.

On appeal, the opinions in the Supreme Court were fractured one to another, adopting a variety of different approaches. Four Justices held that the right to terminate a pregnancy was not a liberty protected by the Constitution, but in the end there was an effective majority of five affirming the central decision in *Roe*. The decisive factor was that the two justices who favoured affirming *Roe v Wade* on its merits were joined by three, who held that it had stood for sufficient time that it would be wrong to overrule it. O'Connor was one of those who, while disagreeing with the original decision, felt it had stood too long to be reversed. She delivered the crucial opinion, in which two of her brethren concurred. To overrule *Roe v Wade* would cause serious inequity to people who, for two decades of economic and social development, had organised intimate relationships and made choices that defined their views of themselves and their places in society, in reliance on the availability of abortion in the event that contraception failed. The ability of women to participate equally in the economic and social life of the nation had been facilitated by their ability to control their reproductive lives.

Those who wished to overrule the original decision in *Roe* pointed to examples of the Court overruling previous decisions, in particular the decision in *Brown*,[13] where the court ordered desegregation and overruled the earlier decision in *Plessy*[14] that, if equal facilities were provided to blacks and whites, they could be segregated. The majority upholding *Roe* met this argument by pointing to the sea change in social circumstances, which had occurred in the seventy years between *Plessy* and *Brown* and justified overturning the earlier decision; in the case of *Roe v Wade* there had been no such social change.

Between the decision in *Roe* and 1992 progress in medical care of pregnant women had led to a change in assessment of the moment when a foetus became viable, which could be at 23 weeks into pregnancy. This led to a majority decision to reject the three-stage analysis in *Roe* and substitute a two-stage framework dividing at viability.

Ginsburg has remained consistent in her defence of women's rights. In *US v Virginia* she concurred in a majority opinion that a policy of the Military Institute of Virginia to admit only males was in breach of the equal protection provision

---

[12]   505 US 833 (1992).
[13]   Above ch 19.
[14]   ibid.

in the Fourteenth Amendment.[15] On other occasions, in dissenting opinions, she has delivered trenchant criticisms of her brethren's attitude to women's issues. In *Ledbetter v Goodyear Tire and Rubber Co* a woman employee complained that her employers had discriminated against her by under-assessing her worth and paying her less than male employees.[16] The majority opinion defeated her claim, because she had delayed too long in bringing it. Ginsburg, dissenting, said that 'the court does not comprehend, or is indifferent to, the insidious way in which women can be victims of pay discrimination.' In *Gonzales v Carhart* a challenge was mounted to a federal Act banning a method of birth control called 'partial birth.'[17] The majority of the Court upheld the statute, but Ginsburg dissenting, criticised them for adopting 'ancient notions about women's place in the family and under the Constitution—ideas, which have been discredited.'

This account does not do justice to the many opinions in which these two justices have participated. Their opinions demonstrate an intellectual stringency independent of gender. Nevertheless, their appointments will feed the aspirations of many young women—there are now two further female Supreme Court judges. Changed perceptions of role contribute as much as anything to the making of a nation.

---

[15] 518 US 515 (1996).
[16] 550 US 618 (2007).
[17] 550 US 124 (2007).

22

Epilogue: Barack Obama

NOTHER TO BREAK a glass ceiling is **Barack Obama**,[1] when he became the first black President of the United States, yet racial issues have plagued his presidency. On the 12 July 2016 he attended a memorial service in Dallas, Texas, for five police officers shot dead by a sniper five days earlier. The officers were white and the sniper African-American. He was apparently angered by white police officers shooting two young African-American men in separate incidents—Alton Sterling in Baton Rouge, Louisiana and Philando Castile in Falcon Heights, Minnesota. These deaths continued a series of incidents in which young African-American men died at the hands of police. The Dallas shooting was yet another multiple killing that had occurred on this President's watch.

Addressing the service, the President acknowledged the suffering of the people of Dallas and across the country and the need to try to find some meaning amidst this sorrow:

> For the men and women who protect and serve the people of Dallas, last Thursday began like any other day. Like most Americans, each day you get up, probably have too quick a breakfast, kiss your family goodbye, and you head to work. But your work and the work of police officers across the country is like no other. For the moment you put on that uniform, you have answered a call that at any moment, even in the briefest interaction, may put your life in harm's way.[2]

The President sounded weary, trying to sound hopeful when it was almost impossible.

His father, Barack Obama senior, came from the Luo tribe in Kenya to study at the University of Hawaii, where he met a young woman of English ancestry but now from Kansas, Stanley Ann Dunham, in a Russian language class. They married and Barack junior was born in August 1961. The couple separated early on and were divorced in 1964. Barack was brought up largely by his mother's parents in Hawaii. He went on to study political science and international relations at Columbia College, New York. After participating in a number of social projects, he was admitted to Harvard Law School in 1988, became President of the *Harvard Law Review* and graduated with distinction in 1991. He then held

---

[1] Generally see B Obama, *Dreams from My Father* (New York, Random House, 2004); D Maraniss, *Barack Obama: The Story* (New York, Simon and Schuster, 2012).

[2] The transcript of this speech is available at www.whitehouse.gov/the-press-office/2016/07/12/remarks-president-memorial-service-fallen-dallas-police-officers.

academic posts at the University of Chicago Law School and practised in a firm specialising in human rights cases and neighbourhood development. It was at Chicago University that he met his First Lady, Michelle, who was also a lawyer. He became a state Senator in 1997 on the Democratic ticket and similarly a national Senator in 2005. The Democratic Party nominated him as their presidential candidate in 2008 and he became President in 2009. When he visited Dallas he was nearing the end of his second term.

In his first election campaign, he adopted the slogan 'yes we can.' It was not long before he found that he 'couldn't always'. He hit the same fault line that bedeviled the administration of President Clinton. In Britain, the Prime Minister is appointed on the basis that he commands a majority in the House of Commons, even if that is by coalition (though Harold Wilson did govern for a short time as a minority government). In Congress, the President of the United States may find himself without a majority either in the House or the Senate or both. This can happen particularly after mid-term elections. For much of his Presidency, Obama has not had majorities in Congress and pleas for cross-party support have fallen on deaf ears.

In 2009 he introduced a plan for healthcare with a government investment of 900 billion dollars, the so-called public option. The House of Representatives passed a Bill, which did have such a public option. Instead of approving it, the Senate passed their own healthcare bill without the public option. In the end a compromise Act, the Patient Protection and Affirmative Care Act, 2010, narrowly passed. It has a complicated mechanism, which includes some government subsidy of the poorest, incentives to employers to provide healthcare, and tax penalties upon those who fail to take out the minimum medical insurance cover. It was not as far reaching as Obama would have hoped.

On 11 September 2001, planes were used by members of the Al Qaeda organisation to destroy the twin towers of the World Trade Center in New York. The two Houses of Congress passed a joint resolution authorising the President to use all necessary and appropriate force against organisations and persons he determined were responsible for the attack. Militia forces in Afghanistan captured Salim Ahmed Hamdan, who was alleged to have been the chauffeur to the leader of Al Qaeda, Osama Bin Laden, and handed him over to United States forces. In 2002, he was transported to the detention centre in the United States Naval Base at Guantanamo Bay in Cuba, constructed to house suspected terrorists captured in Afghanistan and Iraq. The site had been leased in 1903 from Cuba, which retained ultimate sovereignty, so it was argued that the ordinary protection of United States law would not apply to those detained there. At its height, the complex contained nearly 800 detainees.

In the Revolutionary period, the Second Continental Congress, having authorised the establishment of a Continental Army, drew up Articles of War, governing its conduct. Article 15 authorised the establishment of military commissions to try prisoners accused of offences against the laws of war. The Secretary for Defence, Donald Rumsfeld, now set up such commissions to try those detained in Guantanamo Bay. Hamdan was about to be tried by such a commission and challenged its jurisdiction on a writ of *habeas corpus* in a case that eventually came before the Supreme Court in 2006—*Hamdan v Rumsfeld*.[3] The Detainee Treatment Act of 2005 provided that no court had the power to consider an application for *habeas corpus* brought by a detainee at Guantanamo Bay, but the Supreme Court held that the terms of the Act were not sufficiently specific to their jurisdiction and assumed it. The Court gave the opinion that the military Commission due to try *Hamdan* lacked the power to proceed, because its structure and procedures violated both the United States Uniform Code of Military Justice and the Geneva Conventions 1949, to which the United States were signatories. *Habeas corpus* was granted. Thereafter the Military Commissions Act 2006 sought in different ways to exclude the jurisdiction of domestic courts over the Guantanamo Bay centre, but in 2008 in *Boumediene v Bush* the validity of that Act was challenged.[4] The Supreme Court gave the opinion that, even if the government of Cuba retained sovereignty over the base at Guantanamo, the United States had de facto control over it and the Court had jurisdiction to grant *habeas corpus*.

In his 2008 election campaign one of Barack Obama's principal pledges was to close the Guantanamo Bay complex. He secured the passage of an Act increasing procedural protections for those appearing before military commissions and gradually the numbers detained fell, but the President met apparently insuperable difficulties in the way of finally closing it. In the view of military intelligence, some of those detained remained very dangerous. The countries to which they might be returned, for instance Yemen, could not offer sufficient security to ensure they remained in detention. The only alternative was to hold them in the United States and President Obama ordered that a prison in Illinois be prepared for that purpose. Congress, however, opposed holding any of the detainees on American soil and refused funding. By the beginning of 2016 there were still about 90 detained in Guantanamo. It appears that, while President Obama has done much to reduce the numbers detained in the Bay, he will not be able after eight years in office to keep his campaign promise.

His attempts to restrict gun crime seem to have been even less successful. In January 2016 he issued a number of Executive Orders seeking to reduce gun crime in the United States. There has always been a strong lobby opposing any attempt to restrict the constitutional right to bear arms. This has effectively prevented any legislation controlling the use of guns. The Fact Sheet issued when the President made the orders stated that over the past decade more than 100,000 people had died in the United States as a result of gun violence and millions more had suffered as a result of crimes in which guns had been used.

The use of Executive Orders goes back to the Presidency of George Washington. Article II Section 1 of the Constitution vests the executive power of the State in the President and Section 3 requires him to 'take care that the laws be faithfully executed'—the so-called Faithful Execution clause. It is under these powers that Executive Orders are justified, but they are clearly limited to executing laws

---

[3] 548 US 557.
[4] 553 US 723.

already in force. The Executive Orders issued in January 2016 tried to curb gun crime, first by ensuring that legislation requiring background checks on those buying certain firearms were strictly enforced and secondly that all those selling weapons were properly licensed for that purpose. New funding was to be provided for treatment of mental health and for research into improving the safety of weapons. Republican spokesmen reacted harshly to these measures. Their Republican then-candidate for the Presidency, Donald Trump, said that, if elected, he would unsign the orders fast. Paul Ryan, Speaker of the House of Representatives, has accused the President, rather than focusing on criminals and terrorists, of going after law-abiding citizens.

President Obama has had his successes. His administration came to power at a time of financial recession and, though it took time, America has returned to prosperity. His widening of healthcare provision was in itself a landmark. Some of his judgements in foreign policy have been questioned, but he is a holder of the Nobel Peace Prize. It is too early judge how much he could be said to have contributed to the making of America. It is easy to see, however, why he seemed wearied as he attended the memorial service in Dallas. Here were gun deaths on both sides of the racial divide. He continued his speech:

> The deepest fault lines of our democracy have suddenly been exposed, perhaps even widened ... faced with this violence, we wonder if the divides of race in America can ever be bridged. We wonder if an African American community that feel unfairly targeted by police, and police departments that feel unfairly maligned for doing their jobs, can ever understand each other's experience ... I understand. I understand how Americans are feeling. But, Dallas, I am here to say that to say we must reject such despair. I'm here to insist that we are not as divided as we seem. And I know that because I know America. I know how far we've come against impossible odds.[5]

In November 2016, probably the most divisive election campaign in American history took place. The lawyers were trumped; the electorate chose, albeit by a narrow margin, a businessman. His election was greeted by street protests in a number of cities. It seems inevitable that Obamacare will bite the dust and there will be no further gun control.

Commentators say that Donald Trump was elected on the back of a protest vote by white male blue collar workers. On the 26 May 1776, John Adams wrote to James Sullivan as follows:

> It is certain in Theory, that the only moral Foundation of Government is the Consent of the People. But to what extent Shall We carry this Principle? Shall We Say that every Individual of the Community, old and young, male and female, as well as rich and poor, must consent expressly to every Act of Legislation? No, you will Say. This is impossible. How then does the right arise in the Majority to govern the Minority, against their will? ... Men in general in every Society, who are wholly destitute of Property, are also too little acquainted with public Affairs to form a Right Judgment, and too dependent upon other Men to have a Will of their own ... Such is the frailty of the human Heart, that very few Men, who have no Property, have any Judgment of

their own. They talk and vote as they are directed by Some Man of Property, who has attached their Minds to his Interest.[6]

Donald Trump is a professional Man of Property. No doubt the metropolitan liberal elite (in Britain post-Brexit as well as the United States) will read Adams' words ruefully. Nevertheless, President Trump will swear allegiance to the Constitution of the United States in a year that marks the 230th anniversary of its signing; let us hope that, despite the divisions of the election campaign, he will find a way to govern in the name of all the people.

---

[6] RJ Taylor (ed), *Papers of John Adams* (MA and London, Belknap Press of Harvard University Press, 1977) Vol IV 208.

Appendix: First Fourteen Amendments to the United States Constitution

Congress of the United States
begun and held at the City of New-York, on
Wednesday the fourth of March, one thousand seven hundred and eighty nine.

THE Conventions of a number of the States, having at the time of their adopting the Constitution, expressed a desire, in order to prevent misconstruction or abuse of its powers, that further declaratory and restrictive clauses should be added: And as extending the ground of public confidence in the Government, will best ensure the beneficent ends of its institution.

RESOLVED by the Senate and House of Representatives of the United States of America, in Congress assembled, two thirds of both Houses concurring, that the following Articles be proposed to the Legislatures of the several States, as amendments to the Constitution of the United States, all, or any of which Articles, when ratified by three fourths of the said Legislatures, to be valid to all intents and purposes, as part of the said Constitution; viz.

ARTICLES in addition to, and Amendment of the Constitution of the United States of America, proposed by Congress, and ratified by the Legislatures of the several States, pursuant to the fifth Article of the original Constitution.

Note: The following text is a transcription of the first ten amendments to the Constitution in their original form. These amendments were ratified December 15, 1791, and form what is known as the "Bill of Rights."

AMENDMENT I

Congress shall make no law respecting an establishment of religion, or prohibiting the free exercise thereof; or abridging the freedom of speech, or of the press; or the right of the people peaceably to assemble, and to petition the Government for a redress of grievances.

AMENDMENT II

A well regulated Militia, being necessary to the security of a free State, the right of the people to keep and bear Arms, shall not be infringed.

AMENDMENT III

No Soldier shall, in time of peace be quartered in any house, without the consent of the Owner, nor in time of war, but in a manner to be prescribed by law.

AMENDMENT IV

The right of the people to be secure in their persons, houses, papers, and effects, against unreasonable searches and seizures, shall not be violated, and no Warrants shall issue, but upon probable cause, supported by Oath or affirmation, and particularly describing the place to be searched, and the persons or things to be seized.

AMENDMENT V

No person shall be held to answer for a capital, or otherwise infamous crime, unless on a presentment or indictment of a Grand Jury, except in cases arising in the land or naval forces, or in the Militia, when in actual service in time of War or public danger; nor shall any person be subject for the same offence to be twice put in jeopardy of life or limb; nor shall be compelled in any criminal case to be a witness against himself, nor be deprived of life, liberty, or property, without due process of law; nor shall private property be taken for public use, without just compensation.

AMENDMENT VI

In all criminal prosecutions, the accused shall enjoy the right to a speedy and public trial, by an impartial jury of the State and district wherein the crime shall have been committed, which district shall have been previously ascertained by law, and to be informed of the nature and cause of the accusation; to be confronted with the witnesses against him; to have compulsory process for obtaining witnesses in his favor, and to have the Assistance of Counsel for his defence.

AMENDMENT VII

In Suits at common law, where the value in controversy shall exceed twenty dollars, the right of trial by jury shall be preserved, and no fact tried by a jury, shall be otherwise re-examined in any Court of the United States, than according to the rules of the common law.

AMENDMENT VIII

Excessive bail shall not be required, nor excessive fines imposed, nor cruel and unusual punishments inflicted.

AMENDMENT IX

The enumeration in the Constitution, of certain rights, shall not be construed to deny or disparage others retained by the people.

AMENDMENT X

The powers not delegated to the United States by the Constitution, nor prohibited by it to the States, are reserved to the States respectively, or to the people.

AMENDMENT XI—Passed by Congress March 4, 1794. Ratified February 7, 1795.

Note: Article III, section 2, of the Constitution was modified by amendment 11.

The Judicial power of the United States shall not be construed to extend to any suit in law or equity, commenced or prosecuted against one of the United States by Citizens of another State, or by Citizens or Subjects of any Foreign State.

AMENDMENT XII—Passed by Congress December 9, 1803. Ratified June 15, 1804.

Note: A portion of Article II, section 1 of the Constitution was superseded by the 12th amendment.

The Electors shall meet in their respective states and vote by ballot for President and Vice-President, one of whom, at least, shall not be an inhabitant of the same state with themselves; they shall name in their ballots the person voted for as President, and in distinct ballots the person voted for as Vice-President, and they shall make distinct lists of all persons voted for as President, and of all persons voted for as Vice-President, and of the number of votes for each, which lists they shall sign and certify, and transmit sealed to the seat of the government of the United States, directed to the President of the Senate; -- the President of the Senate shall, in the presence of the Senate and House of Representatives, open all the certificates and the votes shall then be counted; -- The person having the greatest number of votes for President, shall be the President, if such number be a majority of the whole number of Electors appointed; and if no person have such majority, then from the persons having the highest numbers not exceeding three on the list of those voted for as President, the House of Representatives shall choose immediately, by ballot, the President. But in choosing the President, the votes shall be taken by states, the representation from each state having one vote; a quorum for this purpose shall consist of a member or members from two-thirds of the states, and a majority of all the states shall be necessary to a choice. [And if the House of Representatives shall not choose a President whenever the right of choice shall devolve upon them, before the fourth day of March next following, then the Vice-President shall act as President, as in case of the death or other constitutional disability of the President.* The person having the greatest number of votes as Vice-President, shall be the Vice-President, if such number be a majority of the whole number of Electors appointed, and if no person have a majority, then from the two highest numbers on the list, the Senate shall choose the Vice-President; a quorum for the purpose shall consist of two-thirds of the whole number of Senators, and a majority of the whole number shall be necessary to a choice. But no person constitutionally ineligible to the office of President shall be eligible to that of Vice-President of the United States.

Superseded by section 3 of the 20th amendment.

AMENDMENT XIII—Passed by Congress January 31, 1865. Ratified December 6, 1865.

Note: A portion of Article IV, section 2, of the Constitution was superseded by the 13th amendment.

Section 1

Neither slavery nor involuntary servitude, except as a punishment for crime whereof the party shall have been duly convicted, shall exist within the United States, or any place subject to their jurisdiction.

Section 2

Congress shall have power to enforce this article by appropriate legislation.

AMENDMENT XIV—Passed by Congress June 13, 1866. Ratified July 9, 1868.

Note: Article I, section 2, of the Constitution was modified by section 2 of the 14th amendment.

Section 1

All persons born or naturalized in the United States, and subject to the jurisdiction thereof, are citizens of the United States and of the State wherein they reside. No State shall make or enforce any law which shall abridge the privileges or immunities of citizens of the United States; nor shall any State deprive any person of life, liberty, or property, without due process of law; nor deny to any person within its jurisdiction the equal protection of the laws.

Section 2

Representatives shall be apportioned among the several States according to their respective numbers, counting the whole number of persons in each State, excluding Indians not taxed. But when the right to vote at any election for the choice of electors for President and Vice-President of the United States, Representatives in Congress, the Executive and Judicial officers of a State, or the members of the Legislature thereof, is denied to any of the male inhabitants of such State, being twenty-one years of age,* and citizens of the United States, or in any way abridged, except for participation in rebellion, or other crime, the basis of representation therein shall be reduced in the proportion which the number of such male citizens shall bear to the whole number of male citizens twenty-one years of age in such State.

Section 3

No person shall be a Senator or Representative in Congress, or elector of President and Vice-President, or hold any office, civil or military, under the United States, or under any State, who, having previously taken an oath, as a member of Congress, or as an officer of the United States, or as a member of any State legislature, or as an executive or judicial officer of any State, to support the Constitution of the United States, shall have engaged in insurrection or rebellion against the same, or given aid or comfort to the enemies thereof. But Congress may by a vote of two-thirds of each House, remove such disability.

Section 4

The validity of the public debt of the United States, authorized by law, including debts incurred for payment of pensions and bounties for services in suppressing insurrection or rebellion, shall not be questioned. But neither the United States nor any State shall assume or pay any debt or obligation incurred in aid of insurrection or rebellion against the United States, or any claim for the loss or emancipation of any slave; but all such debts, obligations and claims shall be held illegal and void.

Section 5

The Congress shall have the power to enforce, by appropriate legislation, the provisions of this article.

Changed by section 1 of the 26th amendment.

Bibliography

Abrams D, *Sandra Day O'Connor* (New York, Infobase Publishing, 2009)

Adams CF (ed), *Works of John Adams* (Boston MA, Charles C Little and James Brown, 1850)

Adams J, *Defence of the Constitutions of the Government of the United States of America* (New York, De Capo Press Reprint Edition, 1971)

——, *Papers of*, see Taylor RJ

Adams JS (ed), *John Marshall: An Autobiographical Sketch* (Ann Arbor MI, University of Michigan Press, 1937)

Allen N, *Arsonist: The Most Dangerous Man in America* (Griffins Wharf Productions, 2011)

Andrews CM, *Colonial Period of American History* (New Haven CT, Yale University Press, 1934–38)

Aristotle, *Rhetoric*, see Roberts WR

Arlidge A and Judge I, *Magna Carta Uncovered* (Oxford, Hart Publishing, 2014)

Baker L, *Brandeis and Frankfurter* (New York, Harper & Row, 1984)

Barker RS, 'Natural Law and the United States Constitution' (2012) 66 *The Review of Metaphysics* 105–30

Barry R, *Mr Rutledge of South Carolina* (Salem MA, Duell, Sloan & Pearce, 1942)

Basler RP (ed), *Collected Works of Abraham Lincoln* (New Brunswick NJ, Rutgers University Press, 1953)

Bayer LN, *Ruth Bader Ginsburg* (New York, Chelsea House Publications, 2000)

Beeman R, *Plain Honest Men: The Making of the American Constitution* (New York, Random House, 2009)

Belknap M, *The Supreme Court Under Earl Warren* (Columbia SC, The University of South Carolina, 2005)

Bernstein RB, *Thomas Jefferson* (Oxford, Oxford University Press, 2005)

Billings WM, *The Little Parliament* (Richmond VA, Library of Virginia, 2004)

Blackstone WM, *Commentaries on the Laws of England*, see Morrison W

Boardman RS, *Roger Sherman: Signer and Statesman* (Oxford, H Milford and Oxford University Press, 1938)

Brenner R, *Merchants and Revolution: Commercial Change, Political Conflict and London's Overseas Traders 1550–1563* (Princeton NJ, Princeton University Press, 1993)

Brereton J, *A Briefe and True Relation of the Discouerie of the North Part of Virginia* (London, Eliot's Court Press, 1602)

Browne WH, *George Calvert and Cecilius Calvert: Barons Baltimore of Baltimore* (New York, Dodd, Mead, 1890)

Boyd JP, *The Declaration of Independence, the Evolution of the Text* (Library of Congress/Thomas Jefferson Memorial Foundation, 1999)

——, 'The Disputed Authorship of the Declaration on the Causes and Necessity of Taking up Arms, 1775' (1996) 74(1) *Pennsylvania Magazine of History and Biography*

—— (ed), *Papers of Thomas Jefferson* (Princeton NJ, Princeton University Press, 1953)

Brant I, *James Madison* (Indianapolis, Bobbs-Merrill, 1941)

Burlingame M, *Abraham Lincoln, A Life* (Baltimore MD, John Hopkins University Press, 2008)

Butterfield LH (ed), *Diary and Autobiography of John Adams* (Cambridge MA, Belknap Press of Harvard University Press, 1961)

Calvert JE, *Quaker Constitutionalism and the Political Thought of John Dickinson* (New York, Cambridge University Press, 2008)

Canady HP, *Gentlemen of the Bar, Lawyers in Colonial Southern Carolina* (New York, Garland, 1987)

Canny NP, *Making Ireland British* (Oxford, Oxford University Press, 2001)

Caplan L, *The Tenth Justice: The Solicitor General and the Rule of Law* (New York, Alfred A Knopf, 1987)

Chapman G, Jonson B and Marston J, *Eastward Hoe* (London, William Aspley, 1605)

Chernow R, *Alexander Hamilton* (New York, Penguin Books Ltd, 2004)

Cicero, *Marcus Tullius Cicero on the Law*, see Fott D

Clements KA and Cheezum EA, *Woodrow Wilson* (Washington DC, CQ Press, 2003)

Collier C, *Roger Sherman's Connecticut: Yankee Politics and the American Revolution* (Middletown CT, Wesleyan University Press, 1971)

Collins RKL, *The Fundamental Holmes* (Cambridge, Cambridge University Press, 2010)

Cooke JE, *Alexander Hamilton* (New York, Charles Scribner's Sons, 1983)

Connor M, *The Invention of Terra Nullius: Historical and Legal Fictions on the Foundation of Australia* (Sydney, Macleay Press, 2005)

Craven WF, *The Virginia Company of London, 1606–1624* (Williamsburg VA, 350th Anniversary Celebration Corporation, 1957)

Davenport FG, *European Treaties bearing on the History of the United States and its Dependencies to 1648* (Washington DC, Carnegie Institute of Washington, 1917)

Dewey FL, *Thomas Jefferson: Lawyer* (Charlottesville VA, University of Virginia Press, 1986)

Dickinson J, *The Writings of*, see Ford PL

Dodson S, *The Legacy of Ruth Bader Ginsburg* (Cambridge, Cambridge University Press, 2015)

Donald DH, *Lincoln* (New York, Touchstone, 1996)

Doyle J, *Not Above the Law: The Battles of Watergate Prosecutors Cox and Jaworski: A Behind-the-Scenes Account* (New York, Morrow, 1977)

Dueholm JA, *Lincoln's Suspension of the Writ of Habeas Corpus: An Historical and Constitutional Analysis* (Jo Abraham Lincoln Association, 2008)

Eaton C, *Jefferson Davis* (New York, Free Press, 1977)

Esbeck CH, 'Dissent and Disestablishment: the Church—Settlement in the Early American Republic' (2004) *Brigham Young University Law Review* 1385

Farrand M, *The Framing of the Constitution of the United States* (New Haven, Yale University Press, 1913)

—— (ed), *The Records of the Federal Convention of 1787* (New Haven, Yale University Press, 1911)

Flower M, *John Dickinson Conservative Revolutionary* (Virginia, University of Virginia Press, 1983)

Finkelman P, *Slavery and the Founders: Race and Liberty in the Age of Jefferson* (New York, Routledge, 2014)

Floyd MR, *Abandoning American Neutrality* (New York, Palgrave Macmillan US, 2013)

Fott D (translation), *Marcus Tullius Cicero on the Law* (New York, Cornell University Press, 2014)

Ford PL (ed), *Autobiography of Thomas Jefferson* (New York and London, GP Putnam's Sons, 1914)
—— (ed), *The Writings of John Dickinson* (Philadephia PA, The Historical Society of Pennsylvania, 1895)
—— (ed), *The Writings of Thomas Jefferson* (New York, GP Putnam's Sons, 1893–99)
Franklin J, *Papers of*, see Labaree LW
Franklin JH, *Reconstruction after the Civil War* 3rd edn (Chicago IL, University of Chicago Press, 2013)
Galvin JR, *Three Men of Boston* (Washington DC, Brassey's Inc, 1997)
Gaustad ES, *Benjamin Franklin* (Oxford, Oxford University Press, 2006)
——, *Sworn on the Altar of God, A Religious Biography of Thomas Jefferson* (Grand Rapids MI, William B Eerdmans Publishing Co, 1996)
Gerber SD, 'Roger Sherman and the Bill of Rights' (1996) 28 *Journal of the North Eastern Political Science Association Polity*
Gilbert H, *Discourse of a Discoverie for a New Passage to Cataia* (London, Scolar Press, 1576)
Goebel J, *The Law Practice of Alexander Hamilton: Documents and Commentary* (New York, Columbia University Press, 1964)
Gordon-Reed A, *The Hemingses of Monticello* (New York, WW Norton & Company, 2008)
Gormley K, *Archibald Cox: Conscience of a Nation* (Boston MA, De Capo Press, 1997)
Greene J, *Constitutional Origins of the American Revolution* (Cambridge, Cambridge University Press, 2010)
Hakuyt Jr R, *The Principall Navigations, Voiages and Discoveries of the English Nation* (London, George Bishop and Ralph Newberie, 1589)
Hamilton A, *Papers of*, see Syrett H
Hamilton JGR, 'Southern Members of the Inns of Court' (1933) 10 *North Carolina Historical Review* 274
Hamlin P, 'Legal Education in Colonial New York' (1939) *New York University Law Quarterly Review*
Haw J, *John and Edward Rutledge of South Carolina* (Athens GA, University of Georgia Press, 1997)
Heckscher A, *Woodrow Wilson* (New York, Prentice Hall & IBD, 1991)
Hoeflich M, *American Blackstones in Blackstone and His Commentaries: Biography, Law History* (ed Prest) (Oxford, Hart Publishing, 2009)
Holmes Jr OW, *Common Law* (Harvard MA, Belknap Press, 2009)
Horowitz MJ, *The Warren Court and the Pursuit of Justice* (New York, Hill and Wang, 1998)
Hosmer JK (ed), *Winthrop's Journal: History of New England 1630–1649* (New York, Charles Scribner's Sons, 1908)
Howe MD (ed), *Holmes-Pollock Letters* (Cambridge MA, Harvard University Press, 1941)
Hseuh V, 'Giving Orders: Theory and Practice in the Fundamental Constitution of Carolina' (2002) 63(3) *Journal of History of Ideas* 425–46
Hubbard W, *A General History of New England from the Discovery to MDCLXXX* (Boston MA, Massachusetts Historical Society, 1815)
Hutson JH, *Forgotten Features of the Founding, The Recovery of Religious Themes in the Early American Republic* (Lanham MD, Lexington Books, 2003)
Illick J, *Colonial Pennsylvania—a History* (New York, Kraus International Publications, 1976)

Jackson RJ and Vignarajah T, 'Nine Justices, Ten Years: a Statistical Retrospective' (2004) 118(1) *Harvard Law Review* 510–23

Jefferson T, *Autobiography of*, see Ford PL

——, *Literary Commonplace Book*, see Wilson DL

——, *Papers of*, see Boyd JP

——, *Notes on the State of Virginia* (London, John Stockdale, 1787)

——, *Writings of*, see Ford PL

Johnson HA (ed), *Papers of John Marshall* (Chapel Hill NC, University of North Carolina Press, 2006)

Johnson P, *History of the Jews* (New York, Harper & Row, 1988)

Ketcham R, *James Madison: A Biography* (Charlottesville, University Press of Virginia, 1990)

Kingsbury SM, *Records of the Virginia Company 1606–26* (Washington DC, Government Print Office: Library of Congress, 1905)

Konkle BA, 'David Lloyd, Penn's Great Lawmaker' (1937) 4(3) *Pennsylvania History: A Journal of Mid Atlantic Studies* 153

Krugler JD, *English and Catholic: The Lords Baltimore in the Seventeenth Century* (Baltimore MD, John Hopkins University Press, 2004)

Labaree B, *Colonial Massachusetts, a History* (Millwood NY, Kraus International Publications, 1979)

Labaree LW (ed), *Papers of Benjamin Franklin* (New Haven and London, Yale University Press, 1970)

Larson R, *Daughters of Light: Quaker Women Preaching and Prophesying in the Colonies and Abroad* (New York, Knopf, 2000)

Levin NG, *Woodrow Wilson and World Politics: America's Response to War and Revolution* (New York, Oxford University Press USA, 1968)

Lewis JE and Onuf PS (eds), *Sally Hemmings and Thomas Jefferson: History, Memory, and Civic Culture* (Charlottesville VA, University Press of Virginia, 1999)

Lincoln A, *Collected Works of*, see Basler RP

Link AS (ed), *Papers of Woodrow Wilson* (Princeton NJ, Princeton University Press, 1966)

Lipson E, *The Economic History of England—The Age of Mercantilism* (London, Adam and Charles Black, 1959)

Logan RR, *Collection of Dickinson Papers (Collection 383), the Historical Society of Pennsylvania* (Pennsylvania, Library Company of Philadelphia)

Maccarthy-Morough M, *The Munster Planation—English Migration to Southern Ireland 1583–1641* (Oxford, Oxford University Press, 1986)

MacMillan M, *Peacemakers: Six Months that Changed the World: The Paris Peace Conference of 1919 and Its Attempt to End War* (London, John Murray, 2003)

Maier P, *American Scripture: Making the Declaration of Independence* (New York, Knopf, 1997)

Maraniss D, *Barack Obama: The Story* (New York, Simon and Schuster, 2012)

Marshall J, *An Autobiographical Sketch*, see Adams JS

——, *Papers of*, see Johnson HA

McCullogh D, 'John Adams' (2002) 117(1) *Political Science Quarterly* 1317

——, *John Adams* (New York, Simon & Schuster, 2001)

McDonald F, *Alexander Hamilton* (New York, WW Norton & Co, 1979)

—— (ed), *Empire and Nations* (Upper Saddle River NJ, Prentice-Hall Inc, 1962)

McPherson JM, *Abraham Lincoln* (New York, Oxford University Press, 2009)

Middlekauff R, *The Glorious Cause* (Oxford, Oxford University Press, 1982)

Milhous R (ed), *Public Papers of the Presidents of the United States: Richard M Nixon, 1973* (Ann Arbor MI, University of Michigan Library, 2005)

Miller JC, *The Wolf by the Ears: Thomas Jefferson and Slavery* (Charlottesville VA, University of Virginia Press, 1991)

Milton JR, *John Locke* (Oxford, Oxford University Press, 2004)

Moore R, *The Light in the Consciences: Faith, Practices and Personalities in Early British Quakerism* (Pennsylvania PA, Pennsylvania State University Press, 2000)

Morgan ES and Morgan HM, *Stamp Act Crisis: Prologue to Revolution* (North Carolina, University of North Carolina Press, 1995)

Morison S, *The Story of the Old Colony of New Plymouth* (New York, Knopf, 1955)

Morrison W (ed), *Blackstone's Commentaries on the Laws of England Volumes I–IV* (London, Routledge Cavendish, 2001)

Murchison W, *The Cost of Liberty: The Life of John Dickinson* (Wilmington, ISI Books, 2013)

Newmyer RK, *The Treason Trial of Aaron Burr: Law, Politics, and the Character Wars of the New Nation* (Cambridge, Cambridge University Press, 2012)

Nolan D, 'Sir William Blackstone and the New Republic: A Study of Intellectual Impact' (1975) 51 *New York University Law Review* 283

Obama B, *Dreams from my Father* (New York, Random House, 2004)

O'Connor SD and Day HA, *Lazy B; Growing up on a Cattle Ranch in the American Southwest* (New York, Random House, 2002)

Philbrick N, *Mayflower: a Story of Courage, Community and War* (New York, Viking, 2006)

Powell JH, 'Speech of John Dickinson Opposing a Declaration of Independence' (1941) 65(4) *Pennsylvania Magazine of History and Biography*

Powell WS, *John Pory, the Life and Letters of a Man of Many Parts 1572–1636* (North Carolina, University of North Carolina Press, 1976)

Prest W, *William Blackstone: Laws and Letters in the Eighteenth Century* (Oxford, Oxford University Press, 2008)

Preston RA, *Gorges of Plymouth Port* (Toronto, University of Toronto Press, 1953)

Purvis TC, 'Pattern of Ethnic Settlement in Late 18th Century Pennsylvania' (1987) 70(2) *The Western Pennsylvania Historical Magazine* 107

Rabb TK, *A Jacobean Gentleman, Sir Edwyn Sandys 1561–1629* (Princeton NJ, Princeton University Press, 2005)

——, *Enterprise and Empire: Merchant and Gentry Investment in the Expansion of England* (Cambridge MA, Harvard University Press, 1967)

Rakove J, *James Madison and the Creation of the American Republic* (New York, Foresman/Little Brown, 1990)

——, *Original Meanings: Politics and Ideas in the Making of the Constitution* (New York, Knopf, 1996)

Rice DW, *The Life and Achievements of Sir John Popham* (Teaneck NJ, Fairley Dickinson University Press, 2005)

Roberts WR (trans), *Rhetoric* (New York, Modern Library, 1954)

Sanford C, *The Religious Life of Thomas Jefferson* (Charlottesville VA, University of Virginia Press, 1988)

Sheridan ER, *Jefferson and Religion* (North Carolina, University of North Carolina Press, 2001)

Smith JE, *John Marshall: Definer of a Nation* (New York, Henry Holt and Co, 1996)

Smith P, *John Adams* (Garden City NY, Doubleday, 1962)

Soderland JR, *William Penn and the Founding of Pennsylvania—A Documentary History* (Philadelphia PA, University of Pennsylvania Press, 1983)

Stoebuck WB, 'Reception of English Common Law in the American Colonies' (1968) 10 *William and Mary Law Review*

Syrett H (ed), *Papers of Alexander Hamilton* (New York, Columbia University Press, 1962)

Taylor EGR, *The Original Writings and Correspondence of the two Richard Hakluyts* (London, The Hakluyt Society, 1935)

Taylor RJ (ed), *Papers of John Adams* (Cambridge MA and London, Belknap Press of Harvard University Press, 1977)

Thomas P, The *Townshend Duties Crisis: Second Phase of the American Revolution 1767–73* (New York, Oxford University Press, 1987)

Thompson JA, *Woodrow Wilson* (London, Routledge, 2002)

Tudor W, *The Life of James Otis of Massachusetts* (Boston MA, Wells and Lilly, 1823)

Urofsky MI, *Louis D Brandeis and the Progressive Tradition* (Boston MA, Scott Foresman & Co, 1981)

Vile JR, *Great American Lawyers* (CA, CO and Oxford, ABC-CLIO, 2001)

Warden LC, 'The Life of Blackstone' (1938) *Louisiana Law Review*

Warren C, *History of the American Bar* (Boston MA, Little, Brown and Company, 1911)

Warren E, *Memoirs of Earl Warren* (Garden City NY, Doubleday, 1977)

White GE, *Oliver Wendell Holmes* (Oxford, Oxford University Press, 2006)

Wiencek H, *Master of the Mountain: Thomas Jefferson and his Slaves* (New York, Farrar, Straus and Giroux, 2012)

Wilkes GA, *Complete Plays of Ben Jonson* (Oxford, Oxford University Press, 1951)

Willan TS, *The Early History of the Russia Company* (Manchester, Manchester University Press, 1968)

Willis G, *Inventing America: Jefferson's Declaration of Independence* (London, Athlone, 1980)

Wilson DL (ed), *Jefferson's Literary Commonplace Book* (Princeton NJ, Princeton University Press, 1989)

Wilson T, *The Myriad Faces of War* (London, Polity Press, 1986)

Wilson W, *Constitutional Government in America* (New York, Columbia University Press, 1917)

——, *Papers of*, see Link AS

Index